BROADWAY TO MAIN STREET

BROADWAY TO MAIN STREET

How Show Tunes Enchanted America

Laurence Maslon

OXFORD
UNIVERSITY PRESS

OXFORD
UNIVERSITY PRESS

Oxford University Press is a department of the University of Oxford.
It furthers the University's objective of excellence in research, scholarship,
and education by publishing worldwide. Oxford is a registered trade mark of
Oxford University Press in the UK and certain other countries.

Published in the United States of America by Oxford University Press
198 Madison Avenue, New York, NY 10016, United States of America.

Library of Congress Cataloging-in-Publication Data

Names: Maslon, Laurence, author.
Title: Broadway to Main Street : how show tunes enchanted America / Laurence
Maslon.
Description: New York : Oxford University Press, [2018] | Includes
bibliographical references and index.
Identifiers: LCCN 2017042504 (print) | LCCN 2017034396 (ebook) | ISBN
9780199832538 (alk. paper) | ISBN 9780199832545 (updf) | ISBN
9780190620417 (epub)
Subjects: LCSH: Musicals—New York (State)—New York—History and criticism.
| Popular music—United States—History and criticism. | Original cast
recordings. | Dissemination of music. | Sound recordings—Production and
direction—History.
Classification: LCC ML1711.8.N3 M372 2018 (ebook) | LCC ML1711.8.N3 (print) |
DDC 782.1/40973--dc23
LC record available at https://lccn.loc.gov/2017042504

1 3 5 7 9 8 6 4 2

Printed by Sheridan Books, Inc.,
United States of America

To Steve Ross,
A long-playing champion, with bonus tracks.
LM

I grew up in Evanston, in the suburbs of Chicago, and I was about twelve when the first national touring company of *Oklahoma!* came to town, at the Erlanger Theatre. A friend of mine in junior high school said, "Oh, you absolutely have to go downtown to see it! It's such a wonderful show and every song you hear on the radio is in it!" And I took the train downtown and I got my tickets and I saw it and it *was* wonderful. Except I remember being so disappointed that "Rum and Coca-Cola" wasn't in the score.

—Librettist George Furth, as told to the author

Contents

Acknowledgments

Many people helped me on this journey, nearly all them inspired by a love for show music and a desire to see its profound effect on American culture recognized and celebrated.

This book would not have been possible without the generous souls who shared their perspectives about Broadway and its music with me in extended interviews; their time and their insights are most appreciated: Keith Caulfield, Ted Chapin (who also provided some discreet source materials, in the form of a rare Columbia promotional item); Kim Criswell, Didier Deutsch, Kurt Deutsch, Brian Drutman, Scott Farthing, David Foil, Will Friedwald, Charles L. Granata, Sheldon Harnick, John Kander, Michael Kerker, Deborah Lapidus, Steve Lawrence (who sang to me over the phone), Bruce Pomahac, Harold Prince, Chita Rivera, William Rosenfield, Stephen Schwartz, Thomas Z. Shepard, and Charles Strouse. Messrs. Pomahac and Drutman also provided sensitive and supportive readings of the original manuscript.

I also want to thank some fine folk who helped make a few of those interviews happen: David Garrison, Malcolm Gets, Michael Kantor, and Eric Price.

The staff at Yale University's Gilmore Music Library was exemplary; they could not possibly have been more polite, professional, or helpful. They remain a high-water mark for devotion to research. I want to thank archivist Richard Boursy, Emily Ferrigno, Mary Horn Jones, and their staff.

The Library of Congress's Department of Recorded Sound was also extremely helpful: thanks to Bryan Cornell; also Mark Eden Horowitz from the Music Division; and Sam Brylowski.

Sony Music was a treasure trove and profound thanks to the director of its music archives, Thomas Tierney, for his diligence and attentiveness. Lauren Denney and Toby Silver of Sony Music were also extremely helpful in acquiring digital assets.

At New York University, the Humanities Council deserves thanks—Jane Tylus and Asya Berger for a grant to cover transcriptions; also to Dean Allyson Green and Associate Dean Louis Scheeder of the Tisch School of the Arts for two separate Dean's Grants to assist in research and permissions. The chair of the Graduate Acting Program, Mark Wing-Davey, and Sarah Schlesinger, chair of NYU's Graduate Musical Theater Writing Program were also supportive and gave me an opportunity to share some of my thoughts with the gifted students of their respective programs.

Andrew Solt and his sterling associates over at SOFA Entertainment helped so much to open the door into the fascinating world of Ed Sullivan. They made the research for that section in the book a joy, and SOFA's subsequent generosity is much appreciated.

Dana Levitt and Joanne Levitt were extremely helpful and supportive with memories and memorabilia about their grandfather Jack Kapp. Given that much of the Decca archives vanished in a California fire some years ago, the Levitts helped to fill in some essential gaps in the momentous Decca story.

If this book were a fictional narrative, its hero would be Goddard Lieberson. I am so thankful to the Lieberson estate, particularly Katherine and Kristina Lieberson, for permission to reproduce his voluminous correspondence; I hope they will find much to learn and admire about their grandfather.

I was lucky enough to have support and encouragement from Tom Lindblade (through two drafts), Bert Fink, Lisa Halliday, Andrew Zerman, Charles Kopelman, Amanda Vaill, Richard Barrios, Ira Weitzman, Michael Owen, Jon Burlingame, Howard and Ron Mandelbaum, Matthew Sussman, Kyle Lynch, Salomon Lerner, and the folks at WPPB-FM who keep my radio program, "Broadway to Main Street," on the air every week.

This book wouldn't have made it over the transom without the care and guidance of Karyn Gerhard (who joined the team officially as an expert copy editor), as well as the preparation skills of Lee Aaron Rosen, Erin Lora Chapman, Adrienne Carlile, and Stephanie Queiroz. Diana Bertolini provided valuable research, enthusiasm, and advice.

I want to thank the editorial and production staff at Oxford University Press. Editor Norman Hirschy has a unique blend of precision, perception, and persistence, and I'm grateful for all of those qualities. Joellyn Ausanka joined the project as it moved into production, and I deeply appreciate her kind approach and her meticulous eye.

Steve Ross deserves his own special "bonus track" for going the distance with me. He and his colleagues at Abrams Artists were never less than wise, supportive, and possessed of great humor.

Finally, to my wife, Genevieve, and my son, Miles, much love and gratitude for their tolerance and forbearance. We can't all be the von Trapps—that's fine with me.

CREDITS

"If He Walked into My Life"

From MAME Music and Lyrics by Jerry Herman © 1966 (Renewed) JERRY HERMAN All Rights Controlled by JERRYCO MUSIC CO. Exclusive Agent: EDWIN H. MORRIS & COMPANY, A Division of MPL Music Publishing, Inc. All Rights Reserved *Reprinted by Permission of Hal Leonard LLC*

Quotes from *The Ed Sullivan Show: "The Ed Sullivan Show"* © *SOFA Entertainment.*

Quotes from the correspondence of Goddard Lieberson, courtesy of the Lieberson estate.

Use of Cole Porter letter graciously permitted by the Cole Porter Literary Trust.

Stage directions from *South Pacific* and correspondence from Oscar Hammerstein II, courtesy of the Rodgers and Hammerstein Organization/Imagem.

About the Companion Website

www.oup.com/us/broadwaytomainstreet

The companion website provides more context and a musical landscape through which the reader can better understand the complex decisions at play during this cultural journey. The brief musical MP3 selections, each marked with ⏵, give the listener a chance to hear the various artists and performers who interpreted the Broadway songbook in unique and unusual ways: early Broadway recordings by Al Jolson; radio interviews with George Gershwin; rare dance band arrangements of Rodgers and Hart tunes; ground-breaking renditions of "forgotten" Broadway classics by Frank Sinatra and Ella Fitzgerald; demo recordings of "unsung" musicals written by revered songwriters, and a wide variety of exceptional cover renditions of great Broadway songs by an unexpected cohort of singers, from Bing Crosby to John Legend, and from Eydie Gormé to Jay-Z.

The quintessential 1950s show for the tired businessman, sauciness included. By permission of Sony Music.

House Seat

Music and the Private Space of Broadway

For millions of listeners, the music from Broadway begins when the curtain comes down.

Over dozens of theatrical seasons, from hundreds of shows, thousands of songs from Broadway have been unpacked by the consumer and enjoyed across America, on gramophones, on radios, on televisions, on hi-fi sets, on Walkmans, or on iTunes in living rooms, on subway trains, in coffee shops, gyms, and bedrooms. Broadway show tunes are public performances experienced in private spaces.

Lin-Manuel Miranda, talking about his score to *Hamilton*, said, "So when you have our cast album, you can go home and imagine your own version of *Hamilton* because, frankly, it's tough to get a ticket."[1] *Hamilton* can be seen by only 1,319 people a night on Broadway—which is about 10,000 people a week; the week the cast album was released digitally, it was downloaded by 50,000 people. More than a million people (and counting) have now listened to *Hamilton* in a private space. For enthusiasts of show music, the living room, to paraphrase one of Miranda's lyrics, *that's* the room where it happens.

For me, the room where it first happened was my parents' living room, in front of a battleship gray Garrard hi-fi set. The music came from a 1958 Columbia original cast recording of *Oh Captain!*. *Oh Captain!* was somewhat mechanically adapted from a then-recent Alec Guinness movie about a very proper married British sea captain who philanders his weekends away in another port of call. His wife decides to surprise him one weekend in Paris; she crosses paths with his lubricious mistress, and complications ensue. It was the kind of adaptation of high- or middle-shelf material, often of a British nature, that arrived on Broadway in the wake of *My Fair Lady*. The family legend purported that the album made its way into our living room because we were related to one of the two songwriters who composed the score, Jay Livingston or Ray Evans; no one ever seemed to know which. They were very talented Hollywood songwriters who delivered such massive postwar hits as "Buttons and Bows," "Mona Lisa," "Silver Bells," and "Que Sera, Sera." *Oh Captain!* was the first of the team's two forays on Broadway, an Everest of prestige for Hollywood songwriters, but often a tough and perilous climb.

Even though I grew up forty-five minutes from Broadway, as the song goes, I don't think that my parents even *saw* the show while it was running. The record was not particularly meaningful to our family other than its putative relation to Livingston (or Evans), but when I discovered the album sitting in my parents' record cabinet at the age of six or seven, it was pure enchantment. It didn't matter how the record got into our house, because it soon transported me many nautical miles away from our living room.

The first thing that stirred the imagination of an impressionable six-year-old right away was the album's cover: a saucy wench, obviously French, stirring some, well, *sauce* in a saucepan, wearing nothing but a frilly apron and a captain's hat, set at a rakish angle. Tony Randall starred as the eponymous captain of the title; he sang well enough and certainly put across the show's more jovial material, but even I intuited, at the tender age of six, that this was a different kind of singing than I heard on the radio from Dean Martin or Andy Williams. And the occasional line of spoken dialogue made me laugh, such as Randall's rationalization of his double-life: "It is absurd to imagine that the same woman who can cook up the kippers can kick up the capers." It wasn't exactly Oscar Wilde, but it seemed glamorous and sophisticated nonetheless.

▶   Audio Example F.1, "Three Paradises" (Tony Randall)

I might have referred to the plot synopsis squeezed onto the back of the album once or twice, but *Oh Captain!* worked its magic spell best when it spun and crackled on the phonograph. A six-note brass fanfare introduced the overture, went up a key and repeated, then ushered in a pit full of string players. Over the next 54 minutes (28 minutes on side one, then turn over for Act Two), I was transported to a proper English town, a ship traversing the English Channel, the hot spots of Montmartre's demi-monde, and, by the time the finale was over, to a happy ending.

Oh Captain! had opened and closed on Broadway within six months, but I didn't really need a ticket to see it live. The show that played on the phonograph and that played in my head was just as good—maybe better—as the show that played at the Alvin Theatre. It remained a cherished—and relatively private—memory of my childhood. And then one day years later, in a used record store, I noticed something very curious: there was an album with Rosemary Clooney and José Ferrer on the cover, each wearing captain's hats set at a rakish angle, winking at the buyer: *The Ferrers Sing Selections from the Broadway*

Musical Comedy Oh Captain! What was *that*? Who let Rosie Clooney and José Ferrer in on the secret of *Oh Captain!*?

What it was, I later learned, was the recording industry. There had always existed the imprimatur of Broadway—inaccessible to most, irresistible to many—that could be tapped and exploited by the recording industry for commercial purposes. And one of the easiest ways to peel off and disseminate some of that glamour was through the songs of Broadway; not necessarily, or even preferentially, the full score of a Broadway show, but its songs—its hits, its gems, its "selections." As it turned out, the selections album of *Oh Captain!* also revealed some behind-the-scenes machinations of the record business. Rosemary Clooney, who had been a Columbia mainstay for a dozen years, was married to the Academy Award-winning actor and director José Ferrer, who, not coincidentally, directed *Oh Captain!* on Broadway and co-adapted the show's book. Displeased at how she was being treated by Columbia, Clooney bolted from the label soon after *Oh Captain!* opened; her first move toward independence was recording a dozen or so selections from the score with Ferrer on the relatively new MGM label.[2]

What also became clear was that the Ferrers' album of "selections" was hardly a fluke, or the manifestation of a contractual temper tantrum. A Broadway show like *Oh Captain!*, written in the mid-1950s by two highly profitable songwriters, had the kind of prestige to inspire no less than four other albums "covering" show tunes in its score—"cover" being a useful, if general, term to describe performance renditions subsequent or alternate to any original Broadway rendition. One was an orchestral album by the Bob Prince Quartet called *Dancing with Oh Captain!*; another, far superior, album was a jazz rendition of the score, assembled by Leonard Feather and Dick Hyman with a breathtaking group of sidemen, including Coleman Hawkins and Harry "Sweets" Edison.

The songs from the show were attractive to singers, as well; Clooney had already covered two of *Oh Captain!*'s songs as a 45 rpm single while she was still at Columbia, released before the show even opened. Columbia had a lot at stake with *Oh Captain!*. Its executive vice president, Goddard Lieberson—the genius who had masterminded the blockbuster *My Fair Lady* cast album two seasons earlier—produced the cast recording. Not only would Columbia release the cast album but, based on their healthy relationship over the years with Livingston and Evans and their hit tunes, they invested in the show. Eager to promote their investment, Columbia turned to their A-list stable with a vengeance with the songs from *Oh Captain!*; in addition to Clooney, songs from the score were recorded for popular release by Tony Bennett, Jo Stafford, Vic Damone, the Norman Luboff Choir, and a recent addition to the roster, a young singer named Johnny Mathis.

Mathis released a particularly soothing single version of *Oh Captain*'s final, conciliatory ballad, "All the Time." A few months after the song hit the market, "All the Time" was ganged onto an album collection called *Johnny's Greatest Hits*, a Columbia LP generally considered to be the first "Greatest Hits" album ever released. It would go on to become one of the best-selling albums of all time, sitting on the *Billboard* charts for almost a decade, meaning that a little touch of *Oh Captain!* in the night circulated in pop music and the cultural consciousness for years after the show's demise. Indeed, a tenderly rendered song from *Oh Captain!* impressively transcended the only production of *Oh Captain!*.

▶ Audio Example F.2, "All the Time" (Johnny Mathis)

As *Variety* concisely put it, when reviewing one of the *Oh Captain!* cover albums, these popular recordings provided a "substitute or supplement" for those who hadn't seen the show on Broadway.[3] Another article in *Variety*, which ran the day that *Oh*

Captain!* opened, hinted at the range of American living rooms across the country that might provide a happy haven for *Oh Captain!* product, be it the Broadway cast album or a Johnny Mathis single: "Not only do the sets take off in New York, the point of origination, but in the grassroots, too, where hinterlanders are indoctrinated in Broadway product with extensive newspaper and magazine coverage."[4] If a fairly obscure and forgotten musical such as *Oh Captain!* spawned so many variations of "Broadway product," one can easily project the exponentially larger commercial reach of such hits as *South Pacific* or *My Fair Lady* or *The Sound of Music*.

As a youngster, I was, perversely perhaps, more attracted to *Oh Captain!* than such popular blockbusters; sitting in my living room—with its hi-fi set playing that particular score—I had the best seat in the house. But, as I grew older and expanded my repertoire of musical interests,

Tony Randall, torn apart by two lovers, in *Oh Captain!*. Jacquelyn McKeever (left), as his wife, made the Columbia original cast album. Abbe Lane (center), as his mistress, missed the boat: she was under contract for RCA and they wouldn't release her. Credit: Photofest.

Once the company of *Oh Captain!* arrived at Columbia Studios in February 1958, Abbe Lane had been replaced—for the album only—by Broadway stalwart Eileen Rodgers (left); Randall is still caught between the two ladies. By permission of Sony Music.

I began to wonder about all those other living rooms across America, in the grassroots, in the hinterlands. I wondered how show music—and how *much* show music—was transported to those private spaces; were listeners even aware how much of their music *was* show music? How did that music get from West 44th Street to the West Coast? There seemed to be a lot of highways and byways, expressways and access roads, sudden turns and detours on the caravan from Broadway to Main Street.

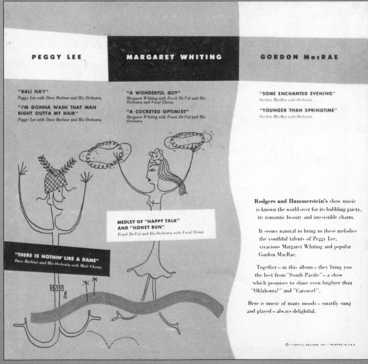

This Capitol set of eight songs from *South Pacific* featured their very deep bench of great singers; these recordings reached consumers in spring 1949, two months before the cast album recording on Columbia. Author's collection.

CHAPTER 1

Turn Over for Act Two

Content and the Context of Broadway

One more thing about *Oh Captain!*: The day the show opened, on February 4, 1958, Jay Livingston and Ray Evans gave a joint interview to *Variety* about what they wanted to accomplish with their score. Given that this was the first crack at a narrative musical from a team that had primarily written one-off hits for the movies or the pop charts, Livingston and Evans knew they had a different set of challenges ahead. "When a show tune becomes a hit, it's mostly accidental," they said. "A show tune is written with an eye and ear to the production value as a whole and not as a single entity."[1]

All songs have content. Tin Pan Alley songs, pop songs, and rock songs nearly always are written with discretely contained content. Their limited parameters are their raison d'etre; they are consciously detachable, and as such, require little or no contextual explanation. However, because they were originally written for shows—"the production value as a whole"—songs from Broadway also have context. They have team spirit—like relay race runners, Broadway tunes pass the baton of narrative from one song to the other, until the show reaches the finish line; if one of those runners fails or falters, the relay cannot be completed and the race is lost. The songs of Broadway are more complex than most: they function in one way when they're "single entities" and in another way when they're part of a larger narrative.

Historically, the songs of Broadway—show tunes unfettered by dramatic context—have caught the attention of the public in advance of their larger narrative, and have held a respected position in popular music for decades, more pertinent and more persuasive than many observers and critics realize. Whether they are conscious of it or not, everyone knows at least one show tune, and for decades practically every family had at least one cast album in the record cabinet or a cassette of show music in the glove compartment of the car. The music of Broadway is not a genre in opposition to pop music; the sound of Broadway was—and remains—popular music.

Many show tunes have become popular standards without even the nominal support of a contextualizing cast recording made during its original production. A large number of these songs from the 1920s, 30s, and 40s were consistently hobbled in their day by technical or commercial considerations that brought them even farther afield from their original context in the production where they were introduced. They were either never recorded while the show itself was running on Broadway; never recorded as intended by the songwriters; never recorded with the original lyrics as written for the stage production; or in some cases, never recorded at all. Occasionally, they were rediscovered later in the century by singers who never performed in a Broadway show and never would. These songs would be reinterpreted in new arrangements, spun in unpredictable ways by performers with their own takes on the material, occasionally contextualized in "songbooks" that highlighted the songwriters, without regard to the nature, order, or intent of the musicals for which they were created.

Granted, theater songwriters wrote in the service of narrative more frequently after World War II, but even in the early 1920s (and even in the revue format), there was always the imperative to write to some sort of context for the stage—even if the rationale was as mundane as "the producer's girlfriend needs a love duet with the boy." Among the best of the stage musicals of the 1920s, 30s, and early 40s—*Show Boat,* certainly, and *Of Thee I Sing, The Cradle Will Rock, The Boys from Syracuse, Lady in the Dark*—songs were tailored by brilliant musical tunesmiths to achieve specific storytelling ends, often with specific performers, even if subsequent generations of musicians and performers have obliterated their original context while transforming the songs into accessible tunes for the popular consumption. Take these three songs, for example: "Can't Help Lovin' Dat Man," "Supper Time," and "Have You Met Miss Jones?." Each has become a "standard" on its own terms, superb examples of craftsmanship that also resonated with musicians, performers, and audiences in a variety of venues. Yet, the original context for which these songs were written dictated character, situation, and narrative in fairly determinate ways. "Can't Help Lovin' Dat Man" (from *Show Boat*) foreshadows the tortured racial background of its supporting heroine. "Supper Time" (from *As Thousands Cheer*) was framed (literally) by the pain and racial isolation of lynching. "Have You Met Miss Jones?" is the way a young man convinces Franklin D. Roosevelt's cabinet members to balance the Federal budget so that he can have enough money to marry his fiancée, the eponymous Miss Jones. (This last is all true, courtesy of Rodgers and Hart's 1937 spoof, *I'd Rather Be Right*.)

With the rise in narrative musicals post-*Oklahoma!*, songs had to tote even more contextual barges than convincing the New Deal cabinet to balance the budget. Of course, there was always room for a romantic ballad to hit the pop charts as a single or as a tune suitable for a dance orchestra, but character, situation, and the relation of one song to another became more complex. By the early 1950s, there was a shift in how show tunes might be marketed for a popular audience. For some Broadway songwriters, it was a delicate balance between the generic appeal of a potential hit single and the specificity of a narrative context that might imperil a song's longevity in the commercial market. In 1959, when Stephen Sondheim brought the lyrics for "Small World," a ballad intended to be sung by Ethel Merman, as a mother with children in Act One of *Gypsy*, to composer Jule Styne—a very commercially minded and highly excitable fellow—Styne supposedly flipped. "It can't say 'Lucky, I'm a woman with children'—for Christ's sake! How is a *guy* supposed to record a cover version of the song?!" This sensible imprecation didn't stop Johnny Mathis from having a huge pop hit when he changed the lyric to "Lucky, 'cause I'd like to have children." When he turned to writing the music and lyrics of his own material in the 1960s and 70s, Sondheim made contextual specificity the hallmark of his work—the pop charts be damned.

In his review of *American Musicals (1927–1969): The Complete Book and Lyrics to Sixteen Broadway Classics* (full disclosure: edited by this author), critic Michael Anderson asserted in *The New Criterion* that "the only songs from the shows in *American Musicals* to become standards in the American Songbook were written by lyricists well-established before the revolution of *Oklahoma!*... Only one Rodgers and Hammerstein song—'Some Enchanted Evening'—enjoyed contemporary popularity."[2] This is an ill-formed assessment that assumes, somehow, after World War II the pop market diverged from the show tune market and left it behind. Not only was "People Will Say We're in Love" from *Oklahoma!*, as recorded by Bing Crosby and Trudy Erwin, a No. 1 hit in 1943 for two weeks in a row, but many Broadway songs recorded years after "Some Enchanted Evening" made it to No. 1 on the charts: "Wish You Were Here" from the musical of the same name; "Hey There" from *The Pajama Game*; even "No Other Love," from an obscure 1953 musical by Rodgers and Hammerstein called *Me and Juliet*. This doesn't even account for the dozens of Broadway songs that proliferated on the pop charts into the 1970s: "So in Love," "Bali Ha'i," "On the Street Where You Live," "I'll Never Fall in Love Again," and, especially, Louis Armstrong's rendition of "Hello, Dolly!," which famously became the No. 1 song in America at the height of Beatlemania.

Certainly, by the time one gets to "Some Enchanted Evening" in 1949, shows (that is, scores from shows) became equally popular with the public as songs. Part of this appeal was a matter of timing; only a few years after *Oklahoma!,* technology provided a platform where songs could be better contextualized within an extended storyline: the long-playing record, or LP. The LP served the narrative needs of the home consumer in much the same way the narrative musical of Broadway's Golden Age served the tastes of the-atergoers who attended the productions. The original cast album soon became a commercial commodity that would transcend generations, tastes, and genres, and provide a rare commonality within American households.

The original cast album, as an amalgam of disparate elements into a narrative context, is not without its own paradoxes as a product for home entertainment. Perhaps the most disjunctive element is the idea of listening to music composed for a theatrical event—with sets, costumes, choreography, spontaneous performance—in one's living room, carved up and repurposed for a secondary, and perhaps inferior, experience. David Byrne, former leader of the Talking Heads and an accomplished composer, wrote about this cognitive dissonance from a rock performer's point of view: "The performing musician is now expected to write and create for two very different spaces: the live venue and the device that could play a recording or receive a transmission. Socially and acoustically, these spaces were worlds apart. But the compositions were expected to be the same!...These two demands seem unfair to me."[3]

Why, then, would recordings of scores from Broadway shows—either as full cast albums, or even as single "cover" renditions—be successful in any way, compromised as they are, worlds apart from their original intent and venue? Unlike a random collection of pop singles, Broadway scores rely on connective narrative tissue. Unlike jazz albums or concert albums, they are almost never recorded in front of the audiences that their creators sought to entertain. Unlike albums built around gifted singing superstars, they deliver a variety of performers—often with varying musical abilities—to the listener. Unlike symphonic or even opera recordings, they are selectively edited down from the scope of their original design. Unlike soundtrack albums, they are not even necessarily definitive.

As Byrne writes in his 2012 book, *How Music Works:* "Recording is far from an objective acoustic mirror, but...to its promoters, it is a mirror that shows you how you looked at a particular moment, over and over, again and again. Creepy...also untrue."[4] Cast albums are imperfect mirrors of a particular moment that has come and gone—limitation is part of their definition, perhaps even of their illusory charm. One of the best Broadway album producers is Jay David Saks, who produced, among many other albums, several of Stephen Sondheim's cast recordings from the 1980s for RCA. He sums up the paradox eloquently: "The best compliment one can receive as a Broadway producer is to hear that it sounds like it's in the theater. In fact, if we actually did it like it's in the theater, it wouldn't sound very good at all, but it creates that illusion."[5]

The important collaborator in that illusion is the listener. As early as 1966, the brilliant pianist and essayist Glenn Gould intuited that the home listener might prefer to play with music than to have music played at him: "At the center of the technological debate, then, is a new kind of listener—a listener more participant in the musical experience…[This] listener is able to indulge preferences and, through the electronic modifications with which he endows the listening experience, impose his own personality upon the work. As he does so, he transforms that work, and his relation to it, from an artistic to an environmental experience."[6]

Few genres of recording are more tolerant of the imposition of personality than music from Broadway, particularly with the narrative construct of the original cast album, which can function as a potent expressway between two destinations: Broadway and Main Street. The original cast album can bring Broadway to the listener's Main Street, a potent reminder, souvenir, and keepsake of a beloved two-and-a-half hours in the theater. According to composer John Kander, "From my point of view, [cast albums] are very happy reminders of the experience. I prefer an album to feel like you're watching the show, a little bit." On the other hand, a cast album can bring the listener from Main Street to Broadway, as the back cover for a 1946 album of 78s for *St. Louis Woman* put it, "for those listeners who will not be able to make the trip to the Majestic Theater to see this masterpiece." Composer/lyricist Stephen Schwartz splits the difference: "I think a good album is one that's a combination: it can stand on its own musically as a recording and invite repeated listenings, and can also convey a sense of the experience of having seen the show."[7]

When cast albums rode the crest of LP technology out of the 1940s, they represented a new commitment to the listening experience; they were not just mindless collections of pop hits to be casually disregarded as background noise while vacuuming the carpet. Attention had to be paid—and millions of consumers did pay attention. Between 1945 and 1969—twenty-five of the most fertile and febrile years in popular music—thirteen different original cast albums hit No. 1 on the *Billboard* charts for *at least* one week—not on the "Cast Albums" chart (which didn't even exist as a separate category during those decades), but on the charts that reflected all the albums in every genre of popular music. Taken together, those thirteen original cast albums—not only *My Fair Lady* and *The Sound of Music*, but lesser-known titles such as *Flower Drum Song* and *Carnival*—tallied more weeks at No. 1 than all of the albums, during those same years, by Frank Sinatra and The Beatles put together. If one factors in the soundtrack albums directly derived from Broadway scores during those same decades (*Oklahoma!*, *West Side Story*, etc.), the number of weeks at No. 1 for albums of Broadway-originated material surpasses all the weeks at No. 1 of albums by The Beatles, Sinatra, Elvis Presley, The Rolling Stones, and The Monkees *combined.*

At a recording session for *Juno* in March 1959, composer/lyricist Marc Blitzstein, producer Goddard Lieberson, and star Shirley Booth listen to playback. Blitzstein and Lieberson, each in his own way, would trailblaze the territory of Broadway recording. By permission of Sony Music

To ask why theater music is so popular in America is a question that can, on one level, be answered very simply by even the briefest sampling of the work of Jerome Kern, Richard Rodgers with Hart and Hammerstein, George and Ira Gershwin, Cole Porter, Lerner and Loewe, Stephen Sondheim, and so on. However, what's more complex are the ways in which that music penetrated the consciousness and living rooms of generations of Americans; how it was produced, performed, formatted, designed, and delivered to the public. The history of this transmission weaves in strands of taste and technology, labor issues and liner notes, publishers and producers, record clubs and royalty arrangements, financing and formats. Over the decades, these attempts to transmit the public excitement of a live Broadway performance to the personal space of a private listener covers a wide range of techniques and media: sheet music, popular "cover" recordings, radio, movies, television, LPs, compact discs, digital streaming, and, of course, original cast albums. Although, for many, cast albums may embody the gold standard when it comes to memorializing Broadway material, they are hardly the only medium to do so, and have to be seen in the context of what came before and what comes concurrently. As technology evolves into the digital streaming age, listeners have more agency to move between songs and story, even to reconstruct what part of the Broadway narrative they want to hear and how they want to hear it.

Distinct among all genres of popular music, show music is the only genre to exist in the *past*—as a souvenir of a production; in the *present*—as a song to be enjoyed in the moment; and in the *future*—as a prospect of a theatrical event yet to be savored. From the stages of Broadway's legacy, a singer from *Cats* implored the listener to "let the memory live again;" Cole Porter exhorted the listener to "use your imagination;" in *A Little Night Music,* Stephen Sondheim tantalized the listener with "perpetual anticipation." Memory, imagination, anticipation—three magic words that have brought the incantation of Broadway to millions of listeners from the very beginning.

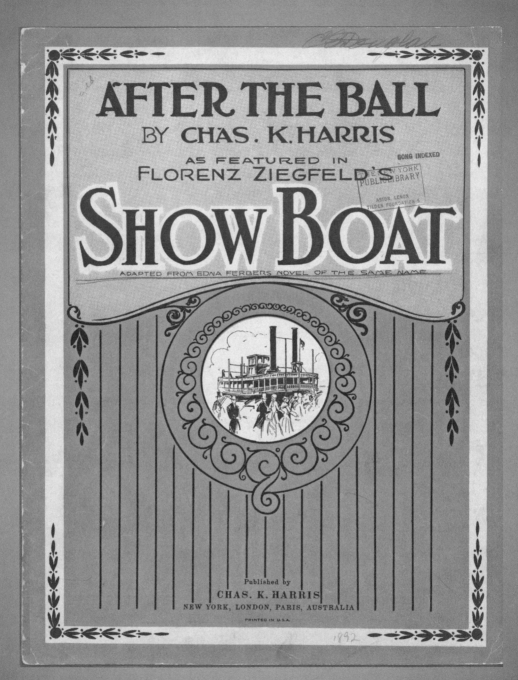

"After the Ball" was one of America's first megahits back in 1893; it hitched itself to the Broadway star of *Show Boat* thirty-four years later. Courtesy of The New York Public Library.

CHAPTER 2

The Jewish Population of Tennessee

Sheet Music and the Imprimatur of Broadway

In spring 1961, stepping out of the shadows of his only two collaborators, Richard Rodgers took the rather bold step of writing his own lyrics to an original stage musical, *No Strings*, a contemporary musical set among the fashionistas and photographers in Paris. The show's romance centered around a white photographer and a black fashion model, whose racial background was never directly mentioned. Her home address, back in the States, was, in Rodgers's lyric: "up north of Central Park."

Perhaps Rodgers was simply being nostalgic; he was raised up north of Central Park, in a brownstone at 3 West 120th Street, the home of his maternal grandparents. "The main object in the [living] room—indeed in the house, indeed in my life—was the Steinway upright near the window," he wrote in his memoir, *Musical Stages*.[1] "It was then that I learned that exciting sounds came from the piano when my mother played it. This was the beginning of my lifelong love affair with music." Growing up in a fractious household during the very beginning of the twentieth century, Rodgers sought some refuge in the living room with the "lovely piano which my mother played so beautifully while she and my father sang." And what did they play and sing?

Songs from the current musical shows on Broadway. Both my parents were avid theatergoers, with a special passion for musicals, and since the complete vocal-piano score was always sold in the theater lobby, Pop never failed to buy a copy. So home would come *Mlle. Modiste, The Merry Widow, The Chocolate Soldier* and all the rest to go up on the piano rack. They would be played so often, both before and after dinner, that I soon knew all the songs by heart.[2]

What kind of alternate musical theater universe might we have inherited if Rodgers's father had only brought the sheet music to the hit songs of those shows—the "gems," as the publishers called them—"Kiss Me Again," or "Vilja," or "My Hero," respectively— each of which were available in convenient copies that cost 40 or 50 cents each? Thankfully his father plumped two whole dollars for the full vocal score, which contained all the major songs of the operetta in question.

The vocal score to Victor Herbert's *Mlle. Modiste* was more than 150 pages long, filled with nearly a dozen songs, plus an overture, several finales, and a ballet. When Rodgers grew up to become one of America's greatest popular composers, he had an instinctive gift for melody that placed him solidly among his rarified peers. What he possessed beyond the talented songwriters of his generation was his ability to understand and master the *architecture* of a musical score—when to create alternations among solos, duets, trios, and ensemble numbers; when to juxtapose a comic number with a ballad; when to add a dance break; when to reprise a musical number and how to do it. Rodgers knew how to *build* musicals because the vocal scores he enjoyed as a youngster showed him the way.

Sitting in his living room, hearing his mother playing the full piano scores, Rodgers was experiencing the fullest possible range of a Broadway score, given the technology of his time: the vocal score was an "album"—a repository of musical memories for home consumption. The journey of show music from Broadway to the living rooms of millions of Americans, even those up north of Central Park, would begin with a family piano, reams of sheet music with colorful covers, and the single-minded entrepreneurs who placed them in the same room.

Shortly before his eighth birthday, Rodgers was brought to his first Broadway show, a Saturday matinee of another Herbert comic operetta, *Little Nemo*, at the New Amsterdam Theatre. This was particularly appealing to Rodgers, as the show was based on the surreal Sunday funnies adventures conjured up by cartoonist extraordinaire, Winsor McCay. The score was one "which I [had] heard my parents play and sing for weeks until I knew every note and word." By the end of the first decade of the twentieth century, Rodgers had not only learned the full scores of the musicals his parents had seen, but skipped eagerly into the lobby of the New Amsterdam to experience a score that had already enchanted him at home.[3]

Following the Civil War, the home became the center of family entertainment. Any middle-class family—or lower middle-class family with aspirations—had a piano in the parlor, just like the Rodgers family. Sheet music had been part of the country's home entertainment culture since the mid-nineteenth century, with various folk tunes, church music, choir arrangements, and Stephen Foster songs making their way into parlors and congregations around the country.

Several economic and social factors combined at the end of the nineteenth century to create a more evolved industry for sheet music, based largely in New York City, and, eventually and more specifically, on a short block of West 28th Street that wended its way through nearly every living room in America: what would be called Tin Pan Alley, a phrase reportedly coined from the profusion of pianos banging away from every open office window, like so many tin pans.

Tin Pan Alley, one of the most rapacious and influential industries in American popular culture, owed its existence to the would-be songwriters and tunesmiths who felt exploited by the more long-standing publishers and sought to protect their own intellectual property—however rudimentary—by founding their own firms. The pioneers of Tin Pan Alley bypassed Boston, Philadelphia, and Chicago—which were the headquarters for tonier musical genres, such as hymnals or classical orchestrations—to set up shop in New York City, the logical epicenter for the popular music publishing business. New York had its fingers on the pulse of popular entertainment of the time, such as music halls, vaudeville, burlesque, and nickelodeons. Equally important, New York began to consolidate the ancillary industries of performance itself: managers, booking agents, costumers, and so forth. By 1900, if a song was going to travel into the front parlors of Appleton, Wisconsin, or Lancaster, Pennsylvania, it would be hopping a train set up for a cross-country tour that pulled out of New York.

The sheet music firm of M. Witmark & Sons built itself in 1886 around publishing novelty numbers and was soon followed by T. B. Harms, the first firm to focus on the bounty of theatrical tunes coming from the New York stage. In 1892, Harms published a volume of vocal selections from Charles Hoyt's phenomenon *A Trip to Chinatown*. The show, which opened the year before, would go on to run 657 performances; it was a mélange of comedy and music, about some humorous misunderstandings born out of a night on the town—it predated Thornton Wilder's *Merchant of Yonkers*, which was predated by an Austrian musical comedy by Johann Nestroy (itself predated by a British opera). Still, the buoyant tunes by Percy Gaunt, along with Hoyt's lyrics, were well-served by the portmanteau quality of the plot and allowed for a free-and-easy compliance to conventional narrative. Harms' collection of songs included "The Chaperone," "The Widow," "Reuben and Cynthia," "Out for a Racket," and its smash hit, "The Bowery," which would be persistent enough to make it into television commercials for New York City's Bowery Savings Bank almost a century after its debut.[4]

A Trip to Chinatown was so successful in its day that it immediately spawned several touring companies. As luck would have it, a run in the Midwest would change the fortunes of an aspiring songwriter named Charles K. Harris and clear the trail for the juggernaut of popular music in the next century. Harris (whose previous novelty numbers included "Bake That Matzoh Pie") was based out of Milwaukee, and, one night when he was visiting an elegant eatery in Chicago, he overheard an encounter between a couple which revealed the end of a love affair, because of a fatal misunderstanding. Harris was inspired by this anecdote to concoct a lilting waltz with the poignant refrain: "Many a heart is aching, if you could read them all / Many the hopes that have vanished after the ball." Harris had gotten nowhere with his song, but through the genius of self-promotion (and some chicanery), he convinced a leading singer of the day, J. Aldrich Libbey, who was appearing in the *A Trip to Chinatown* tour, to interpolate "After the Ball" into the second act. The number stopped the show cold and sparked a spontaneous singalong with the audience.

Harris's story has several punch lines, starting with the fact that "After the Ball" became the first blockbuster "single" in pop music history. Its popularity was so immediately apparent that the Witmark firm in New York offered Harris $10,000 for the publication rights; if they were worth that much to Witmark, Harris reasoned, then the rights should be worth at least $20,000. He underestimated: "After the Ball," published by the Charles K. Harris firm in Milwaukee, sold one million copies of sheet music within its first year, and went on to sell another four million copies, transforming Harris into a millionaire.[5]

▶   Audio Example 2.1, "After the Ball" (Joan Morris)

The second punch line arrived thirty-four years later. When Oscar Hammerstein II and Jerome Kern were engineering the epic sweep of their musical version of Edna Ferber's *Show Boat*, they needed a musical number to be sung from the stage of the Trocadero Music Hall, one of Chicago's finer entertainment establishments, on New Year's Eve, 1904. They were certainly capable of concocting an original song of their own, but in a clever act of storytelling (and a generous act it was as well), they allowed their leading lady, Magnolia, to lead the revelers in a rendition of "After the Ball," cheered on by her father, Cap'n Andy, who has coincidentally wandered into the Trocadero. "After the Ball" was the perfect song to introduce to the crowd for a singalong in 1904, and thereby fulfills an essential narrative function in *Show Boat*.

The third, and perhaps its most enduring commercial, implication of "After the Ball" is its presentation in print. Harms had originally published a nondescript folio of songs from *A Trip to Chinatown* the year before. Harris one-upped them by publishing his own sheet music of "After the Ball" with a robust photo of its acclaimed interpreter, J. Aldrich Libbey, and the words "As sung in 'A Trip to Chinatown'" prominently displayed under the song's title. Thus "After the Ball" became the first song branded and marketed with an all-important consumer trifecta: it promoted a hit song, a hit show, and a celebrity, all on the same page.

As the nineteenth century transitioned into the twentieth, the most popular form of family entertainment was still sitting around the front parlor piano, and the sheet music industry was making its commodity more attractive and more attainable. Cover graphics became bolder and more colorful; there were music stores devoted to the sale of sheet music, and the burgeoning department store business added sheet music counters—between 1893 and 1896, such counters had grown from 50,000 to 250,000 across the country. The individual songs were not inexpensive—they retailed from 40 to 60 cents (although prices dropped by almost 50 percent by the 1920s)—and it cost the publishers roughly $2,500 to print 10,000 copies of sheet music, plus distribution. It was an efficient and bountiful industry; between 1900 and 1910, almost a hundred songs sold more than a million copies.[6]

These immensely popular Tin Pan Alley one-offs required no greater context, nor could they really be shoehorned into an extended narrative—*Show Boat* notwithstanding. American life—its mores, predilections, its rosy-hued vision of itself—*that* was the context. The content of these songs could also be attractive devoid of any specific context. Chaste sweethearts, broken romances, the innocence of youth, the novelty of technology, and the transcendent wisdom of Mother were just a few of the more popular tropes. When all else failed, one could always appeal to the nostalgia of the hometown that one left behind; there were songs about every state in the Union and just about every neighborhood anyone ever lived in. A character in Ring Lardner and George S. Kaufman's 1929 spoof of Tin Pan Alley, *June Moon,* observes, "If song-writers always wrote about their home state, what a big Jewish population Tennessee must have."

Parallel to the explosion of sheet music on the national market, the entertainment form of vaudeville gained prominence on the American scene. As David Ewen put it, "vaudevillians, carrying a song on a circuit touching every major American city and many of the smaller ones, became a powerful agency for promotion. The range could extend nationally and [a song] could be kept in the repertory for years."[7] It was a symbiotic relationship for a performer to get a song and for a song to become linked to a performer. Some of those relationships could last nearly a lifetime—or at least a career. "Some of These Days" by the African American composer Shelton Brooks barely made a ripple when it was published in 1910 with a fairly indistinct cover. When Sophie Tucker picked up the song and put it across, her picture—framed by the line "re-introduced to the American public by the Great and Only Sophie Tucker"—was promptly and prominently added to front of the sheet music. It became a million-plus seller, and she sang it for the next fifty years.

The imprimatur of a touring vaudevillian rested squarely on her or his shoulders, but the cachet of a show emanating out of New York, to quote another hit, from *Madame Sherry,* "had a meaning all its own" and the music publishers did everything in their power to exploit the connection. "Tell Me, Pretty Maiden," the breakout tune from 1900's

Floradora featured a photograph of the famed Floradora girls on the cover. Broadway personalities were similarly promoted: cartoons of George M. Cohan in various jaunty poses adorned the covers of most of his Broadway sheet music. Al Jolson's ingratiating mug was plastered on the cover of "The Spaniard That Blighted My Life," his first big hit song from *The Honeymoon Express* in 1911. Jolson was so integral to a song's success that budding songwriters often cut him in for a royalty and a credit, just to ensure his participation; the bigger a star that Jolson became, the bigger his face grew on the sheet music cover. Perhaps no songs carried more cachet than those from the near-annual *Ziegfeld Follies*. From their inception in 1907, under the careful and tasteful guidance of their producer, Florenz Ziegfeld, Jr., the *Follies* offerings were Broadway's most glamorous and most representative of the commercial potential of the Great White Way; not surprisingly, the songs published from the *Follies* have a sheen and elegance unmatched by their peers. Where a one-off popular hit of the 1914, say, "Down Among the Sheltering Palms," had a literal-minded two-color cover, a song from the *Follies* that year had a beautiful four-color print of an alluring showgirl bending forward into a mirror, the better to inspect her unique beauty and charm.

Ziegfeld, of course, was also renowned for his discovery and promotion of performers who would emerge as the biggest stars on Broadway. "Nobody"—the trademark song of the African American entertainer Bert Williams—had already been published in 1909 before he entered the ranks of the *Follies*, with his face on the cover (blacked-up, as he always appeared on stage). By 1919, with "The Moon Shines on the Moonshine," the anti-Prohibition comedy song that knocked 'em dead in that year's *Follies*, he appeared in full regalia on the cover of the sheet music, which promoted Williams, the song, and the *Follies* affiliation in equal measure. Fanny Brice's trademark number, "My Man," came into the *Follies* repertoire two years later; when Leo Feist published the sheet music in 1921, the song and the show were highly promoted, as was "Sung by Miss Fanny Brice," with a soulful photo of Fanny on the cover. (Feist would repurpose the sheet music with an even bigger photo of Brice to cross-promote a Vitaphone 1928 movie with the same title.)

However, the performer who took the most advantage of the Broadway synergy invoked by the cross-pollination of show, song, and star was Eddie Cantor. Cantor skyrocketed to stardom in the *Follies of 1917* with his unique blend of comedy, sentimentality, and ethnic charm. Although Cantor usually appeared on sheet music covers with his arms folded, in a rakish dignity, "I Want My Mammy"—sung by Cantor in *The Midnight Rounders of 1921*—portrays the star in all his customary blackface goofiness, twenty stories tall among the sparkling marquees of Broadway. It was the kind of trope that would be repeated over and over again as a mythic vision of the Great White Way. Publisher Shapiro, Bernstein & Co. was promoting the magic of Broadway, available for anyone with a piano and pocket change, no matter on which Main Street they lived.

For the first few decades of the twentieth century, the Broadway world exploded with revues like the *Follies* and *The Midnight Rounders*; the rough-and-ready disregard for narrative context made it particularly easy for publishers to place songs with performers and performers with songs in productions. Given that the publishers had full control of a highly valued product—the songs—if they had enough imagination about songwriters and repertory, they could wield a tremendous amount of power in the entertainment industry. The economic juggernaut of Tin Pan Alley brought along its own consequences, which came to a head in 1914, when a delegation of composers, lyricists, and publishers met at New York's pre-eminent German restaurant, Lüchow's, to resolve, among other issues, unfair competitive practices, as well as their clients' rights to copyright protection and royalty payments. The group turned to composer Victor Herbert, the most prominent of the lot, to lead them; they constituted themselves as the "American Society of Composers, Authors and Publishers," known to posterity as ASCAP. The following year, a test case against uncompensated performance went as far as the Supreme Court, where no less august a figure than Associate Chief Justice Oliver Wendell Holmes, Jr. ruled in ASCAP's favor.[8]

This decision would seal the transaction between publishers and the public for the next century. If one wanted to perform an ASCAP product live, one had to acquire performance rights and pay the compensatory royalties required; later on, as technology progressed, if one wanted to reproduce an ASCAP product on a machine—on the phonograph or on the radio—one had to acquire the mechanical rights and pay the compensatory royalties required. It was that simple—although the infinite granular struggles derived from that equation would be a source of constant conflict up until the present day. Still, the existence of ASCAP would transform a disparate group of salesmen, managers, and song pluggers into a powerful and prosperous industry.

There were many powerful Tin Pan Alley publishers—Leo Feist, Witmark, Shapiro-Bernstein, even Irving Berlin—but the most eminent was Max Dreyfus; he would not only represent Broadway's A-list composers for most of the twentieth century, he determined the direction of their careers and, in doing so, help to chart the course of the popular music industry.

Dreyfus was born in Germany and came to America in 1888, at the age of 14. He tried to make it as a piano player and composer, but was forced to take on whatever musical odd jobs he could (Richard Rodgers recounted, somewhat incredulously, that Dreyfus had played cornet on a riverboat).[9] Eventually, he found his way to the T. B. Harms firm, where he made himself indispensible as a song plugger, arranger, and eventually the company manager. By 1904, he had bought out the Harms brothers (while keeping the firm's prestigious name) and started matching composers with material, wielding an acumen that set him above his competitors.

Soon upon assuming the top job, he was approached by a young, classically trained songwriter named Jerome Kern who wanted to expand his talents and learn about the popular music business. As quoted by David Ewen, Dreyfus said, "[Kern] said he wanted to imbibe the atmosphere of music. I decided to take him on, and to start him off by giving him the toughest job I had—selling music."[10] Dreyfus assigned Kern to the Hudson Valley territory. "He was good. He was full of youthful spirit, and with it a certain charm. He sold music," Dreyfus recalled.[11] When a British musical, *The Earl and the Girl*, made its way to Broadway, it was felt some sprightlier American tunes could be interpolated. In 1905, Dreyfus used his clout to get a Kern tune—"How'd You Like to Spoon With Me?"—into the show, and Kern's career was off and running. Kern eventually made so much money for Dreyfus that he became a partner in Harms; for the rest of his four decades as one of America's most successful composers he never worked with another publisher.

Dreyfus's discriminating eye for talent extended to a precociously brilliant young song plugger from Remick's—George Gershwin. Still in his teens, Gershwin had ambitions beyond his years, and the grinding post at Remick's was in his way. He applied to Irving Berlin for a gig as his musical secretary, but Berlin felt that Gershwin was destined for greater things as a composer and encouraged him to move on. Finally, in 1917, Gershwin went to Dreyfus. As he had with Kern, Dreyfus felt he had a creative young man with industry in Gershwin: "He was the kind of man I like to gamble on, and I decided to gamble."[12] Gershwin was hired for $35 a week as a kind of research and development man, without any fixed duties other than the obligation to send any worthwhile tunes into, as it were, Harms's way. Within two years, Dreyfus's investment paid off: Gershwin contributed to the score of *La, La, Lucille* in 1919 and by the end of the decade had a phenomenal hit with "Swanee," once Al Jolson picked it up and added it to his repertoire. Again, Dreyfus would remain Gershwin's trusted consigliere and promoter for the rest of his life. He soon added Cole Porter, Vincent Youmans, Irving Caesar, Buddy DeSylva, Lew Brown, Ray Henderson, and Sigmund Romberg to the Harms stable.

With such a track record, it was no surprise that a teenaged Richard Rodgers thought of Harms as "the Tiffany of the music publishing business."[13] Through a family connection, Rodgers got an appointment with Harms to play some of his music for Louis Dreyfus, Max's brother, who also was a gatekeeper of the firm. The brother suggested that Rodgers go back to high school instead. After Rodgers had teamed up with lyricist Lorenz Hart in 1919, he spent most of the early 1920s looking for his big break. A producer with an interest in Rodgers brought him back to Harms in 1924, this time to audition for Max Dreyfus himself, and the eager Rodgers played through his portfolio, including the breezy number that would eventually become "Manhattan." "You couldn't tell by looking at him whether he liked something," Rodgers told a journalist decades later. "He was not very enthusiastic."[14] In fact, Dreyfus opined that there was "nothing of great value here" and passed.

A minor hit from a major venue: the bright lights of Broadway appealed to consumers on Main Streets across the country. Author's collection.

Rodgers was crushed; not only were his idols handled by Harms, "to have a T. B. Harms label on the songs of Rodgers and Hart [would be] an unqualified sign of prestige."[15] A year later, Rodgers and Hart became the darlings of Broadway with "Manhattan," placed in the *Garrick Gaieties* and a book musical set in Revolutionary War New York, *Dearest Enemy*. The composer was immediately summoned to Harms by Dreyfus and offered a spot in the illustrious stable. But why, Dreyfus, wondered, had Rodgers not played "Manhattan" for him when they met last year? Rodgers, emboldened by his hard-earned acceptance, replied that Dreyfus didn't think much of the tune. Dreyfus shrugged, and began a decades-long relationship with Rodgers. "He said nobody could tell if a song would become a hit but that it might become one if you worked to sell it," said Rodgers. "He knew how and where to promote a song."[16]

Dreyfus was, along with his more discriminating publisher comrades, the creator of a role that would become prominent in the recording field years later: the artist and repertory producer, or the A & R man. In Dreyfus's case, he was more of a "W & R" man: writing and repertory. Dreyfus knew that hits were not born, they were made. The music publisher emerged as the first industry leader to wield judgment over how a song could be packaged and repurposed, designed and realigned. Moreover, in the growing empire of popular music—which would soon include the phonograph and the radio—the song was a weapon to wield in order to win a commercial war. The endgame of that war was to launch a song—preferably a salvo of songs—into every living room in America.

Music publisher extraordinaire Max Dreyfus (l.) working with lyricist Ira Gershwin, perhaps selecting which songs from *Park Avenue* (1946) might make it to the Hit Parade; alas, in this rare instance, none did. Credit: Photofest.

The collaboration between Rodgers and Dreyfus, as composer and promoter, would extend five decades into the future. They would continue to place Broadway songs and scores in living rooms, using ever-evolving media, so that generations of families could enjoy Rodgers's tunes "played so often, both before and after dinner," as he said about his own experience in the living room, "that I soon knew all the songs by heart."

Jolson was such a big star that the ordinary dull brown envelopes that usually contained 78s were "Gus"-sied up for his celebrity. Author's collection.

CHAPTER 3

Face the Music (and Dance)
The Gramophone and the Voice of Broadway

For nearly three minutes, a time-capsule of the 1920s is captured on a recording of a toe-tapping Fred Astaire, accompanied by his hard-driving, yet perfectly fluent accompanist, George Gershwin. In the middle of the unexpected dance break of the "'The Half of It, Dearie,' Blues," Astaire calls out:

"How's that, George?"
"Pretty good, Freddy!"
"That's *fine*!"

The effusive repartee is startlingly spontaneous—as is Astaire's "woo-hoo!" toward the end of the song. Gershwin playing, Astaire dancing, a great tune from *Lady, Be Good!*: together, it's a moment of pure, unadulterated Broadway joy at its most effervescent.

▶   Audio Example 3.1, "The Half of It, Dearie, Blues" (Fred Astaire and
     George Gershwin)

Except it really has nothing to do with Broadway. That particular once-in-a-lifetime rendition of "'The Half of It, Dearie,' Blues" was actually recorded in London one week after *Lady, Be Good!* opened its West End engagement. The Astaires had taken New York by storm with *Lady, Be Good!* two years earlier in George and Ira Gershwin's first full-length score for a book musical. The songs for that production included "Fascinatin' Rhythm" and "Hang on to Me"—both successful duets for the Astaires. Yet none of that score was recorded in New York during the run of the show; instead, the number was recorded in London on April 20, 1926, at Columbia Studios, while George was overseas to help mount the show. The two disks of Gershwin/Astaires renditions from the London *Lady, Be Good!* wouldn't be commercially available in New York, unless they were brought over by some good-natured traveler on the Normandie. When and if those recordings became available for Broadway connoisseurs, *Lady, Be Good!* would be long gone from the boards. Fred and Adele Astaire—perhaps Broadway's most beloved performance couple of the 1920s—wouldn't record a Broadway song in the United States until 1931, nearly fourteen years after their New York stage debut.[1]

This paradox was central to the confused and contradictory world of recording Broadway show tunes in the first three decades of the twentieth century; anyone seeking coherence or consistency would be bitterly disappointed. The technology and the exploitation of early sound recording was both so complex and so exponentially popular that it outpaced even the most basic rules of the nascent entertainment business. The contemporary niceties of upholding the integrity of a Broadway score were subsumed by the oncoming waves of a limited technology, followed by the shifting currents of popular tastes of the time.

The sale of sheet music was a fairly simple and discrete industry. Various firms owned the rights to various material from various songwriters; if one wanted the music of, say, Jerome Kern, you had to buy the product from T. B. Harms. Once the product was brought home, anyone could play it or sing to it or dance to it; it was egalitarian in that regard. Sheet music was also beyond technological evolution; it was always exactly *that* and no publishing company was significantly involved in the commercial possibilities of producing and selling the pianos on which to play the product.

The recording industry was after the consumer in a completely inverse way. What they initially owned, and invested in, was the technology—the various gramophones, phonographs, and Victrolas. It was only after getting their product into the American home that the industry threw itself into the art of the recordings themselves. Initially those recordings were perceived more as novelties than as works of art, but they soon acquired distinct qualities for the consumer. It was all well and good to have Al Jolson's picture on the sheet music in your living room, but if you wanted the *voice* of Al Jolson in your living room, you had to purchase it from whichever company had expended significant capital to arrange for the exclusive use of Jolson's services. (In the mid-1920s it was Brunswick.)

In this way, recordings demonstrated a different type of consumer egalitarianism. Anyone with a quarter or two could buy a piece of sheet music, but not everyone could play it. The record industry enabled any consumer to have music in his or her home—this is why, for example, the phonograph appealed particularly to immigrants recently arrived in America at the dawn of the twentieth century. Both the sheet music industry and recording industry relied on promoting the songs of Broadway as its musical product, but the recording industry added something new and essential to the mix: only a recording could promote the idiosyncratic voices of those hard-working celebrities who sold those songs nightly on the Great White Way.

The long and tortured journey to putting these celebrity avatars in America's living rooms began with Thomas Edison in 1877. Edison invented a way of reproducing sound by engraving acoustical sound waves via a large horn onto a rotating cylinder, which could be played back with a stylus. A decade later, Emile Berliner found a way of creating acoustical reproduction by deploying a flat disk and a stylus that would move side-to-side (as opposed to up and down, like Edison's cylinders). Both Edison and Berliner were initially devoted to reproducing human speech for business correspondence on their respective machines, but it was soon apparent that recorded music, rather than speech, was what consumers wanted. Edison called his machine the "phonograph," and Berliner called his the "gramophone."

In 1893, Berliner transferred his patent rights to Eldridge Johnson, a manufacturer of gramophone machines, and the two started a business that would evolve into the Victor Talking Machine Company. By 1900, 32,000 musical reproduction machines made by either Edison or Berliner were sold; by 1911, the number had approached 750,000 and thousands of records were being pressed daily to supply listening material.[2] Due to its efficient factory based in Camden, N.J., Victor was in the superior position to press and market the records themselves. Victor further solidified its market share in 1902, when it signed an up-and-coming opera tenor named Enrico Caruso, who would go on to record hundreds of opera arias over the next two decades, earn millions for Victor, and become the medium's first commercial superstar and name celebrity.

Victor's success with phonograph records forced Edison to give up his cylinder product, and his company faded away as a commercial force, but its eminence was challenged by the Columbia Phonograph Company, which had its manufacturing plants based in Bridgeport, Connecticut (where they continued to press records until the mid-1960s). By 1901, Columbia was making disks out of a durable shellac; three years later, the United Kingdom branch of Columbia (the unit that would eventually record Gershwin and Astaire) pioneered the double-sided disk, an innovation that, when adopted in general use by the end of the first decade, would enlarge the depth of musical repertory in the recording industry. Although another entrant to the field, the Chicago-based Brunswick-Balke-Collender, came on the scene in the 1920s, promoting jazz and dance bands throughout the twentieth century, the field of popular recording would belong largely to the rival companies, Victor and Columbia.

Much of what these companies recorded in the early years were musical renditions that appealed to the customer's regard for novelty, rather than aesthetics. This was largely due to the technological restrictions in acoustic recording in rudimentary studios, where instruments and singers were grouped uncomfortably around an acoustic horn (singers had to move out of the way for instrumental solos). The longest records in the 78 rpm world (the consistent speed for most phonograph/gramophones) were not much more than two minutes, and musical compositions of a sophisticated nature had to be truncated, revised, or cut up into several smaller units. However, the limitations of the recording industry were liberating for popular songs originating from vaudeville and the early Broadway musical, and for the personalities who graced their stages; 150 seconds of novelty was just enough—yet not too much—to suit their purposes admirably.

One might suppose that the Broadway star with the most personal brand of ebullience during the early years of acoustic performance would find a natural home on the gramophones of America, but George M. Cohan was, for all intents and purposes, completely absent. Cohan came to explosive prominence with *Little Johnny Jones* in 1904, demonstrating his far-ranging talents as a singer, dancer, composer, lyricist, and playwright. Yet his reedy tenor voice didn't transmit the full force of his personality, and during the course of his four-decade career, he recorded only ten songs (all in 1911) and none of his major hits.

Luckily, there was someone in the wings ready and available to become Cohan's avatar. Denver-based Billy Murray recorded his first wax cylinder in 1897 and by 1903, moved to New York to become a professional "recording artist." He sang for practically every nascent musical label, and by 1910 he was recording cylinders for Edison and disks for Victor simultaneously. Murray had a pleasant voice, distinct enough to render the hits of the day with enough clarity and verve to overcome the rudimentary technology. He would record most of Cohan's major songs within months of their Broadway debuts, particularly, "Give My Regards to Broadway," "The Yankee Doodle Boy," and "Forty-Five Minutes from Broadway." As his long career of more than 300 recordings progressed, Murray also recorded several early Irving Berlin show tunes. He was, at the very least, the first "cover" artist in American recording; but apparently his vast audience didn't feel cheated or put out that they weren't getting the "original artist." As critic and scholar Will Friedwald put it, "People would go to see shows, and they'd want to hear the songs from the shows, but nobody really got all the way around to the idea that you had to put the [actual] performer from the show doing it. Recording was thought to be a whole other separate medium that had no connection with performance."[3]

▶ Audio Example 3.2, "Yankee Doodle Boy" (Billy Murray)

For the discriminating home listener who *did* care who was singing the song, the stars of the *Ziegfeld Follies* made their consumer experience an especially satisfactory one, neatly paralleling the way in which they entered the family parlor on a sheet music cover. Bert Williams may have well been the first major American stage performer to commit his major body of work to recording; he started to record cylinders with his initial vaudeville partner, George Walker, in 1901. By 1906, Williams had recorded his signature number,

"Nobody," that had premiered in the all-black musical, *Abyssinia,* for Columbia. After Williams was hired to perform in the *Follies* in 1910, he recorded several of his *Follies* specialties (including a re-recording of "Nobody," which had been interpolated into the 1913 edition of the *Follies*) over the years, while continuing a robust relationship with Columbia, pretty much up until the day he died in March 1922.

Fanny Brice's shtick made it to a crossover listening audience as early as 1916, several seasons after her *Follies* debut, with renditions of "Becky Is Back in the Ballet" and other numbers written to showcase her unique personality for Columbia and Victor. In 1921, she gave posterity one of its earliest recorded examples of a celebrity matched with an indelible piece of material from Broadway: the recording of her signature number, "My Man," introduced in the *Ziegfeld Follies of 1921*; she'd go on to record the song about a half dozen more times throughout her career.

Eddie Cantor recorded most of his *Follies* specialties from 1919 on, a season after his debut on the New Amsterdam stage. Every season for the next decade, he could be relied upon to set down a song or two from whatever new musical comedy in which he was starring; when he broke out in his own vehicle, *Make It Snappy,* in 1922, he recorded six songs from the score, including those of other cast members, which was an extensive amount for a Broadway performer to devote to his own show. Cantor had a robust recording career throughout the 1920s on Columbia, at the salary of $1,000 per song (about $14,000 today), alternating Tin Pan Alley novelty songs with material from the various Broadway contraptions concocted for his antic persona. Cantor may have well been the first performer to take a popular hit recording, place it into a Broadway show, and turn it into an even bigger hit. A radio personality named Tommy Lyman picked up the 1924 one-off "My Blue Heaven" (written by a pal of Cantor's and a frequent collaborator, Walter Donaldson) as his theme song and it soon attracted Cantor's attention. Cantor was then starring in the *Ziegfeld Follies of 1927*, and, a few months after it opened, he interpolated "My Blue Heaven" into his solo spot in the first act, rewriting some of the lyrics to reflect his domestic life with a wife and five daughters.[4] While Cantor was delighting audiences with that number at the New Amsterdam, a Victor recording artist named Gene Austin released a 78 rpm recording of the song in 1928; it went through the roof, staying at No. 1 on the charts for fifteen weeks and selling five million records—by far the largest amount up to that time.

As hard-working as Cantor and his fellow Ziegfeld stars were—putting it over the New Amsterdam footlights at night, then committing the same songs to the acoustical horn in an airless studio the next morning on their day off—they were indolent lazybones compared with the full wattage personality who worked for the competition: Al Jolson.

"He literally acts and feels his parts; he puts his whole heart and soul into his work. You will find every one of his Brunswick records interesting—one stimulates laughter, another portrays pathos—but all of them amusing," ran a 1924 advertisement promoting Jolson, after the Brunswick company had signed him away from Victor to make two dozen records for an advance of $100,000—nearly $1.4 million today, and an astronomical sum back then.[5] But Jolson was one performer who always gave his audience—on stage or by the living room phonograph—their money's worth. Once he had become a headliner at the Winter Garden in 1911, Jolson immediately crossed over to the studio. While he apparently recorded some cylinders for Edison as early as 1910, he was recording disks for Victor in New Jersey and performing on Broadway by 1911; from a forgotten stage vehicle entitled *Vera Violette*, he set down "That Haunting Melody" (written by George M. Cohan) and "Rum Tum Tiddle." The next year, he had two hits, "That Lovin' Traumerai" from *The Whirl of Society*, along with "Ragging the Baby to Sleep"/"Movin' Man, Don't Take My Baby Grand," a non-show-specific record that nonetheless sold more than a million copies.

By 1913, with the show *Honeymoon Express*, Jolson had become a Broadway freight train—simultaneously local and express—starring in a show every season, then taking it on the road across America, frequently continuing his performances after the curtain came down with an impromptu concert down by the footlights. Through 1926, he recorded practically every major number he performed in his shows, loosely arranged vehicles such as *Robinson Crusoe, Jr.*; *Sinbad*; *Bombo*; and *Big Boy*. However, it would be foolhardy to acknowledge these recordings as in any way indicative of what the actual musical was about or what it contained. Usually, Jolson played the "character" of Gus—simply his overly ingratiating, wisecracking, black-faced archetype—and sang whatever showstoppers his songwriting pals had crafted for him whenever he wanted. If the number "Where Did Robinson Crusoe Go with Friday on Saturday Night?" had any narrative connection to the 1916 vehicle *Robinson Crusoe, Jr.*, it has been wiped away by the sands of time. (Although one wonders about Jolson's apparent follow-up, "Who Played Poker with Pocahontas (When John Smith Went Away)?")

▶ Audio Example 3.3, "Where Did Robinson Crusoe Go with Friday on Saturday Night" (Al Jolson)

It hardly mattered: tunes such as "Rock-A-Bye Your Baby with a Dixie Melody," "Toot, Toot, Tootsie," "April Showers," and "Swanee" (the biggest financial success of George Gershwin's career) all debuted on the Broadway stage and were sold to the American public by the tireless entertainment crusade known as Al Jolson. He made more than one hundred recordings in less than two decades—including show tunes introduced by others, such as "Ol' Man River" and "Liza."[6] His ability to lend a veneer of Broadway razzle-dazzle to the commercial appeal of his various recording companies was so impressive that his name and visage were dramatically branded on the normally dull and functional brown paper wrappers that held the era's 78 rpm recordings—one could practically hear Jolson before you put his record on the phonograph.

Jolson's mantle as the prodigious king of the acoustic phonograph recording was mitigated toward the end of the 1920s by a technological advance that gave his relative sparkling clarity a run for its money and eventually beat him at his own game: electronic recording.

After years of experimentation, condenser microphones were created in the early 1920s that could transmit the sound of the voice as electrical current; boosted by vacuum tubes, that sound could be replicated with greater fidelity through enhanced speakers on a home phonograph. It would transform the economics of the industry and the nature of performer who could succeed in it. By 1924, Western Electric, the company that had perfected the system, allied its technology to the Columbia Phonograph Company; within two years, the entire industry had abandoned acoustical recording.[7]

By the mid-1920s, the recording industry was facing advances and setbacks, both in technology and public tastes, from all sides. The market for phonographs themselves had stalled, and the industry (worth almost $200 million in 1920) diverted its attention to selling records and creating and exploiting what we would now call "niche markets," including jazz, and nurturing the appetite for African American performers within the African American community: "race records" as they were called back then. But, the major change in how Americans engaged with popular music during this period was the introduction of social dancing as a cultural phenomenon; by the early years of the 1920s, dance music had surpassed any other genre or novelty in recorded music. A tune rendered by a dance band orchestra—whether from Tin Pan Alley or a Broadway show—was now judged by a simple criterion, employed again some thirty years later on television's *American Bandstand*: did it have a good beat and could you dance to it?

If consumers bought records in the 1910s because they were enchanted by the novelty of amusing or engaging performers, they now traded them in for a rhythmically sophisticated bandleader and his players; these were the new musical celebrities. Favorites included the Casa Loma Orchestra, the Ben Selvin Orchestra, Leo Reisman and His Orchestra, George Olsen and His Music, and towering above them all, Paul Whiteman and His Orchestra.[8] Each of these bands had its own sound, due to skillful arrangements done by fine artisans in that field; discriminating listeners could pick out which orchestra was playing with their eyes closed. These bands may well have co-opted dozens of songs from the Broadway musical theater of the 1920s and 30s; they may have stolen songs from the talented folks who originated them; they may have even pushed the lyrics far back into the recording—or even eliminated them entirely—but in many ways, they were the best friends the early Broadway musical ever had.

The bandleaders had willing and able comrades in the songwriters and performers who packed the Theater District in the 1920s and 30s with dozens of revues and musical comedies every season. A new generation of songwriters such as the Gershwins, Cole Porter, Rodgers and Hart—among many others—joined the field pioneered before 1920 by Irving Berlin, Jerome Kern, Oscar Hammerstein II, and Sigmund Romberg, while ace performers from the vaudeville stage, such as the Marx Brothers, Bob Hope, Jimmy Durante, and Sophie Tucker would get their chance to transition into big, gaudy Broadway revues and musicals tailored to their sensibilities; these were the boom times for the American musical.

There were millions of listeners eager to hear the music of Broadway and dozens of dance bands eager to share it with consumers. What the dance bandleaders wanted, though, was not a legendary performance from the Great White Way etched for posterity; they wanted tunes that could be artfully rearranged and presented for their audiences, audiences that followed them live, on recordings, and eventually on the radio. Variety was key to their appeal; dancers (and listeners) needed to change up the rhythm of their dance card—even recordings of the foxtrot could get pretty boring when played in rapid succession. Show music aficionados might grouse that the integrity of a full score by, say, the Gershwins or Jerome Kern was seriously compromised, but the simple fact is that, in this era, no one wanted to hear ten songs from the same show in a row—they rarely wanted to hear ten similar consecutive recordings of *anything*.

The taxonomy for recordings of show tunes in the 1920s up through 1935 reveals several different categories, some that continue into the present, but many which were unique to their time. The largest category of show recording during this era was probably that of the arrangement for dance orchestra. Typically, the arrangers would create an upbeat foxtrot tempo for a Broadway tune—for example, "Manhattan," or "The Man I Love," or "Make Believe"—and the orchestra would take a spin through 32 bars, then an often anodyne vocalist would take over the reins for a chorus, so that listeners could hear the lyrics, then back to the orchestra for a final play-out. Hundreds, if not thousands, of show tunes were made into dance orchestra recordings; in many cases they were the only versions that listeners beyond Broadway would have heard. These dance orchestra renditions ushered countless show tunes into American living rooms, providing the ever-fascinating rhythm that would exalt the pantheon of the American Songbook.

Bestriding the universe of dance orchestra recordings like the colossus he sometimes resembled was Paul Whiteman. Whiteman had broken into recording as the 1920s began and availed himself of the breadth and depth of the Broadway catalogue, turning songs into national and international hits. His recordings ranged from the *Follies*—"My Man," without the signature voice of Fanny Brice—to the groundbreaking 1921 black musical *Shuffle Along*—"I'm Just Wild About Harry" and "Gypsy Blues;" from operettas such as *Rose-Marie*—"Indian Love Call"—to the latest Rodgers and Hart smarty-pants ballad, such as "You Took Advantage of Me" from *Present Arms* in 1928. Whiteman's reputation was burnished for eternity by his relationship with George Gershwin. He commissioned and conducted the piece that would be revealed as "Rhapsody in Blue" for a concert in 1924, but Whiteman and Gershwin would have shared an ideal relationship even if "Rhapsody" had never happened. Whiteman conducted the pit orchestra for *George White's Scandals* of 1922, which featured Gershwin's magnificent tune, "I'll Build a Stairway to Paradise," later recorded as one of the most rousing foxtrots of the 1920s by Whiteman; he'd go on to record dozens of Gershwin tunes.

Despite Whiteman's reliance on the tunes more than the lyrics, he showed a real nose for song interpreters. Among the band vocalists he spotlighted were Mildred Bailey, Ramona Davies, Johnny Mercer, and, beginning in 1926, a group from Spokane called "The Rhythm Boys." The signature singer in that trio was Bing Crosby, and, while still under the baton of Whiteman, Crosby would record songs from *Show Boat*, as well as "Let's Do It," "Makin' Whoopee," and a very credible "March of the Musketeers" from Rudolf Friml's 1928 operetta, *The Three Musketeers*.

▶ Audio Example 3.4, "March of the Musketeers" (Bing Crosby)

One of the stranger show tune taxonomies of the dance orchestra era was the medley. The medley was nothing new as a consumer enticement—small chamber groups would frequently string together the best classical melodies or opera arias as part of the salon music phenomenon in hotels and tea rooms in the late nineteenth century. Instead of offering a full Broadway score with more than a dozen numbers, record labels, singing groups, and bandleaders came up with the express train version, a crash course in three or four of the best songs of a Broadway score, compressed into less than four minutes. This musical buffet was popular as early as 1909 with Victor's own "house" singing group, the Victor Light Opera Company. Throughout the 1910s, they worked through most (though not all) of the operetta hits of the day then segued into the works of the more essential songwriters of the 1920s. They were nothing if not prodigious; they "covered" the scores to nearly one hundred shows. In 1925 and 1926, they recorded "gems" from a dozen different scores as far-flung as *Sunny*, *The Cocoanuts*, and *The Desert Song*. Their selections from *The Cocoanuts* would have been the only major recording of anything from Irving Berlin's score for the Marx Brothers' 1925 Broadway pandemonium—in fact, it's the only contemporary recording of anything from the Marx Brothers' Broadway offerings.

In his autobiography, Richard Rodgers called the Victor Light Opera Company medleys "the closest thing to an original cast album,"[9] and they devoted one of their recordings to gems from *Dearest Enemy*, the 1925 book musical that Rodgers wrote with Lorenz Hart. Rodgers may have felt a kind of gratitude to the Victor Light Opera singers for preserving at least some of *Dearest Enemy*, but it's unlikely that any of the creators of *No, No,*

Nanette would have felt that the Light Opera represented anything remotely connected to their breezy Jazz Age confection; in the Light Opera rendition, "Tea for Two" is so regimented and lugubrious that it sounds as if it's from *The Chocolate Soldier* instead.

▶ Audio Example 3.5, "Gems from *No No Nanette*" (Victor Light Opera)

There were other medley singing groups, including the Revelers, a quartet of earnest male singers who covered several Gershwin medleys, including the 1930 *Strike Up the Band*, a wonderful score that was sadly neglected during the Depression. These reductive renderings, however, paled beside the technical challenges of capturing an entire Broadway score. The 10″ or 12″ 78 rpm shellac disks of this era were heavy, and although automatic record changers had been introduced to the U.S. market as early as 1927, they were extremely cumbersome, even for those few who might have wanted those twelve consecutive songs from *Show Boat*. Those same 78s were also not promoted to the public in the colorful, attractive way that sheet music had been. Usually slotted into brown cardboard or dull paper liners, the main attraction was the open circle that allowed companies to paste distinctive, color-coded labels in the center of the disk. But through some time-honored contractual arrangement—created no doubt, by the music publishers—the label nearly always specified not only the genre of the tune, but its Broadway provenance. For example, the label for a 1927 recording by George Olsen on Victor 21034-A reads: "MY HEART STOOD STILL"—Foxtrot (From "A Connecticut Yankee").

Given that 78s were essentially a binary affair—they had two sides—it was frequently the case that a Broadway show got a twofer: two songs promoted from the same show. In some cases, this was simply common sense. Helen Morgan had only two real songs of her own when she appeared in *Show Boat*—"Can't Help Lovin' Dat Man" and "Bill"—and each one appears on a side of her 78 release for Victor in 1928. (She repeated the trick in 1929, with two standards from her starring vehicle *Sweet Adeline*: "Why Was I Born" and "Don't Ever Leave Me.") In other cases, it was a question of making an educated guess about what song was destined to become popular. When the Paul Whiteman Orchestra recorded "Anything Goes" in 1934, it made sense to have the title tune of that show, but "All Through the Night" was put on the B-side. Perhaps it was for variety's sake, or the song's suitability as an intimate foxtrot, but it was certainly not Cole Porter's most famous tune, nor even one of the most enduring from that particular show. Most of the decision-making around which song would be promoted on a record with another was made on an instinctive hunch—usually before the show itself even opened--by the music publishers, who still had a huge stake in which song was going to be a hit, either on a recording or as a piece of sheet music or both.

Once the potential hit song, or songs, or even "gems" were placed by the publishers with the record labels, the recording artists originally attached to those songs frequently—though not consistently—had the opportunity to record them. Early vaudeville and music hall performers committed their signature ditties to the acoustic recording device as early as the 1880s—the peripatetic DeWolf Hopper set down his "Casey at the Bat" in 1906 and the leading lady of *Irene* in 1919, Edith Day, dedicated her "Alice Blue Gown" to acoustic posterity. When the larger personalities of the revue stage and musical comedies of the 1920s—Williams, Brice, Cantor, and Jolson—became distinctly associated with certain numbers, they were given opportunities to record them, as were Fred and Adele Astaire, although their Gershwin performances were invariably recorded when these shows visited the West End.

In general, the British were much more assiduous about committing their stage performers to recordings; in fact, there were several multiple 78 rpm record albums that attempted to cover partial theatrical scores as early as 1898. By the mid-1920s, with both homegrown productions of Gilbert and Sullivan and American imports such as *No, No, Nanette* and *The Desert Song,* fuller recordings—often with six or eight disks—appeared on the British market. Why this tradition flourished in the UK, but not in America at the time, remains a bit of a mystery. Some of the reason, no doubt, has to do with more sedate home listening habits in England; also, the distance from the West End stage to the British living room was shorter and more comfortably circumscribed than from Broadway to, say, the Main Streets of California. Perhaps it's because the tradition began in England during World War I, and the comforting sounds of a familiar West End musical in such trying times sealed a nostalgic bond between recording and consumer.[10]

Whatever the reasons, the theatrical legacy of the interwar era of the British musical was well represented. Composer/lyricist Noel Coward merited an extraordinary contract with HMV in London, setting down nearly all of his seminal compositions—often recording songs that he had written, but were sung in revues by others. There are even recordings of Coward acting in scenes from his plays, most notably in *Private Lives,* with the incandescent Gertrude Lawrence. Lawrence was held in such esteem in London that she recorded two discs of 78s that included several songs and medleys from Cole Porter's West End *Nymph Errant* in 1933, a show that never made it to New York. When West End stars came to visit Broadway, they continued the tradition; during her 1926 Broadway run in Gershwin's *Oh, Kay!,* Lawrence made an excursion to Camden, New Jersey, to record "Do-do-do" and "Someone to Watch Over Me" for Victor. Fred Astaire eventually got the chance to record one of his original Broadway creations; when he was starring (solo) in Porter's *Gay Divorce* in New York in 1932, he set down "Night and Day," backed up by the Leo Reisman Orchestra: it went on to become one of the most popular songs in the country.

Broadway leading ladies tended to fare better than their male counterparts, largely because they were the torchbearers of the era's vogue for torch singers. Helen Morgan recorded her major torchy material from *Show Boat*; Ruth Etting set down her classic "Ten Cents a Dance" from Rodgers and Hart's *Simple Simon* (twice, in fact—in 1930 and 1935); Libby Holman, whose personal life was one long torch song, recorded four of the baleful ballads she originated in various Schwartz and Dietz shows, including "Moanin' Low," and "Something to Remember You By." Special mention, however, should be given to Paul Robeson; although he never appeared in the 1927 Broadway version of *Show Boat*, he did play it in the West End in 1928 and recorded "Ol' Man River" while in England, in two separate versions. It became the song most connected with his titanic personality, and he recorded it twice again in America in the early 1930s, before appearing in the 1936 film version. (Robeson wrestled with what he considered to be the demeaning self-references to blacks in the lyrics, although he recorded practically every permutation.)

Given that there actually were a number of recordings of Broadway songs by the original artists from the period, it's maddening to consider what is missing or what has been misappropriated. When Rodgers and Hart wrote their first (and only) show for Florenz Ziegfeld, *Betsy*, in 1926, it starred Belle Baker, a highly emotive performer who already had chalked up a not-unimpressive history recording 78s, usually of an ethnic Jewish bent. Baker decided at the last minute that she needed a starrier number, so Ziegfeld brought in Irving Berlin to craft a number for his expensive star, practically as the curtain was about to rise. The number was "Blue Skies" which made Ziegfeld, Baker, and audiences happy; Rodgers and Hart, however, were furious at everyone involved. One would think that at least a rendition of "Blue Skies" by Belle Baker for the ages would have made the whole experience tolerable, but she never recorded it.

The recording studio could be an unforgiving fortress; many Broadway stars were denied the opportunity to memorialize the tunes they made famous on stage and often were replaced by lesser lights. Astonishingly, Marilyn Miller, Ziegfeld's leading lady and one of the most adored musical comedy stars of the 1920s, never recorded a single number that was released (two songs recorded in the studio were scrubbed by Columbia) so the magical pixie who originated "Look for the Silver Lining" in *Sally*, with Jerome Kern's immortal tune, had to endure Marion Harris's charmless rendition with the Isham Jones Orchestra. William Gaxton and Victor Moore, Broadway's comic duo par excellence, who headlined *Of Thee I Sing, Let 'Em Eat Cake,* and *Anything Goes* during this period, never recorded a single note or lyric while these shows were running. The pair of ingénues who, respectively, introduced two of the most successful songs in American history back in 1925—Sterling Holloway and June Cochrane, with "Manhattan" in the

Garrick Gaieties and Jack Barker and Louise Groody with "Tea for Two" from *No, No, Nanette*—never got near an electric microphone; those songs were left to the dance orchestras and their anodyne house singers (and neither song was ever recorded as the duet that its composers originally intended).

Sometimes, it wasn't even enough to be a Broadway star with recording chops. Ethel Merman made her career-igniting smash in 1930 with "I Got Rhythm" in *Girl Crazy* and would have seemed a natural to put it on disk, but, alas, this is one that got away (along with "Sam and Delilah," her other big number from the show).[11] In the meantime, she had to sit back and listen to her big number on 78s by Adelaide Hall, Ethel Waters, and Kate Smith. The next season, Merman introduced "Life Is Just a Bowl of Cherries" in *George White's Scandals* of 1931, but it was her castmate, Rudy Vallee, who had the chart-topping hit in 1931, even though he never sang the song on stage. (Merman did record it for Victor, but it was only done as a test recording and never released at the time; perhaps the folks in the technical department weren't advanced enough to contain her voice.) By 1932, she was in *Take a Chance* and recorded her big number "Eadie Was a Lady" for Brunswick on *both* sides of the disk; a six-minute performance by one singer was nearly unheard of. Two years later, she recorded "I Get a Kick Out of You" and "You're the Top" from *Anything Goes* and never looked back.

▶ Audio Example 3.6, "Eadie Was a Lady" (Ethel Merman)

By the time *Anything Goes* opened in fall 1934, the Broadway score had gotten a bit more sophisticated, and the perceived injustice of only extracting a song or two from an entire evening in the theater felt more pronounced; the fuller breadth of a songwriting team's intentions was only reaching the folks who bought tickets to see the show in New York. In the final week of 1931, the Gershwins had opened the first musical to win the Pulitzer Prize, *Of Thee I Sing* (with a book by George S. Kaufman and Morrie Ryskind), a complex narrative mixture of romance and political satire. Six weeks later, Irving Berlin teamed up with the hot new comedy writer, Moss Hart, to skewer the Depression from a metropolitan point of view with *Face the Music*. It would be reasonable to assume that the topicality of these thoughtful, yet tuneful, musicals, delivered by the masters of the era, would be enough to assure some archival semblance of these masterpieces for the home audience; in fact, they only yield a medley of missed opportunities.

Face the Music was given one of the more extended medleys of the period on Brunswick, an eight-minute survey of the score (that is, one suite of songs of each side of the 78—to get the full effect, one had to flip the record on the phonograph very, very swiftly). The Victor Young Orchestra—one of the bands that picked up Whiteman's baton in the 1930s—played two of the songs, rather relentlessly, with Bing Crosby covering "Soft Lights and Sweet Music" on the A-side and members of the Brunswick Studio

Orchestra sang "Let's Have Another Cup of Coffee" the B-side; it might have been better if Crosby had sung both.

Of Thee I Sing was, to its credit, far too sophisticated a piece in terms of context, structure, and musical architecture to be reduced to anything coherent for generic consumer consumption, given the recording conventions of the era. Still, *Of Thee I Sing* deserved better. The title number and the jaunty duet that captured the era's desperate attempt at optimism, "Who Cares?," were paired twice on recordings: first, on Columbia by Ben Selvin's Knickerbockers dance band with a vocal assist from the Rondoliers; second, on Victor by the Arden-Ohman Orchestra, with vocals by Frank Luther. Each version was upbeat and tuneful in its foxtrotty way, but surely Gershwin's score merited a first-rate singer or two; it would be two decades before most of the score would be even committed to disk, and more than a half century before this masterpiece was given a recording that matched its stature in the musical theater canon.[12]

Face the Music and *Of Thee I Sing* were so successful on Broadway that each team rolled up its figurative sleeves and produced follow-ups for the next season: the revue *As Thousands Cheer* was Berlin and Hart's extended look at the effects of the Depression on a more global scale; *Let 'Em Eat Cake*, by the Gershwins and Co., was a more literal sequel to the adventures of their screwy politicians and their travails.

Given its episodic structure, *As Thousands Cheer* didn't need a complex recording format, the way that *Of Thee I Sing* did; what it *deserved*, however, was for its intentions to be preserved—as the most sophisticated, tuneful, personality-driven, and popular revue of its day. A series of 78s, with such gifted and marketable performers as Ethel Waters, Clifton Webb, and even Marilyn Miller—if she could have been convinced to appear before a studio microphone—would not have been unreasonable, even within the limitations of the era. It would have also gone a long way to buoy the reputation of a show that, even now, has gone unrecorded with a full orchestra or its full original score.

Instead, *As Thousands Cheer*'s score was atomized over several different labels and formats, in a rather maddening patchwork quilt of recordings. Ethel Waters did record two of her major songs from *As Thousands Cheer* for Columbia in 1933, in terrific versions: "Heat Wave" and "Harlem on My Mind." (Another number, entitled "To Be or Not to Be," about a wife who's leery of her husband's theatrical ambitions, appears on a YouTube segment of undisclosed provenance.) Yet the masterpiece of the score, "Supper Time," the excoriatingly plaintive song that Waters had originated in the stage production while framed by a headline that read "Unknown Negro Lynched by Frenzied Mob," went unrecorded by her. It wasn't that the song was too incendiary—that didn't stop such dimmer stars in the recording firmament as Thelma Nevins (with Leo Reisman and His Orchestra), Gertrude Niesen (with Isham Jones), as well as Bee Sharp and Orchestra from tackling

"Supper Time" in the early 1930s. Waters eventually rendered a highly lachrymose version of the song on *The Perry Como Show* on television in the early 1950s, but a seminal moment of Depression-era Broadway history was lost to posterity.

Clifton Webb, the leading man of *As Thousands Cheer,* made three recordings from the show—"Not For All the Rice in China," "How's Chances?," and a particularly popular version of "Easter Parade"—on the Victor label, all with Leo Reisman and His Orchestra. Even though "Easter Parade" (originally performed by nearly the full company in an all-sepia-toned production number set at the turn of the century) would become nearly ubiquitous in the next fifteen years, in different film renditions, the original sophisticated choral intentions for "Easter Parade" as it appeared on stage were lost. What remains is a foxtrot by Leo Reisman and his Orchestra, with a "vocal refrain by Clifton Webb" (in even smaller type).

In one of the few—if only—inside jokes in the 1930s recording industry, the Paul Whiteman Orchestra released what it called a "tabloid version" of the *As Thousands Cheer* score on RCA Victor—amusing, if you knew that the central conceit of the Berlin/Hart revue was that each song or skit was framed by a tabloid newspaper headline. The Whiteman disk was also one of the few products of the time to capture some semblance of Broadway excitement. It was released as a 12″ picture disk, a brief fad at the time. Embossed directly on the disk with a picture of two cast members—Clifton Webb and Marilyn Miller but without their actual participation on the recording—the picture disk was an attempt to advertise the show with some kind of graphic, absent an actual cover design. Since *As Thousands Cheer* was a non-narrative revue, there was no need to gang the numbers together in a coherent way, and Whiteman's extended four-and-a-half minute medley was a much more sophisticated product than the Victor Light Opera medleys of the previous decade. "Easter Parade" appears, as does the not-so-spectacular closing number, "Not for All the Rice in China." Whiteman adds "How's Chances?," a terrific Berlin ballad that never really got its moment in the pop culture sun; however, "Supper Time," as rendered by Whiteman's female house singer, Ramona Davies, carries none of the emotional weight of Waters's extraordinary performance: what could?

The flip side of the Whiteman picture disk features a series of selections from *Let 'Em Eat Cake,* which would seem to be an even less likely candidate for a decent representation in the recording world; it was born in the shadow of its predecessor's achievements, and died there as well, running one-fifth the number of performances and earning little of *Of Thee I Sing*'s critical approbation. Still, there was interest in the sequel from the recording industry. Both Leo Reisman and Emil Coleman's Riviera Orchestra each performed lackluster versions of "Let 'Em Eat Cake" and "Mine," the latter a delightfully contrapuntal duet, but rendered, in these cases, with only one melody line. What's remarkable is the

Paul Whiteman and His Orchestra covered two groundbreaking Broadway scores from 1933: *Let 'Em Eat Cake* and *As Thousands Cheer.* Alas, this is as close as the original stars got to being on a recording of the shows. Courtesy of the University of Buffalo Music Library.

extent to which Whiteman teases out the complexities and context of *Let 'Em Eat Cake*'s score as an intelligent tour through its highlights, with two large choral numbers—"Union Square" and "On and On and On"—added to the title number and "Mine" (with the contrapuntal melody line restored for the reprise). The inclusion of the choral numbers—politically trenchant in the context of the show, but completely useless for foxtrotting or casual listening—is really quite extraordinary. Even though the original performers (William Gaxton, Lois Moran, and Victor Moore) only get as close as their pictures on the disk, this version feels as if Whiteman is committed to telling listeners that the score to this show was different and even important; the recording defies contemporary convention as much as the show itself did on stage.

▶   Audio Example 3.7, "*Let 'Em Eat Cake* (medley)" (Paul Whiteman Orchestra)

When George Gershwin enthusiastically accompanied Fred Astaire on the "'Half-of-It-Dearie' Blues," he and his brother were just beginning their Broadway careers together. Less than a decade after *Lady, Be Good!* opened, the Gershwins—along with their talented peers—had transformed the Broadway musical into something much more sophisticated and complex, as represented by the score of *Let 'Em Eat Cake,* the last musical comedy that Gershwin would write for Broadway. However, the recording industry and its market for Broadway scores would barely mature at all during that decade, still living comfortably with the bandstand sounds of the dance orchestra and their flavorless vocalists. "Posterity is just around the corner," mocked Ira Gershwin in *Of Thee I Sing*; when it came to memorializing the great Broadway performances and the groundbreaking scores of the 1920s and 1930s, posterity was a lot further away than that.

Eddie Cantor makes funny with the radio microphone, prior to his game-changing appearances on *The Chase & Sanborn Hour,* 1932. Credit: Photofest.

CHAPTER 4

The Majestic Theater of the Air

Radio and the Personality of Broadway

For Eddie Cantor, all the world was a Broadway stage—even the radio broadcast studio.

In fall 1931, when Cantor claimed the hallowed grounds of *The Chase and Sanborn Hour*—an NBC variety show sponsored by the coffee company—by taking over as its host and lead performer, live radio programs were still intimidated by the public they were trying to serve. Radio studios were hermetically sealed off from the live audiences that attended their broadcasts, even for variety programs. Performers fulfilled their chores in a booth with a thick glass window, and frequently there were illuminated signs asking audiences NOT to applaud. For Cantor, that setup was at best counterintuitive; at worst, anathema. None of the technical and physical limitations of radio should be allowed to keep him from his appointed rounds, which were to entertain the hell out of the customers.

He demanded a real-life audience, right in front of him and—given that he was the most popular performer in the country, having conquered the stage, popular recordings, and talking pictures by 1931—the sponsor, somewhat anxiously, gave in to his request. Cantor leapt right in; hamming away at the studio audience, rolling his eyes, milking laughs and applause. He would run into the audience and grab someone's hat; goose his shapely female guest stars; jump on someone's back and initiate a "chicken fight." The New York studio audience would erupt in pandemonium; listeners from Topeka to Tacoma would often sit in their living rooms, clueless as to what antics provoked such laughter. Critics at the time thought that those audiences might be resentful—it's more likely the mystifying, unseen laugh cues only made them more curious and attentive.[1]

Eddie Cantor understood something essential about the new medium of radio. He ran the numbers: "Say you played in a Ziegfeld show at the New Amsterdam Theatre, which seats 1,600 [people]," he reflected in his memoirs. "In a week, you play to 13,000. Play that Ziegfeld show for 50 weeks, you would play to 650,000. If you played it for ten years, you'd play to 6 1/2 million. In 20 years, it would be 13 million. And if you played it for *forty* years, to packed houses, standing room only, you'd play to less people in 40 years than you played to in one night on the *Chase and Sanborn Hour*."[2] Eddie Cantor brought the razzle dazzle of the Broadway musical theater into homes across the country in a new and exciting way. While sheet music might allow Cantor to share his tunes with America, and while records might allow him to share his voice, only radio would allow him to share his *personality* with millions of devoted fans.

As in the history of recorded sound, radio struggled with limited technology during its embryonic days. It was largely a hobby until 1920, when a Pittsburgh radio station carried election returns and snippets of the news; the next year, a Chicago station joined the fray by carrying local advertising and news. The race was on to create a coast-to-coast network, through which various affiliates across the country could carry the same broadcast simultaneously; in 1924, an informal network of stations carried a speech by Calvin Coolidge. The National Broadcasting Company was formed in 1926; under the visionary leadership of "General" David Sarnoff, it would soon aggregate four dozen national affiliates and provide coast-to-coast variety programming by 1928. That same year, William S. Paley reorganized the Columbia Phonograph Company into the Columbia Broadcasting System and began to take the course of its broadcasting empire westward. By the end of the decade, 40 percent of all Americans had radio consoles in their homes; not surprisingly, the number reached 58 percent for households in New York City, the headquarters of both networks.

To be invited into America's homes, radio used music as its most effective calling card. This burgeoning industry necessitated many hours of programming to fill the airwaves, and the most accessible programming was music. It couldn't be just any kind of music; the networks' bills were paid by commercial sponsors who demanded successful shows, and therefore executives had to be sensitive to listeners' predilections. Paley personally mandated a ratio of CBS programming in the early days that included 26 percent of airtime to "symphony/opera/chamber music" and 29 percent to "popular music." This proved to be an unparalleled opportunity for the music from Tin Pan Alley and Broadway. As scholar Philip Eberle wrote: "It was to the most familiar segment of the established show business structure—vaudeville and musical comedy performers and dance orchestras—which radio turned for its first program fare."[3]

The easiest thing for metropolitan-based stations to do was to tap into the vast array of dance orchestras that had already laid claim to the public's enthusiasm (and pocketbooks) since the beginning of the 1920s. Dance orchestras and their charismatic band leaders usually had some kind of home base at a local hotel ballroom (and hotels were conveniently located in tall buildings for maximum broadcast reception), so it was a comparatively easy task to run a remote broadcast unit from the hotel to provide a couple of hours of accessible music programming in the evenings. Given the nature of their repertoire, the popularity of dance orchestras on the air tipped the scales of contemporary tastes further toward popular music and jazz. Radio enabled jazz music in particular to enjoy a new kind of egalitarianism in American culture, vaulting over segregated markets, and providing the beginning of the crossover market in American music.[4] Throughout the 1920s, though, most people wanted to hear the music that had originated on Broadway, or at the very least, by the songwriters who dominated Broadway. "Without radio, those American classicists, the musical comedy composers, would have reached far fewer appreciative ears. Radio was the megaphone through which Cole Porter, Rodgers and Hart, and George Gershwin, were able to be heard and thus contribute to the musical appreciation of untold thousands," wrote Eberle.[5]

In 1927–28, out of the top ten songs played on the radio, more than half were from Broadway shows: "Blue Skies" (*Betsy*), "Hallelujah" (*Hit the Deck!*), "Ol' Man River" and "Can't Help Lovin' Dat Man" (*Show Boat*), "'S Wonderful" (*Funny Face*), and "The Varsity Drag" (*Good News*). It's nearly impossible to find a scientific way to go back and compute an exact list from those early days, but, by conflating several sources, among the top ten songs of radio's first active decade included such entries from Broadway revues and musicals as "Fascinatin' Rhythm," "Tea for Two," "One Alone" (*The Desert Song*), "Someone to Watch Over Me" (*Oh, Kay!*), "With a Song in My Heart" (*Spring Is Here*), "You Do Something to Me" (*Fifty Million Frenchmen*), "Life Is Just a Bowl of Cherries," "Brother, Can You Spare a Dime?" (*Americana*), "Night and Day" (*Gay Divorce*), and "Easter Parade."

That is not to say that other songs directly from Tin Pan Alley weren't popular—novelty items such as "Yes, We Have No Bananas" or "The Music Goes 'Round and 'Round," which seem to have been invented solely to entice customers into buying them, also filled the airwaves. Of course, after 1928, the list of Broadway songs at the top of the charts was further diluted by songs and themes from Hollywood—but even many of these had some sort of Broadway provenance, or were written by Broadway composers. At the beginning of the Great Depression consumers were getting songs from Broadway in three forms: sheet music, records, and on the radio, transforming the music industry into a growing family of squabbling siblings. As the 1920s began, records were the consumer medium of choice: 105.6 million were sold in 1921. Five years later, that number would dwindle to nearly half that: 59.2 million records. During the same period, the number of radio sets sold went from less than 500,000 to two million. Consumers could now have access to the music of the finest of bands, orchestras, and singers—and they didn't have to venture outside to hear it or purchase it.[6]

Radio programs enabled listeners to hear about the world of Broadway in addition to listening to its musical "lullaby" and, given that both NBC and CBS had access to the major performance talent in New York City, it was only natural that the networks would tap into Broadway—as a concept, as an industry—in order to garner talent and prestige. Broadway conveyed a unique glamour and excitement to radio audiences, at least until the mid-1930s, when Hollywood muscled in on the singular allure of Broadway with similar kinds of programs trading on Tinseltown talent and mythology.

There were a number of radio programs in the early 1930s that traded on their association with the glamour of the Great White Way: *Ziegfeld Follies of the Air*; *Manhattan Merry-Go-Round*; *First Nighter*. Later in the 1940s, *Tonight on Broadway* and *Johnny Mercer's Music Shop* also appeared on the air. (Alas, *Broadway is My Beat* was a cop show, not an entertainment show, but it has a certain panache as a title anyway.)[7] Mention should be made of someone whose beat was, indeed, Broadway: Walter Winchell, the voice that meant Broadway for Mr. and Mrs. North America ("and all the ships at sea," to use his tagline). The Broadway gossip columnist for the *Daily Mirror*, Winchell had a radio platform for almost two decades in a series of fifteen-minute shows; his famous staccato delivery of Times Square tidbits—framed by the rat-a-tat-tat spurts of a telegraph signal—brought the lives and legends of Broadway to millions.

But, it was the radio variety show, broadcast out of New York with the best of Broadway's talent merely a few blocks away, that provided radio listeners with their most edifying glimpse behind the plush red velvet curtain. During the 1933–34 radio season, four of the top five programs were variety shows with some kind of Broadway provenance; the most popular of these was led by one of the most influential figures of the broadcast era. Only one day before the stock market crash, onto the broadcasting studio strode one Hubert Prior Vallee, a former saxophonist who attended Yale and led his dance combo under the name of Rudy Vallee.

Fleischmann's Yeast Hour is generally considered to be the first sustained variety show on the radio. Vallee was ideally suited to be its main performer and its host, as someone who could lead a "straight dance combo" and additionally bring along the kind of distinct personality that 1920s audiences began to demand of their recording artists. His patrician good looks, genial manner (on stage), and relative soft sell made him an attractive performer who had a nonchalant way with a song. He formed his own combos, the Heigh-Hos, then the Yale Men, and eventually earned a radio spot in New York, sponsored by a local jewelry store. When it was suggested to Vallee that the Yale association might be alienating to some (including other Yale men), Vallee sought inspiration from the Broadway stage. Valle had caught the Rodgers and Hart musical *A Connecticut Yankee* at the Vanderbilt Theatre in 1928, a few months into its year-long run. Smitten by such "viable melodies as 'Thou Swell' and 'My Heart Stood Still,'" as he recounts in his autobiography, "As I came out of the theater after the matinee I suddenly realized its title wouldn't be the worst in the world for naming a band. I could picture exactly how the billing would look on a marquee or on a record label." Henceforward, he and his band would achieve fame as Rudy Vallee and His Connecticut Yankees.[8]

Vallee was radio's first matinee idol; "his appeal to women and to his style of singing feminized the airwaves," in the view of media historian Susan Douglas.[9] Vallee's appealing style would help usher in the beginning of new age of "synergy" in popular music. Vallee noticed that a "mystifying thing happened" when sheet music salesmen reported to their publishers that there was a rush of requests for specific songs at various five-and-dime stores in the Northeast. "There was only one clue to the enigma; the five-and-ten-cent girls reported that their customers said the songs were being broadcast by a performer called Rudy Vallee. Now, the songs the buyers were clamoring for were perfectly good tunes. We possessed some magic power that enabled us to interest listeners in almost any song we played—and we had a radio outlet."[10]

That "radio outlet" might have been helpful for the dozens of published songs that Vallee sang on the radio, but if the recording industry had in general given the sheet music business a black eye, the radio broadcasting enterprise was delivering an uppercut. "The gal in Kalamazoo don't buy sheet music any more," a touring musician was quoted as saying, "The radio can make a song—sure! But let me tell you, it can kill it just as quick."[11] Irving Berlin, who was still presiding over a large publishing house as well as producing annual revues and musicals at the Music Box Theatre (which he co-owned) throughout the early 1920s, put it more sympathetically:

> We have become a world of listeners, rather than singers. Our songs don't live anymore. They fail to become part of us. Radio has mechanized them all. In the old days, Al Jolson sang the same song for years—until it meant something—when records were played until they cracked. Today, Paul Whiteman plays a song hit once or twice or a Hollywood hero sings them once in a film and the radio runs them ragged for a couple of weeks—then they're dead.[12]

Still, the radio would give Broadway tunes and tunes by Broadway songwriters unprecedented exposure to the nation's consumers. Even Berlin would become a major recipient of radio's "mechanized" largesse; for example, his "I've Got My Love to Keep Me Warm" (introduced in the 1937 film *On the Avenue*) was the most-played song of the week of April 16th—it was performed by a variety of artists on different evening programs thirty-four times times, an extraordinary number in the pre-AM radio days.[13]

The "golden age" of broadcast radio provided an unprecedented opportunity for Broadway songwriters to meet the public. Sheet music might occasionally feature their picture on the cover; on the label of a record, their credits were minuscule. Radio allowed for some discourse about their work (along with the hyperbolic introductions invariably provided by the host/sponsors/copywriters), a way of getting to know how they plied their trade and perfected their craft. Eddie Cantor in the full flush of his Broadway stardom had made his radio debut on *Fleischmann's Yeast Hour* with Vallee in February 1931, but performers such as Cantor and other musical talent were a radio variety show's bread and butter; their participation was obligatory. However, when George Gershwin spent eight minutes with Vallee in fall 1932, it brought the experience of Broadway to a new level.

Gershwin's music had been a presence on the radio since the medium's infancy; the ever-gregarious composer himself had already appeared on several radio shows: *The Eveready Hour*, an early attempt at variety in 1930, and *The Majestic Theater of the Air*. What Vallee provided for his large audience was an introduction to the magic and the mystery of being the most discussed and admired composer of his era. The host quizzed Gershwin on "what Americans want to know" about his early career, his latest project (*Pardon My English*), and, of course, the eternal question about which comes first, the music or the lyrics. Gershwin also obliged by playing several of his songs. When Cole Porter appeared on Vallee's show two years later ("the man of the hour with his smash hit *Anything Goes*"), he did Gershwin one better by singing his own tune "You're the Top"— with a special lyric for his host: "You're the boy who dares / Challenge Mrs. Baer's / Son, Max / You're the Russian Ballet / You're Rudy Vallee / You're Feen-a-lax!" Porter was pointedly poking fun at Gershwin's latest project—his own radio program, sponsored by Feen-a-mint laxatives. The twice-weekly, fifteen-minute show entitled *Music by Gershwin* began in spring 1934. Although he was under tremendous pressure at the time to finish the score to *Porgy and Bess*, Gershwin served as both performer and host, playing and introducing an ambitious selection of his own music, while earning $2,000 a week; a 30-minute version of the program was broadcast in the fall for several months.[14]

▷ Audio Example 4.1, *The Fleischmann Yeast Hour* (Rudy Vallee / George Gershwin)

The greatest conflation of Gershwin's notoriety with the alchemy of the airwaves in the 1930s was, alas, born out of tragedy. On the coast-to-coast network of NBC, the dean of radio announcers, Milton Cross, was heard intoning on the morning of July 11, 1937:

This morning, the world heard the tragic news of the untimely passing of George Gershwin. . . . The radio audience on countless occasions has thrilled to his melodies. . . . He is a colossus with one foot planted in Carnegie Hall, and the other in Tin Pan Alley.

NBC devoted its airwaves that day to an extraordinary series of programs and remote hookups; a bereft Al Jolson sang "Swanee" from a New York studio, accompanied by Lennie Hayton, while Paul Whiteman stood in front of a microphone in Fort Worth, Texas, where his orchestra was on tour, mourning "the passing of one of my best friends." Fred Astaire, who had known Gershwin since 1915, when they were both trying to make a name for themselves, gave a characteristically minimal but elegant statement to NBC Radio from Hollywood. The masterworks of Gershwin's stage career—songs from *Of Thee I Sing, Lady, Be Good!,* and *Porgy and Bess*—mixed with his "brilliant compositions" of the concert hall: "Rhapsody in Blue," "Cuban Overture," and so on filled the NBC airwaves for the better part of the evening.

The Mutual Broadcasting System offered similar programming, a far-ranging amalgam of classical compositions and show tunes rendered in memoriam to the composer. Harold Arlen, Hoagy Carmichael, George White, and others gave eloquent eulogies. Ethel Merman appeared live to sing "I Got Rhythm"—perhaps the first time the radio listening public had heard Merman perform the number that skyrocketed her to fame—and in a timorous (yes, timorous) voice, she introduced a heartfelt rendition of "They Can't Take That Away from Me."

▶   Audio Example 4.2, "They Can't Take That Away from Me" (Ethel Merman)

If it hadn't been for radio, the American public might have shrugged off Gershwin's untimely death—he'd have been a name on the front of some sheet music or a theater program, or some tiny words in the middle of a spinning record. But radio allowed for the music of Gershwin—and his spirited, talented brotherhood and sisterhood of songwriters—to be heard by millions of Americans in the context of how creative, influential, clever, and generous he was, as well. Perhaps not until the death of Franklin D. Roosevelt in 1945 did the airwaves devote so much time to the consequence of one individual's passing.

Even for a celebrated composer of lesser magnitude, the airwaves had an obvious appeal. Sigmund Romberg, without Gershwin's witty magnetism (and saddled with a Hungarian accent) took a more academic route: the same year that *Music by Gershwin* debuted, Romberg had a radio program where he discussed musical selections with the critic William Lyons Phelps; this was followed by three more musical series hosted by the operetta composer, all the way into 1948 when "An Evening with Romberg" was a summer replacement for NBC.[15]

A number of other ambitious programs sought to create broadcast events inspired or built around entire narrative musicals. One of the most successful shows of the early 1930s—in fact, the No. 2 program on the air for two seasons—was based on a Broadway musical: *Show Boat,* or as it was officially known, *The Maxwell House Show Boat.* Airing first in 1932, *Show Boat* didn't take its literal cue from the Kern-Hammerstein master-piece, but it sure looked awfully similar to anyone standing on the levee, as it sailed along the airwaves for five seasons. Charles Winninger, who had played Cap'n Andy in the original 1927 production (and in the 1936 film) hosted as "Captain Henry" who skippered his show boat into ports along various rivers and harbors across America. In addition to various soap operas played out among the "show folk," marginal black characters appeared, played—at one point or another—by Jules Bledsoe, the original Joe on Broadway in 1927, and Hattie McDaniel, the Queenie of the film version.

In 1935, NBC did *Show Boat* one better, producing a colossal radio extravaganza based on the reigning colossal stage extravaganza of the time: *Jumbo*, the Rodgers and Hart circus musical produced by Billy Rose at the immense Hippodrome Theatre on Sixth Avenue. *The Jumbo Fire Chief Program* premiered on the air two weeks before the musical opened and, essentially, extended the musical's thin plot about rival circus owners into an ongoing soap opera with songs and music. Jimmy Durante played the lead in both the musical and the radio program; broadcasting at 9:30 p.m. on Tuesday nights from the Hippodrome stage—ostensibly Durante's evening off from the stage show. It all sounds exhaustingly ambitious—in our age, a myriad of unions would have shut the whole thing down before it started. The radio program "left town" within half a season, but the actual musical kept running for another two months.

A radio show inspired by a new musical wasn't the worst idea in the world: a radio show that attempted to produce a new musical every week was another, more problem-atic, story. In fall 1934, Procter & Gamble premiered a new radio show, perhaps the most ambitious of its time. *The Gibson Family* recounted the weekly domestic distractions of the eponymous characters; the parents didn't do much, but the son and daughter—and the daughter's amorous swain—worked through their problems in musical numbers. As *Time* magazine reported, the week after the program premiered in mid-September, "The music for each program will be as new to the public as the music at the opening night of a theatre musicomedy [*sic*]. If radio audiences particularly like any Gibson Family songs, they will be able to buy sheet copies, which may plug them into hits."[16]

The sponsors had alighted on Arthur Schwartz and Howard Dietz, who—despite being at the height of their creative powers with five successful revues in as many years—had hit a dry spell. Luckily for both men, Procter & Gamble offered them $1,250 a week each; the catch was that they had to come up with three songs a week—for not terribly interesting characters, at that. "We wrote 94 songs in the next 39 weeks," recounted Dietz in his memoirs. "In that period, it seems to me, I never came out of the shower without a new lyric. And Arthur always had a tune for it."[17] Six months into the heavily promoted show, bored audiences turned the dial to other programs; toward the end of the run, the sponsors brought in Charles Winninger (who had left *The Maxwell House Show Boat* in a contract dispute) to transform the Gibson family into performers in a tent show entertainment. By March 1935, the program was cancelled. Dietz and Schwartz were clever enough to repurpose "If There Is Someone Lovelier Than You" into their next stage musical, *Revenge with Music*, and left the Procter & Gamble project exhausted, but thousands of dollars richer (and with, one assumes, a lifetime supply of Ivory Soap).

A product giveaway of any kind would have been a nice perk for Rodgers and Hart in 1935. While *Jumbo* was still in rehearsal, they were part of an unmitigated disaster on CBS Radio. Apparently undeterred from the uphill battle of *The Gibson Family*, a producer named Howard Brenner thought an original weekly musical could still be feasible. He commissioned Rodgers and Hart to write two songs (although they are reprised so often, it feels like two hundred) for an hour-long program called *Let's Have Fun.* The second half was your run-of-the-mill variety show, but the first half concerned a Broadway songwriter transported back to Ancient Egypt to consort with Cleopatra, played by none other than Helen Morgan. This basic conceit had already been rendered more skillfully by Rodgers and Hart in the 1920s with *A Connecticut Yankee* (and time travel to the ancient world was rendered even better in the Eddie Cantor musical film, *Roman Scandals,* two years earlier). Rodgers and Hart turned in some of their least inspiring work—"A Little of You on Toast" and "Please Make Me Good"— and the leads were baffled and bewildered. The whole thing was cancelled after its one broadcast on October 22, with the mildly risible line spoken by Cleopatra to the songwriter—"What is this 'Broadway' of which you speak?"—as the only amusing takeaway from this disaster.

Rodgers and Hart were working too busily and too well in the Theater District to have their careers threatened by these ambitious missteps on broadcast radio. A year later, they wrote a brief dramatic oratorio called "All Points West"—a musical monodrama about a peripatetic train conductor—conducted by Paul Whiteman for the Philadelphia Orchestra; it was broadcast in January 1937 on New York NBC affiliate WEAF, to great acclaim. Rudy Vallee would subsequently include it as part of a nightclub act at the Hotel Astor (much to the chagrin of Rodgers, who felt the dramatic heft of the material was above Vallee's paygrade). What radio gave to Rodgers and Hart—what it gave to all of their Broadway cohorts—was a national stage and a kind of prestige that had previously been bordered by Sixth Avenue and Eighth Avenue.

Of course, it was the songs themselves that did the best job of selling Broadway to Main Street. And the opinions of Main Street—rather than, say, the predilections of a sponsor or some Ivy League, pipe-smoking producer in Manhattan—made their presence felt on NBC, Saturday evening, April 20, 1935:

Once again the voice of the people has spoken to select the tunes of *Your Hit Parade*.... You've told us by purchasing sheet music and records, by your requests to orchestra leaders, by the tunes you listen to on your favorite programs. That's why the Hit Parade is *your* own program.

Your Hit Parade (originally called *Lucky Strike Sweepstakes*) was the brainchild of someone on the payroll of George Washington Hill, the president of the American Tobacco Company. Hill was an enormously powerful sponsor with millions at his disposal, and he, literally, called the tune. Among his preferences were for "songs that made Broadway Broadway. Not the songs that are making Broadway Broadway ... songs that have rung so in the public ear that they mean something, recall something, start with a background of pleasant familiarity."[18] *Your Hit Parade* would play along to that formula for more than three decades.

It was the first successful radio program to promote a "ranking" of hits—a format that still primes the pump of much commercial radio in the twenty-first century. Exactly how the songs were selected to be on *Your Hit Parade* was a matter of much conjecture—there wasn't the technology yet to monitor consumer purchases objectively—and it was rumored that money had changed hands under the table. Still, *Your Hit Parade* burnished the idea that American music didn't simply have standards: it had "hits." This may have upset Irving Berlin but, in this case popularity trumped longevity and gave the American public at least the impression of egalitarianism, even if the music industry and corporate sponsors were pulling strings behind the scenes.

The imprimatur of Broadway and its aura of "pleasant familiarity" was part of the program from the beginning: the No. 1 song of the week that *Your Hit Parade* premiered was "Soon," written by Rodgers and Hart and sung by Bing Crosby in the film *Mississippi*. Another Broadway song to make the top ten on the program in its first season was "I Won't Dance" from *Roberta*. Other Broadway chart toppers on *Your Hit Parade* in the following five years were "It's De-Lovely" (*Red, Hot and Blue!*, 1936); two Rodgers and Hart "second-place" winners—"Where or When?" (*Babes in Arms*, 1937) and "This Can't Be Love" (*The Boys from Syracuse*, 1938). "All the Things You Are" from *Very Warm for May* was a No. 1 song in 1940.

The performances on *Your Hit Parade*—by a popular, but not particularly challenging, repertory company of five soloists and two vocal groups, backed up by the Lucky Strike Orchestra under the baton of Lennie Hayton—were pleasant and comfortable; they conveyed a generic accessibility that seemed appropriate for a hit song. That would all change when a hot young singer out of the Tommy Dorsey orchestra joined the repertory company: Frank Sinatra. Sinatra was the lead singer on *Your Hit Parade* for almost two years, beginning in February 1943.

Radio was an important part of Sinatra's career, just as it was for his predecessors, Vallee and Crosby. The intimacy of the microphone—and their respective talents at mastering its technology—was essential, of course. But personality and personal connection—that is, being the interlocutor between the material and the audience—counted for a lot as well. Sinatra always had a high respect for Broadway composers and lyricists, and saw their material as a high-water mark in American entertainment. Indeed, he honored the Broadway songbook and its craftspeople throughout his entire career. In 1964, during a tribute to Cole Porter, he told the story that when he was just starting out, in 1938, singing multiple sets at a New Jersey roadhouse, the composer stopped in for a drink with a small entourage. Sinatra, dazzled by Porter's reputation, decided to point out the songwriter to the audience (Porter preferred just to have his drink, thank you very much); not content to leave it at that, Sinatra had the bright idea of honoring Porter by singing "Night and Day"—except that he forgot all the words.[19]

By the time he was appearing on three radio programs simultaneously in fall 1943, Sinatra wasn't in a forgetful state of mind at all; he remembered his roots by crooning standards by Rodgers and Hart, Porter, and Vincent Youmans. On an October 1943 broadcast of *Songs by Sinatra*, he even recalled a seminal moment in his sentimental education:

> When I was a kid, back in the Buster Brown stocking days over in Jersey, somebody in the Sinatra tribe who had a spaghetti-and-vino friendship with some of the big shots in music, took me around to a hotel suite, where a pink-faced gentleman with wonderful white-hair and a smile that made you feel good all over was handing around club sandwiches and coffee. Some of the stage people, I believe, may have skipped the coffee for champagne. All I know is that I was impressed by two things: the nice man and the wonderful club sandwiches. That man was Victor Herbert. I only regret now it couldn't happen to me again, when I wasn't such an icky infant. All of which is by coming in on a flanking movement to take over one of Mr. Herbert's best-known songs, "Kiss Me Again."[20]

Without knowing it, Sinatra was linking his musical roots with those of Richard Rodgers, who had also experienced Herbert as an impressionable young man. Sinatra carried on Vallee's tradition of honoring contemporary songwriters, but Vallee, of course, was more of their generation, so his banter tended to be playful while Sinatra was more reverent and awestruck. In that same *Songs by Sinatra* program, he set up one classic from Oscar Hammerstein II and Sigmund Romberg's *The New Moon*, "Lover, Come Back to Me:" "The Oscar Hammerstein who wrote *Show Boat* and the Oscar Hammerstein who wrote

Bing Crosby, Dinah Shore, Frank Sinatra, and Judy Garland (l. to r.): Not one of them ever appeared in a Broadway musical—and yet the four of them did more to popularize Broadway music than any dozen shows. Credit: Photofest.

the present great hit *Oklahoma!* has a gentle touch of beauty and seems to get it in the lyric. And when you add Sigmund Romberg, who uses his heart as a canvas and his genius as a brush—well, you really have something."

▶ Audio Example 4.3, "Lover Come Back to Me" (Frank Sinatra)

Sinatra would continue on the radio regularly into the 1950s, bringing all sorts of Broadway songs, old and new, to listeners. He carefully guided them through the provenance of the songs, their place in the story, their musical value, and their context. He functioned as pop culture's seal of approval for Broadway. During a live broadcast from the Hollywood Bowl in 1945, Sinatra even flagged the complexity of the most recent masterpiece from the relatively new team of Rodgers and Hammerstein:

Here now is a song—it's more than a song, it's a wonderful piece of material, it's from another great show I was lucky enough to catch on Broadway, *Carousel.* It's called "Soliloquy" and it hasn't been heard frequently enough. It concerns a rather robust kind of fellow, but he's a good guy on top of it all and his lovely little wife tells him she's about to have a baby.[21]

When Eddie Cantor bounced around NBC's Radio City studios in the early 1930s, using his particular brand of hijinks to sell ground coffee to the masses, he was also selling the brand of Broadway for its time: energetic, ebullient, and inconsequential. When Sinatra was selling Broadway to the masses, a decade and a half later, he was selling a different brand of Broadway: something more mature, more consequential, more in need of contextualization. Cantor and Sinatra couldn't have been more different as performers, but home listeners sitting by the Philco relied upon them both to act as ambassadors of the airwaves to that mythic kingdom in New York known as Broadway.

Top: Jack Kapp (right) conferring with (a toupeeless) Bing Crosby at a Decca session, after the war. Kapp would be the first visionary of the Broadway cast album empire. Credit: Photofest. Bottom: American Federation of Musicians president James Petrillo, making a pointed remark before Congress, 1948. Credit: Photofest.

CHAPTER 5

The Farmer and the Cowman Should Be Friends

Album Sets and the Narrative of Broadway

For two fierce rivals fighting over the same territory, they were astonishingly similar.

In the middle of World War II, Jack Kapp, the president of Decca Records, squared off against James C. Petrillo, the president of the American Federation of Musicians, in an epic national labor battle that would, in many ways, determine how Broadway theater would be recorded and embraced by the American public.

They were both from working class immigrant families—Kapp's came from Russia, Petrillo's from Italy—who settled down in Chicago, where both were born and raised at the turn of the century. Though neither was a trained musician, they both grew up in the music business; Kapp was a clerk for Columbia Records, where his father was a salesman, and Petrillo was a mediocre cornetist, working weddings to make ends meet. Dynamic, clever, and magnetic leaders who ran their domains with no interference from above, Kapp and Petrillo were autodidacts with little formal schooling, making up their craft as they went along. They were also principled and intransigent, especially in the service of their respect fields: Kapp at building a legacy of musical excellence for his record company and Petrillo at ameliorating the lot of the thousands of musicians whose livelihood he was sworn to protect.

The territory of popular music that Kapp and Petrillo were fighting over had gotten increasingly complex by the end of the 1930s. A showdown between capital and labor was inevitable. Back in 1906, John Philip Sousa had decried what he called "canned music"—that is, music reproduced without the presence of live musicians—and by 1940, canned music had become ubiquitous. Phonograph records were enjoying an upswing of popularity; RCA Victor and Columbia had been joined by Kapp's rival Decca Records in 1933 and, taken together, they accounted for the sale of 50 million records in 1939. Electrical transcription disks (ETs) of radio variety programs—initially derided as a cheat by popular bandleaders and radio stations alike—were now played by affiliates all over the country, displacing a wide swath of live musicians. Hollywood had obviously used studio musicians for its soundtracks—live orchestras for film presentations had died out more than a decade earlier—and jukeboxes were becoming a national preoccupation, with more than 400,000 across the country, utilizing 78 rpm recordings of popular songs that were played for a nickel a pop by the habitués of restaurants, taverns, and bars: venues that had once been fertile platforms for live music.[1]

The livelihood of a trained musician was increasingly and seriously compromised by this rapid progress in media technology. Another group of talented musicians—the songwriters whose works were being played more and more on the radio, as well as these other venues—were also feeling squeezed out. Back in 1914, Victor Herbert and his fellow tunesmiths formed the American Society of Composers, Authors, and Publishers (ASCAP) as a way of protecting themselves and their work from unauthorized performances or performances without remuneration. Ten years later, as radio became ubiquitous, ASCAP would come to an agreement with the major broadcasters to receive royalties for its members based on the amount of times a song was played; in fact, ASCAP was in the business of monitoring the performance of work on the air (and on recordings), collecting residuals from the broadcasters and parsing out the payments to its songwriting members according to a fairly arcane rating system. From the mid-1930s on, ASCAP was locked in a series of negotiations with the National Association of Broadcasters (NAB)—whose heavy hitters were NBC and CBS—over an increase in the residual rate for its members. Sheet music sales had plummeted since the height of the early 1920s, and ASCAP members, the crème de la crème of Broadway and Tin Pan Alley (Berlin, Kern, Gershwin, Rodgers and Hart, Romberg, Youmans, and so on), who had lost out on sheet music residuals were eager to get some piece of the ever-expanding pie of musical offerings on the radio.

Now, as the 1930s were segueing into the 1940s, and the country—still unable to get the mud of the Depression off its boots—was contemplating the ramifications of war in Europe, a complicated tangle of commercial and artistic issues was engulfing the music industry. ASCAP was threatening to pull its goods from the broadcasting market, leaving an unknown landscape for radio listeners.[2] (Indeed, for a few months in 1935, Warner Bros., which had purchased Harms and several other firms in 1929, had pushed to take ASCAP songs off the radio.) The American Federation of Musicians (AFM), the leading musicians' union, was fighting for higher wages and greater benefits from the recording industry. For two decades, the public had been enjoying a better quality of music from a better quality of performer on a better quality of technology. Now it might all come crashing to a halt.

Compounding this potential catastrophe was the fact that songwriting for musical theater on Broadway was also at the peak of its development. Although many songwriters had decamped to Hollywood in the very early 1930s, several of them came back to Broadway—even if only for brief stays. Broadway was a place where, although a theater writer's reach might exceed his grasp, the reach was admired and appreciated. Nearly all of those who returned, with the exceptions of Jerome Kern and Cole Porter (who each enjoyed, in his own way, the climate and the lifestyle of the West Coast) knew this instinctively. George Gershwin had ventured back to the West Coast at about the same time that Rodgers and Hart returned to Broadway, but in 1935, he and his brother (and DuBose Heyward) had given New York *Porgy and Bess* as a farewell present. That same year, Kurt Weill emigrated from Germany to America. Although several of the seasons between 1935 and 1940 produced only meager financial successes, the imagination of the American musical was bounteous indeed.

During this period, musicals began stretching their boundaries to become relevant in content: *Pins and Needles*, penned by Harold Rome and performed by youthful members of the International Ladies Garment Workers Union, captured the spirit of New York's socially conscious proletariat; Weill contributed *Johnny Johnson* and *Knickerbocker Holiday*, two politically charged scores; even the normally apolitical team of Rodgers and Hart tackled FDR and his policies in *I'd Rather Be Right*. Rodgers and Hart also pushed the form, incorporating major swaths of ballet into *On Your Toes*, and Elizabethan comedy—courtesy of Shakespeare and George Abbott—into *The Boys from Syracuse*. At the very end of 1940, after a few somewhat trivial shows about college football and whatnot, they contributed *Pal Joey*, the first musical to deal with, as Rodgers put it, "the facts of life."[3]

All of this pushing of boundaries was evolutionary—even when it wasn't revolutionary—and ambitious and honorable. The scope of it, however, was not recoverable by the non-theatergoing listening public.

The ambitions of the musical stage in the late 1930s vastly outpaced the comparable innovations in recording technology. Folks still had to flip over cumbersome shellac disks onto their turntables every three and a half minutes, unless they had a Capehart spindle, which would provide only an additional whopping ten to twelve minutes of music. As Broadway turned out more mature work, in which the context was increasingly complex—how to picket a garment factory, or the intricacies of the New Deal—the distance between songs that were easily extractable and songs that existed organically to serve the narrative of the show was growing. Of course, there were still songs from musicals that were recorded and became popular—"September Song," "This Can't Be Love," "All the Things You Are"—but some excellent theater songs from the period, such as "My Funny Valentine" and "The Lady Is a Tramp" (from *Babes in Arms*), "Have You Met Miss Jones?" (from *I'd Rather Be Right*) or "It Never Was You" (from *Knickerbocker Holiday*), or even "Begin the Beguine" (from Cole Porter's jovial *Jubilee*), would have to wait years to be truly discovered, rendered sensitively, and admitted to the canon of the popular songbook.

In addition, an entire generation had grown up since the carefree, often knuckle-headed ditties of the 1920s, and the Depression had toughened the taste of the American public, even as it still craved escapism. The arc of the theatrical universe in American musicals bends toward narrative, and thoughtful, extended stories occasionally achieved a surprising popularity. An outlier that captures the anxieties and aspirations of the era was "Ballad for Americans," a ten-minute cantata written by composer Earl Robinson and lyricist John La Touche for inclusion in the 1939 Federal Theatre Project show, *Sing for Your Supper*. Six months after the show closed, radio producer Norman Corwin brought Paul Robeson into a CBS studio to perform the cantata with full orchestra for a prime-time radio program. A complex epic of boisterous populism, "Ballad for Americans" was a wide-ranging tapestry of American history and lives: "Well, I'm everybody who's nobody. I'm the nobody who's everybody," intoned Robeson. Apparently, the studio audience was so impressed that it applauded Robeson for twenty minutes. In 1940 Robeson recorded the piece for RCA Victor on two disks to great commercial success; months later, Bing Crosby followed suit by recording the piece for Decca, also released as a two-disk set. The release of "Ballad for Americans" on two separate multi-disk sets demonstrated an audience for theatrical music transitioning into more extended forms with complex storylines.

There had been attempts to wrangle the technology of 78s to showcase a full score as far back as 1931. Victor released two 78s of the Dietz and Schwartz score to *The Band Wagon*, starring Fred and Adele Astaire. The release is really a collection of four separate medleys of songs from the production, one medley per side, under the baton of Leo Reisman: some energetically sung by Fred and/or Adele, some merely played as instrumentals. Reisman himself "introduces" the recording, following the overture; after some tentative "hellos" from the Astaires, he tells the listener, "Due to this record playing twenty minutes we are able to present a rather comprehensive presentation of *The Band Wagon* score . . . you may turn me over on my back for the second act." It's more admirable as a record of what this fabulous duo sounded like in performance than an archival presentation of the score.

In 1940, Columbia marketed a series of four 78s of previously released recordings from Brunswick as an anthology of *Show Boat* renditions entitled *Here Comes the*

Showboat. The performances were a mixture of original artists (Helen Morgan), replacements (Paul Robeson), commercial singers (popular tenor James Melton, Countess Albani), and the Victor Young Orchestra. In the album set, the records are grouped not by the narrative demands of the show, but by artist; Helen Morgan's two songs, recorded back in 1932, are grouped on the same disk, even though they appear in two separate acts in the show. Likewise, the Countess Albani—an exotic singer with a brief career—recorded "Why Do I Love You?" with Frank Munn in 1932, although two other songs performed in the show by the same character (Gaylord Ravenal) are performed on the anthology by James Melton. Columbia must have known that it was, in some way, pulling a fast one; the back cover of the attractively designed album proclaimed "Remember how vividly *Show Boat* came to life in Florenz Ziegfeld's original production?…For many of us, this new Columbia album brings back fond, fond memories…" More of an *aide-memoire* than an "original cast album," *Here Comes the Showboat* (the album set doesn't even call itself *Show Boat*) could only capture the hits, not the full scope of the original score.

The first successful attempt to capture that full scope of an original show into a set of recordings—an album set, with multiple disks in separate sleeves, bound by a sturdy cover—came not from one of the grand theatrical endeavors of the hallowed writers of the ASCAP pantheon, but from one of the great outliers of the Broadway musical, Marc Blitzstein's 1937 *The Cradle Will Rock*. The story of the opening night of Blitzstein's self-described combination of "realism, romance, vaudeville, comic strip, Gilbert and Sullivan, Brecht, and agitprop"[4] on June 16, 1937, has become part of the American theatrical mythology: how the Federal government closed the WPA-sponsored production down; how director Orson Welles and producer John Houseman managed to find a new theater at the last minute; how Blitzstein narrated the show at a piano on a bare stage; how the cast members—enjoined by their union from appearing on stage—sang their material from the audience; how the extraordinary rallying cry of hard-working artists performing a show about hard-working steelworkers made the front pages of newspapers across the country.

But, when the dust had settled, *The Cradle Will Rock*, emboldened by the publicity it engendered and the enthusiasm of progressive audiences who saw its opening night triumph as a metaphor for "fighting City Hall," continued performances for several weeks in the hot summer of 1937 in its opening night version, with Blitzstein at the piano and the cast performing from the audience. "There has always been the question of how to produce a labor show so that an audience can be brought to feel that it is part of the performance," Houseman told the *New York Times*. "This technique seems to solve the problem."[5] In January of the following year, *The Cradle Will Rock* moved into the Windsor Theatre, an intimate house on West 48th Street run by the Labor Stage, and settled in for a four-month run, again with Blitzstein framing the action.

Although it was impressive that the show continued to interest audiences, *The Cradle Will Rock* was hardly a blockbuster and Blitzstein's score—which worked extremely well within the context of his objectives—had no extractable commercial appeal. In addition to the occasional "Jesus!" and "bastard" in the lyrics, the character with the best ballad ("Nickel Under the Foot") was a prostitute and, of course, the entire musical was an attack against capitalism. Still, if any recording company was an appropriate metaphor for the show itself, it was Musicraft Records.

Musicraft had been founded in 1937 in Manhattan as a bargain-basement company that would produce accessible masterpieces of Western music, performed by anonymous orchestras and chamber groups, pressed onto 10-inch discs and sold for 29 cents (less than half the usual price for a 78) at drugstores and chain stores. At some point, during *The Cradle Will Rock*'s run at the Windsor in early 1938, Blitzstein and the entire cast were brought by Musicraft into a rented studio. They recorded nearly the entire show on seven 12-inch disks—fourteen sides, more than had ever been accorded to a Broadway musical before. Very little of Blitzstein's score was compromised for the recording—the recording contained more than a dozen numbers—and there was a fair amount of dialogue as well. Just as he had done every night on stage, Blitzstein narrated the proceedings (in fact, the few elisions to the show are papered over by some capsule narration by Blitzstein). What the Musicraft recording of *The Cradle Will Rock* resembles more than anything is a radio program with music; one gets the full story, with the narrative alternating between dialogue, song, sound effects, and actual narration, with a beginning, middle, and an end. The final product was unwieldy—one had to turn records over in mid-scene—but there was no dancing around what it provided. If you wanted to know what the full architecture of *The Cradle Will Rock* sounded like—indeed, if you wanted to know what the original production sounded like, cast members, underscoring, sound effects, and all—Musicraft Records release #18, all 57 or so minutes of it, delivered.

It's difficult to know now what attracted Musicraft to *The Cradle Will Rock* beyond its reputation. Its previous seventeen releases had all been traditionally revered classics—Mozart, Bach, Brahms, etc.—and one release of Carl Sandburg reading his own poetry. As time went on, Musicraft released more Sandburg, along with poetry and folk songs, so perhaps the company saw Blitzstein as part of a progressive American folk tradition. Although the album cover was as plain as could be, Musicraft included a short booklet explaining to listeners what to expect, as well as a capsule history of the musical's opening night:

Since then, thousands who were carried off their feet by the dramatic force of the play have been clamoring for a recorded version. Others who have not been so fortunate will now have their first opportunity to hear this "play in music."

The opera is recorded just as it was performed on Broadway. The comparatively few deletions do not affect the continuity, which is performed in a running narration by Marc Blitzstein, so that, for all practical purposes, the performance can be considered a complete one. We may add that all of the well-known songs, as published by Chappell & Co., have been included.

The idea of "all of the well-known songs" may have been wishful thinking, but the sophisticated intentions of *The Cradle Will Rock* were perfectly captured in the first real original cast album.

▶   Audio Example 5.1, "Finale" (*The Cradle Will Rock* original cast)

To paraphrase a line from its finale, by the time *The Cradle Will Rock* hit stores in the late spring of 1938, the stormbirds were certainly circling the music industry. The real labor struggle in the music industry was the money at stake between the NAB and ASCAP, which increasingly relied on revenue for its members from their works being performed on the radio. ASCAP members still weren't being compensated for the amount of putative airplay their songs were getting on the thousands of jukeboxes across the country. Even with the recession of 1937, broadcast radio was big business. In 1939, sales from advertising had brought in more than $165 million, with NBC taking in over $45 million and CBS earning $35.5 million in sponsorship fees. ASCAP, for its part, had only received $4.3 million in royalty payments for the vast amount of member music on the airwaves. The only intelligent way to change the way the wind blew, it seemed to ASCAP, was to ask the NAB for an increase of more than double its royalties to 7½ percent.[6]

For the broadcasters, anxious about how the impending war in Europe might diminish revenue, this was a non-starter. In 1939, they enlisted the services of a CBS corporation lawyer named Sydney M. Kaye to find a way out. Kaye came up with an ingenious solution, which was, essentially, for the broadcasters to take their football and go home— or, rather, Kaye's plan was for the broadcasters to devise their own alternate football. Plans were quickly set up to create Broadcast Music Inc., a separate licensing firm for composers and lyricists, which the NAB underwrote to the tune of $400,000; the broadcasters would, in turn, own the exclusive rights to all songs licensed and arranged by BMI. Throughout 1940, BMI hired arrangers, offered favorable rates to songwriters whose contracts with ASCAP expired, cultivated relationships with new songwriters, and lured away music publishers from the ASCAP fold. Although the networks were not necessarily unified—they had thousands of affiliates in 48 states, each with its own local rules—they did a better job of getting their houses in order than ASCAP did, whose often fractious leadership made the mistake of underestimating the plans of BMI.[7]

Through BMI's organizational plans, the networks were able to build up a considerable store of alternative music for potential airplay. The Broadway and Tin Pan Alley pantheon belonged exclusively to ASCAP, so BMI had to set its sights elsewhere. It snagged two important music libraries, Southern Music and Edward B. Marks, which brought an entirely new repertoire of Latin music, "hillbilly" music (what we'd call "country western"), and other regional sounds that had been mostly ignored by mainstream radio. Clever arrangers and bandleaders also made hay with songs in the public domain in new and original treatments: Glenn Miller scored big with a version of "The Song of the Volga Boatman," and the melody of the pop hit "Tonight We Love" was borrowed from Tchaikovsky. Having stocked their rations sufficiently, the radio networks called ASCAP's bluff on midnight, December 31, 1940, and effectively boycotted their entire catalog. More than one million ASCAP songs vanished from the airwaves overnight.

For many, this wasn't necessarily a bad thing: the ASCAP boycott did a great deal to diversify mainstream musical tastes, and BMI would go on to become an effective business model in American entertainment that is still robust today. But for the handful of songwriters who had just opened musicals on Broadway, it was a disaster. These included Rodgers and Hart, whose *Pal Joey* had opened on Christmas Day, and Kurt Weill and Ira Gershwin, whose *Lady in the Dark* would debut in January 1941. Both shows were sophisticated with complex characters at their centers—an amoral nightclub singer and a conflicted magazine editor, respectively—which might have put record executives off, but the music itself represented those artists at their zenith. Yet, without the possibility of airplay, it didn't really matter how good the songs were.

The star of *Lady in the Dark*, Gertrude Lawrence, would issue a three-disk set of songs on Victor, late in 1941; the show's featured phenomenon, Danny Kaye, would record a similar set for Columbia (singing, as was often the case, songs sung by others in the show). However, the score to *Pal Joey*, rather astonishingly, was never recorded during the eleven-month run of the show—and, of course, it couldn't be played on the radio. The concession stand in the lobby of the Ethel Barrymore Theatre pushed the sheet music—"They can't bar [the music] from your piano"[8]—but it would be more than a decade before the breadth of Rodgers and Hart's achievement—"I Could Write a Book," "Den of Iniquity," and "Bewitched, Bothered, and Bewildered"—would be understood and appreciated by the American public. There were a couple of hurried dance orchestra recordings of

"I Could Write a Book" and "Bewitched," but nothing comparable to the kind of coverage that was obligatory for Rodgers and Hart.

Perhaps the most lamentable Broadway casualty of the ASCAP boycott was *Hold on to Your Hats*, which opened in September 1940. It was the first theater score by Burton Lane and Yip Harburg—not only that, it would be Al Jolson's first time on the Broadway stage in a decade. The droll tale of a radio actor whose portrayal of a cowboy hero is taken far too literally, it had all the makings of a smash, especially with the ebullient Jolson, who was still enjoying a vast popularity of his own. Years later, Lane recalled with dismay, "There were three songs in *Hold on to Your Hats* that had begun to develop hit potential: 'There's a Great Day Coming Mañana,' 'The World Is in My Arms,' and '(Love Is a Lovely Thing) Don't Let It Get You Down.' One minute after midnight, 1940, those songs went off the air."[9] Although Buddy Clark and Frank Sinatra would record pop versions of the first two songs, Jolson never recorded anything from the show, and the score vanished into near-complete obscurity. The greater listening public would have to wait another seven years for a recording of a score by Lane and Harburg: *Finian's Rainbow*.

Harburg may have been hoping that Decca Records would come to the rescue; in 1939 it released a four-disk set of various cover recordings of Harburg and Harold Arlen's score for *The Wizard of Oz* featuring two songs performed by Judy Garland, a Decca artist. Although the album set was not an accurate record of the film, Decca's head, Jack Kapp, was the closest thing the recording industry had at the time to a visionary, and in the early 1940s, he advanced the cause of capturing the Broadway experience at home.

Kapp had been born in 1901; his father had worked as a salesman for Columbia Records, out of Chicago. Kapp took his early jobs with the firm, becoming a shipping clerk, and eventually taking and completing orders. By the early 1920s, he was working as a producer for Brunswick on its Vocalion line, where he hustled to bring a number of innovative black jazz musicians to the label and began blockbuster collaborations with the Guy Lombardo Orchestra and with Bing Crosby, once he started his solo career. Kapp was committed to expanding his horizons: he left Brunswick and in 1933 formed Decca, a company that would sell records at a cheaper price—35 cents per disk, as opposed to the 75-cent product sold by RCA and Columbia. The savvy producer brought along Lombardo and Crosby, whose contracts with Brunswick were up; following soon to the new label were Ethel Waters, the Mills Brothers, and eventually Judy Garland and Ella Fitzgerald.[10]

Kapp was frequently beset by commercial and technological troubles, but he persevered. By the end of the 1930s, Decca was making a tidy profit and had joined the ranks of the top three record companies; out of the 50 million records sold in 1939, 18 million were 35-cent records cut by Decca. Crosby himself contributed two million of those. In an August 1940 profile of Kapp in the *New Yorker*, the writer concluded that Kapp's best quality was his ever-inquisitive spirit: "He doesn't know what the next musical vogue will be, or where it will come from."

One vogue that Kapp brought forward was the American musical. He felt that, if properly packaged with a colorful cover, photographs, explanatory notes, and framed correctly with the Broadway imprimatur, a more expensive set of disks might prove commercially attractive. In 1940, Kapp assembled several members of the original cast of the 1935 *Porgy and Bess* to record selections from the opera, backed by Alexander Smallens and his orchestra, on a four-disk album set. The photographs on the inside included portraits of the performers in the Decca studio, contrasted with production shots from the original show. But at that point, *Porgy and Bess* was long gone from the Broadway stage (although a revival would come along in 1942 that Decca would also record). Kapp created an early brand of "synergy" with the release of *The Wizard of Oz* album set; you can see the movie, then run out and buy the recording with at least one of the stars. Later in 1939, he moved even closer to his commercial objective with the release of Decca Album Set #33: six sides of the Rodgers and Hart smash hit from the 1938–39 season, *The Boys from Syracuse.*

The Boys from Syracuse album set was not entirely without the quirks associated with the period. None of the actual Broadway cast was on the recording, but consumers were no doubt attracted to the appearance of Rudy Vallee and Frances Langford, a very appealing and versatile singer whom Vallee had introduced on his radio show (and who by then had a Decca contract). Vallee and Langford covered the songs that already had some prominent airplay and recording history—"This Can't Be Love," "Sing for Your Supper," and "Falling in Love with Love," which had been on *Your Hit Parade*—but, more interestingly, they also covered songs that, while important to the score and indicative of the skill of Rodgers and Hart, would seem to have little value as commercial releases, such as "Oh, Diogenes!," a troubled plea to find an honest man, jauntily delivered by Vallee. One can infer that Kapp felt that the full breadth of the score—or at least the six songs included— was larger than the sum of its hits.

Such an inference is confirmed by the copy in a booklet included in the set:

> Decca, abreast of the demand for records from this sensational musical production, is happy to present herewith—in an attractive permanent souvenir album—the six most popular numbers from this exceptionally appealing Rodgers and Hart score— these records will…serve also as a most appropriate memento of this production in the years to come.

The front and back covers to the set featured not Vallee or Langford, but a collage of pictures from the original Broadway production with "THE BOYS FROM SYRACUSE" featured prominently, along with credit for the director, George Abbott, and as well as the signatures of Rodgers and Hart.[11]

▶ Audio Example 5.2, "Oh, Diogenes!" (Rudy Vallee)

Decca continued to support the work of Rodgers and Hart, issuing four sides of Shirley Ross performing songs from the 1940 *Higher and Higher* (some of which she originated on stage, others not) and the cabaret singer Hildegarde performing four songs from their 1942 hit *By Jupiter* (in which she did not appear). By the time those songs came out in July 1942, the ASCAP boycott had been settled for seven months. The broadcasters had agreed to take on the job of collecting royalty fees and ASCAP ratcheted down its royalty demand to 2½-2¾ percent; BMI survived the boycott and prospered.[12] But the ASCAP boycott was just the entr'acte to the big finale of labor disputes in the musical industry in the 1940s.

The roots of the American Federation of Musicians strike were, in some ways, the same as the ASCAP boycott: the disenfranchisement of active artists by huge corporations that were making tremendous profits from previously recorded music. But where the ASCAP leadership was neither unified nor charismatic, the AFM had a leader who meant business and had the disposition to fight to the bitter end, no matter what public relations debacle(s) he left in his wake.

James Caesar Petrillo had been a local musicians' union leader as early as 1915; by 1923, he was the local head of Chicago's chapter of the AFM. Even in the corrupt environment of Chicago during the Capone era, he kept his union dealings scrupulously clean—he also delivered for his members. In 1940, he ascended to the presidency of the national union, while still maintaining his local leadership in Chicago. Petrillo was considered a "czar" by virtue of his mandate: the leader of 140,000 working-class musicians—one of the ten largest labor unions in America (he sensibly wondered why executives like NBC's David Sarnoff and CBS's William Paley were never called "czars" by the press). In 1947, he was interviewed by the *New York Times,* which summed up Petrillo's mantra masterfully: "The musicologist may be concerned whether the instrumentalist has talents; Petrillo wants to know if he has groceries."[13]

In spring 1942, Petrillo announced an end run for the purposes of creating awareness for his rank-and-file: on August 1, the union would forbid any of its members to enter a recording studio. For the recording industry, this would be the second major setback of the spring: the War Production Board, now in its fifth month of wartime oversight, had cut the industry's supply of shellac—a resin imported from India used to make record disks—by 70 percent. Columbia, RCA Victor, and Decca now had to make fewer records available to the general public; if Petrillo had his way, however, they would have practically no product to deliver, either. He showed little sign of backing down. He threatened a deadline of midnight on July 31 for the strike, although he offered no conditions under which he might avert it. The record companies were reduced to a six-week scramble to record as many instrumental performances as they could in order to stockpile records. The recording logs for Decca reveal a dense back-to-back schedule for sessions in studios on both coasts during the last few days of July; in fact, the very last thing that Decca recorded in New York before the strike was a final session for the album set featuring Irving Berlin's patriotic extravaganza, *This Is the Army*. [14]

When the strike came—and it did, as Petrillo promised—the record companies had to resort to some fleet-footed strategies. In addition to the stockpiled records, they issued songs that had previously been deemed unreleasable or reissued old songs from their back catalogs. Rudy Vallee's 1931 rendition of "As Time Goes By" (originally written for a Broadway musical, *Everybody's Welcome*) became a hit all over again, spurred by the release of the film *Casablanca* in 1943; no new cover version of the song was possible. The record producers even devolved to *a cappella* recordings of glee clubs or choral groups backing up lead singers. Petrillo professed himself none too pleased with the last stratagem—but, then, he was none too pleased with anything. Newspaper opinion writers, editorial cartoonists, member of Congress—all of them begged him to change his stance, especially as the country's morale, mired in a world war, could use a little musical uplift. No dice, he claimed; he worked for his members, not for the morale board, nor even for the American people. Petrillo wanted records used only for enjoyment at home, where no one would dream of having a live professional musician; performance without compensation anywhere else— on jukeboxes, or on electrical transcription disks, or on the air—was not acceptable.[15]

By spring 1943, the recording industry was running out of options. Obviously, the recording of Broadway material had ground to a halt. One of the few consolations was that there wasn't much first-rate material originating on Broadway during the strike. *By Jupiter* had only just opened when the strike began, and although Hildegarde got her few previously recorded numbers into the mix, a wider range of songs from that score never happened. Ethel Merman had triumphed in Cole Porter's *Something for the Boys*, but no one could claim it was a major Porter score.

All that changed, of course, on March 31 when *Oklahoma!* opened at the St. James Theatre. The debut of the Rodgers and Hammerstein songwriting team was a triumph; the production and the score were met with unbridled enthusiasm in the press, and the show quickly exploded into a hit of unprecedented sustainability. The week after opening, the advance sale—something fairly rare on Broadway at the time—was $25,000 (this, when the top ticket price was less than $5.00), which meant the show would be financially comfortable for a long while; in fact, *Oklahoma!* was sold out for the first four years of its run.[16]

As if the objective financial information didn't indicate that *Oklahoma!* had made a strong connection with its audience, the songs from the score confirmed it. Although nothing in the score met urban audiences with the kind of knowing cleverness of *Pal Joey*, *Lady in the Dark*, or even *By Jupiter*, the songs were so expansive and emotionally resonant (and geared to affirm innocence and nativist spirit, which were extremely important in wartime) that they were guaranteed to become popular on a mainstream level, despite their specific references to a culture decades removed and thousands of miles away from the Theater District and the broadcast studios of Manhattan. The quandary was simply, given the AFM strike, how to get this commercially attractive music out to the American public.

Decca and Columbia each solved that problem in similar ways; they brought in *a cappella* groups to back up their leading singers, Bing Crosby and Frank Sinatra respectively, and produced 78 recordings with "People Will Say We're in Love" on the A-side and "Oh, What a Beautiful Mornin'!" on the B-side. Crosby sang the first as a duet (as it's done in the show) with Trudy Erwin (supported by the Sportsmen Glee Club), while Sinatra went solo, backed by the Bobby Tucker Singers. Both versions are lugubriously weighed down by the backup singers and neither evinces any of the snap and crackle of the original performances in the show itself, but consumers, fascinated by *Oklahoma!*, were in no mood to be picky. By the time the single recordings hit the market in mid-September 1943, the sheet music for "People Will Say We're in Love" was among the best-selling in the country. *Billboard* magazine welcomed the Sinatra rendition with effusive acclaim on September 18:

> More than usual interest must be manifest in any waxed music from the score of Broadway's hit musical, *Oklahoma!*. With "People Will Say We're in Love" already among the song leaders in radio plugs and sheet music sales, the disk marts face an eager market for any waxed version of this highly original and smartly tailored love ballad... In ordinary times, the market would be overwhelming, with a dozen or more versions of this hit show tune.

But it wasn't an ordinary time and Jack Kapp had more concern about "overwhelming" markets than his competition. RCA Victor was backed by NBC and Columbia by CBS; they had boards of directors and trustees and battalions of lawyers to whom they had to answer. Kapp didn't—he only wanted to start recording again. On September 30, on behalf of Decca, he signed an agreement with Petrillo and the AFM, basically agreeing to contribute a royalty percentage to a pension fund run by the union. The week he signed the deal, Crosby's version of "People Will Say We're in Love" was No. 3 on the charts, and Sinatra's was at No. 7.

⊙   Audio Example 5.3, "People Will Say We're in Love" (Bing Crosby & Trudy Erwin)

Kapp moved quickly to get *Oklahoma!* into the recording studio. Typically—as with the *Boys from Syracuse* album set—the musical arrangements would be commissioned for a studio or popular orchestra, but, as luck and posterity would have it, Kapp didn't have the time to create new arrangements for the recording. The cast album of *Oklahoma!* would be the third project Kapp would record in New York after he signed his deal with the AFM, right after he got bandleaders Guy Lombardo and Charlie Barnet back into the studio. The studio date was set for October 20, only three weeks after lawyers ratified the AFM deal (there was a second session on October 25, as Joan Roberts, who played Laurey, had gotten sick and missed the first recording date.)[17] The entire theater orchestra at the St. James—all AFM members—would be hired for the studio date. Jay Blackton, the show's original conductor, remembered the recording session years later:

> We brought the whole gang into Decca's studio on West 57th Street. Jack Kapp supervised the recording with the help of his brother Dave.... Sometimes a song we'd be recording would time out too long for the record side and Jack would come out of the control booth and say, "How about it, a little faster, maybe?" So, I'd speed up the tempo a bit to fit the record.[18]

Blackton recalled that each side of the 78 had to be no more five minutes; on the final product, no song from *Oklahoma!* runs longer than three and a half minutes. In fact, most of the twelve songs recorded for the "Selections from the Theater Guild Musical Play OKLAHOMA!" (as the cover states) were cut and condensed in some way from their Broadway renditions. In addition, three songs, a reprise or two, and the extraordinary ballet sequence that concluded Act One from the original score were left off the album set.

It's a revealing exercise to listen to the songs in that first album set alongside the actual show. Many of the songs are so well-integrated into the book by Hammerstein that there is always some kind of connective dialogue between verses to extend (or contrast) the dramatic moment with the song: none of that appears on the recording. Several songs— "Surrey with the Fringe on Top," "I Cain't Say No," "Pore Jud," "All or Nothin'," even "People Will Say We're in Love" and "Oklahoma!"—have verses or choruses cut from the original versions. The dance break to "Kansas City" is moved earlier and the structure of "Out of My Dreams"—in which the local girls give Laurey advice to make up her mind— is strangely inverted, so that Laurey's mind appears made up (she sings the concluding verse first) before the girls get a chance to sing the "advisory" passage. And, although Blackton and Kapp begin the album set with an Overture—something without precedent—they glue together a finale that doesn't happen in the theater: a reprise of "Oh, What a Beautiful Mornin'" (sung by the leads Alfred Drake and Joan Roberts, instead of by the chorus); followed by what appears to be play-off music; then a reprise of "People Will Say We're in Love" that occurs a scene earlier in the actual show.

Perhaps even more injurious to the original intentions of *Oklahoma!,* the songs not included in the original album set are the ones that give a darker, more complex texture to the social and cultural shifts in the Oklahoma territory that Rodgers and Hammerstein were eager to include. "The Farmer and the Cowman" provides a wider portrait of the oppositional conflicts on the prairie (as well as a relief from the four romantic leads); "It's a Scandal! It's an Outrage!" is the only major musical moment given to the character of the (clearly Jewish) peddler; and "Lonely Room," Jud's aria of alienation and revenge is the show's most serious—and, in the right hands, most touching—moment. Devoid of these numbers, the listeners of the original album set might mistake *Oklahoma!* for a purely upbeat, optimistic story of romantic couples and their feudin', fightin', and makin' up in the end. The original creators had something more nuanced in mind. Perhaps it's not too much to say that the reputation of the show was done something of a disservice by the original album set, the complexity of its score overwhelmed by the ebullience of a product edited and captured on only six 78 disks.

However, one doesn't want to use the limitations of the original album set of *Oklahoma!* as a cudgel with which to beat its enormous influence. Kapp put together a tremendously attractive set, given the context of the era, with a two-toned color cover, a "souvenir" album set of the highest order. The twelve songs included were produced and recorded not through the lens of posterity, or even integrity, but through the commercial standards of the music industry of the day. If one wanted a detailed replication of an original Broadway show, one could buy *The Cradle Will Rock*—at drugstores around town—if it was still in print by 1943. If one wanted the excitement of a Broadway phenomenon as performed by the original cast, in accessible songs rendered in a manner in sync with performances on the radio or on popular recordings of the time, then the Decca album set of *Oklahoma!* was the purchase for you.

The Decca album set of *Oklahoma!* was clearly the purchase for a lot of consumers during the war. Anticipation for its release reached a kind of fevered pitch. On September 30, the day that Decca settled its agreement with AFM, Bing Crosby had been rushed into the Los Angeles studio to record a new song, "I'll Be Home for Christmas." Obviously, it was a time-sensitive release and would do well with holiday airplay, but Decca technicians and employees were working around the clock to get *Oklahoma!* into the hands of reviewers, disk jockeys, and consumers. The album set took precedence over everything else in Decca's catalog; the release of Crosby's single (and several other scheduled Decca singles) didn't happen until a week before Christmas. Kapp got advance copies of the album set out by Thanksgiving week; on the evening after Thanksgiving, host Martin Block played all thirty-six minutes of the album set on his *Make Believe Ballroom* radio program out of New York and was besieged by phone calls and postcards to play it all again, which he did, on his Monday morning broadcast.[19]

With advance sales nearing 60,000 copies, the original cast album set of *Oklahoma!* hit stores on December 1. It was an immediate success, so much so that it climbed on the singles chart, where, as a five-dollar purchase, it performed mightily against records that cost one-tenth the price. In New York, the album set was the No. 1 record; never had a multi-disk product competed on this level. By Christmas week 1943, *Oklahoma!* had sold 125,000 units and Jack Kapp played Santa Claus by stopping by the St. James Theatre and giving the cast and musicians each a small royalty check. No wonder the Decca album set seemed like the perfect present for the holidays. Besides, after the Kapp handshake with Petrillo and the AFM, Decca had a clear field for original material in the recording industry; RCA and Columbia still wouldn't agree to Petrillo's terms for almost another year.

Oklahoma! had been running on Broadway for nine months; its fame had spread across the country in magazines and newspapers, its songs were still sung on popular recordings and on the radio (Sinatra had added "Surrey with the Fringe on Top" to his repertoire), and a national tour was being put together, with its first stop in Chicago. The ubiquity of the music of *Oklahoma!,* captured in various forms and formats (there were a number of orchestral and dance band arrangements of its tunes, including several by Tommy Dorsey and His Orchestra), informed a generation of listeners and grew out of an organic relationship between the New York stage and the vast musical outlets—recordings, radio, sheet music—available to Americans during the 1940s.

Even the comparative failures of the *Oklahoma!* score were successes: "Boys and Girls Like You and Me" was cut from Act Two during the Boston tryout, and subsequently sold to MGM for inclusion in the 1944 release *Meet Me in St. Louis*. It was filmed with Judy Garland singing the number, then cut from the final print. When selections from the film were released as an album set—on Decca, per Garland's contract—her rendition was nonetheless included.

In May 1944, the pure success of the *Oklahoma!* album set (or his own success with the additional album of *Porgy and Bess* material in 1942) brought Jack Kapp and the original cast back to the recording studio for an unprecedented encore. This time, Decca would record a two-disk addendum to the *Oklahoma!* score, featuring the songs left off the original set: "The Farmer and the Cowman" (two sides, including the dance break); "It's a Scandal!," and "Lonely Room." "Lonely Room" was not sung by Howard Da Silva, who played the part of Jud, but by Alfred Drake, who had originated the role of Curly; by the time the second recording session happened in 1944, Da Silva was back on the West Coast, having reupped his Hollywood contract. The presence of Joan Roberts was not required at all for the new recording, but it certainly sounds like Celeste Holm, as Ado Annie, offering up her one line in "The Farmer and the Cowman."

▶ Audio Example 5.4, "The Farmer and the Cowman" (*Oklahoma! Volume Two*)

By the time *Oklahoma! Volume Two* was released to the public in January 1945, much had changed on the national landscape. The Allied forces were contemplating victory in Europe; Roosevelt had been elected to an unprecedented fourth term as president. In the music field, RCA Victor and Columbia settled with AFM in November 1944 and were recording again after a hiatus of twenty-eight months. Sheet music sales were on the upswing, largely because of radio shows such as *Your Hit Parade*; the country had absorbed a barrage of patriotic songs on the homefront and was looking for something fresh; a new generation of songwriters—including Frank Loesser, Jule Styne, and Leonard Bernstein—had achieved success during the mid-1940s; and Rodgers and Hammerstein were hard at work on their next achievement, *Carousel*. During the thirteen months that elapsed between Volume One and Volume Two of *Oklahoma!*, Decca had become an original cast album machine, vacuuming up the scores to more than a half-dozen other shows. Decca must have known something had changed in terms of the nature of how Americans were now listening to show tunes. In the souvenir booklet tucked into Volume Two, the copy read:

> [This volume] completes the record collector's program of song hits from the historic musical show—now no longer a "Broadway production" but the spiritual property of Americans everywhere, thanks to a road company's United States performances, and those of a USO cast that brought this amazing Theatre Guild musical play to the service men [*sic*] and women in the South Pacific. By the same token, Decca carries the *Oklahoma!* music into any and all American homes on records; these two albums together permitting enjoyment of the play from start to finish—right in your own easy-chair—with members of the original cast, chorus, and orchestra.

Unfortunately, neither Decca nor its successor label, MCA, would conflate the selections of Volume One and Volume Two together until the CD age (that obvious task was accomplished first on LP by the Time-Life Records subscription club, but not until 1981), but at least Decca understood what it had accomplished with the two album sets—the enjoyment of the original cast with a full orchestra, pretty much from start to finish, right in your own living room.

Billboard magazine realized the immense influence the original cast album set would have. As an editorial in the December 11, 1943, edition, put it:

> All this Broadway promotion is built around one show [*Oklahoma!*] and on one recording company [Decca], with other shows yet to be proven as big hits on platters.

The demand for the *Oklahoma!* recording was so great that Decca produced a sequel with three more songs from the show more than a year after the show opened. By permission of Universal Music Group/Library of Congress.

If and when the other major disk companies settle their differences with Petrillo, there's likely to be a new field for their wax wares—hit tunes from hit shows for the hinterlands, sold as packaged albums. That is, of course, if Decca in the meantime hasn't managed to grab off all the cream of the project. In any event, the road will profit, Broadway will profit, the Guild, Decca, and Chappell Music (sheet music purveyors) will profit from the current sales phenomenon—and the gravy will be thick everywhere.

"Territory folks should stick together," as the lyric goes in "The Farmer and the Cowman." By the mid-1940s, the territory for cast recordings from Broadway shows now stretched from West 44th Street to the hinterlands to the West Coast; if capital and labor could manage to be "pals," there would be a lot of cream and gravy to go around for everyone.

A magazine advertisement for Decca Records, circa 1946, which used *Annie Get Your Gun* to tout a new cottage industry. Courtesy Brian Drutman/permission of Universal Music Group.

CHAPTER 6

Every Home's a First Night

The Long-Playing Record and the Commodity of Broadway

On the day before Thanksgiving, 1943, *Variety* whetted the appetite of its readers with a small paragraph about the impending, long-awaited release of the *Oklahoma!* cast recording. Looming high above that paragraph, celebrating the achievement of Rodgers and Hammerstein's new score, was the obituary of Lorenz Hart, who had died only two days earlier in Manhattan at the age of 48.

The *Variety* obit made much of the success of the revival of Rodgers and Hart's *A Connecticut Yankee*, which debuted the week before, proving that, in addition to Hart's talent as a lyricist—"whose expert and literate wordage, so expertly wedded to Richard Rodgers' melodies, had long since set a new high standard for the music business and the world"—he was relevant as well. There was one small mistake in the obit, the mention that the team had "split up two years ago" when Rodgers worked with Oscar Hammerstein II on *Oklahoma!*. Whatever Rodgers' private apprehensions, Rodgers and Hart were still a team. It was up to Decca Records to commemorate that team's final work.

By the recording and marketing standards of the time, the five-disk *Connecticut Yankee* set was a fine encomium to Rodgers and Hart. In addition to including an overture and a finale, the set contained the show's several new songs: "You Always Love the Same Girl," "Can't You Do a Friend a Favor?," and Vivienne Segal's showstopping "To Keep My Love Alive." The cover to the album was festooned with a two-color poster; inside and on the back cover were photographs from the production "showing the principal actors," and "candid photos from the recording session." Even more compelling, the booklet insert contained a plot summary, an introductory essay by Rodgers himself, and lyrics to all the songs. One would have never known from all this salutary jollity that the fellow responsible for the show's witty lyrics had died only three months before the release of the record. Still, *A Connecticut Yankee* represented, in early 1944, a high-water mark for what listeners and consumers would expect from the very best cast album packages in the decades ahead: extended musical numbers, essays, lyrics, plot synopses, production photos, and "backstage" shots in the studio. Short of full-color photographs or a souvenir poster, it's hard to think of what else would—or could—be included to produce the ultimate home listening experience. The only thing missing was continuity. Segal's number—the last thing Hart ever wrote—was easily the longest single song recorded from a Broadway show at the time; two complete choruses and two encores that chronicled the escapades of a serial murderess, totaling almost seven minutes. However, to hear the whole thing, you'd have to flip over the record. Segal's acclaimed performance was literally sliced in two by the limited technology of the day.

⊙ Audio Example 6.1, "To Keep My Love Alive" (Vivienne Segal)

As the market for original cast recordings burgeoned after the settlement of the AFM strike and the end of World War II, and the major record labels climbed aboard the Broadway bandwagon, there was still an unrealized quest for that essential quality available for anyone who actually attended a performance: narrative continuity.

"Every home's a first night" was Jack Kapp's motto, according to *Variety*. Journalist Abel Green went further, asserting that Kapp "felt that what Puccini was to Italy, Wagner to Germany, Strauss to Austria, Debussy to France, etc., that's what American songsmiths were to America, and he proceeded to give voice and permanency—via wax—to the living American songwriters."[1]

Under Kapp, Decca simply vacuumed up every halfway decent Broadway show in its path during the mid-1940s—and even added some scores that had been bypassed in the 1920s and 30s. Even before the release of *Oklahoma!*, Jack Kapp was going full-throttle on the original cast initiative. Two weeks after the *Oklahoma!* recording sessions, he (and his brother Dave, a fellow producer) brought Mary Martin and the cast of Kurt Weill and Ogden Nash's *One Touch of Venus* into the studio for a five-disk album set. By the end of December 1943, Decca would also record three more album sets: Moss Hart's patriotic show, *Winged Victory*; selections from *The Merry Widow*, featuring Kitty Carlisle; and the *Connecticut Yankee* revival. In quick succession, over the next 30 months, the company would produce album sets of *Carmen Jones*; Cole Porter's *Mexican Hayride*; the second volume of *Oklahoma!*; Arlen and Harburg's *Bloomer Girl* (in a huge 16-side album set, with accompanying booklet—Arlen even sings on two of the songs); *Up in Central Park; Carousel; Call Me Mister;* and *Annie Get Your Gun*, all with their original casts and usually with the show's orchestra. In addition, selections from *Babes in Toyland, Roberta,* and *The Desert Song* were produced with studio casts, including Alfred Drake and Kitty Carlisle (she was having an affair back then with the married Jack Kapp, but that's another story for another time).

Kapp had a clear field of the World War II-era Broadway shows and set the standard so high that the other major companies would be playing catch-up for years. One of Decca's only real bungles of the period was its bizarre drawing-and-quartering of the score to *On the Town,* which had opened in December 1944, at the height of Decca's dream of conquest. As opposed to recording the selections with the original cast in one or two sessions, Decca set up three separate sessions over eight months to capture only six songs from the show—only half of which were recorded by the original cast. Nancy Walker released a single, with "I Can Cook Too" and "Ya Got Me" (as a solo); the show's book and lyric writers, Betty Comden and Adolph Green, recorded "Carried Away" as a B-side; the A-side was the opening number, "New York, New York" as rendered by the Lyn Murray Chorus. It was up to Mary Martin, of all people—a Decca artist—to record "Lonely Town" (with a new introductory verse) and "Lucky To Be Me." It's difficult to know why Decca wouldn't just go all in with *On the Town*; the Bernstein score might have intimidated lesser producers (as it did with MGM, when it bought the film rights), although it is nice to hear Walker, Comden, and Green singing with the ebullient timbre of their youthful enthusiasm.

With RCA Victor and Columbia out of the picture until November 1944, when they finally settled with the AFM, it's tantalizing to look at the other scores that got away from any recording studio at the time: Vernon Duke and Howard Dietz's *Sadie Thompson* (written for Ethel Merman, but performed by June Havoc); Cole Porter's scores to *Seven Lively Arts* and *Around the World*; Kurt Weill and Ira Gershwin's *The Firebrand of Florence,* featuring Lotte Lenya in her American debut; George S. Kaufman's reimagining of Gilbert and Sullivan, *Hollywood Pinafore or The Lad Who Loved a Salary* (with William Gaxton and Victor Moore); and *The Day Before Spring,* the first all-Lerner and Loewe show to reach Broadway. During the post-*Oklahoma!* gold rush of the 1940s, only one other recording company provided any kind of competition with Decca in the "o.c." field, and, ironically perhaps, its founder was one of the finest lyricists the American Songbook would ever know.

Johnny Mercer, who hailed from Savannah, Georgia, came to New York in 1928 to be an actor and performer, but before long found himself contributing songs to the *Garrick Gaieties* and to one of Paul Whiteman's many radio show incarnations. From 1935 into the wartime years, he was in Hollywood, ensconced at various studios, writing delightful and enduring songs with composers such as Richard Whiting and Harold Arlen ("Too Marvelous for Words," "Hooray for Hollywood," "Blues in the Night") for extremely forgettable movies. One of Mercer's hobbies was stopping by an eclectic and expansive record store on Sunset and Vine, called Music City, run by a friendly genius named Glenn Wallichs, who quickly became an intimate of Mercer's.

Mercer and Wallichs would frequently bemoan the fact that all of the major recording companies were on the East Coast while there was plenty of top-flight musical talent in Hollywood. They decided to form their own record company, with Mercer as president in charge of selecting artists and their material, and Wallichs running the business and distribution end. Capitol Records was formed in April 1942. Mercer was also a fine composer when he needed to be, but on this occasion his timing was off—the new company was in existence for only four months before Petrillo would lower the boom on the record industry. However, Mercer and his fellow executives at Capitol saw no reason to press their luck with the AFM; the company—now armed with such impressive talents as Paul Whiteman, Peggy Lee, and Margaret Whiting—followed Jack Kapp's lead and struck its own deal with Petrillo in October 1943. For a fledging company (that also procured some quick-and-dirty access to that highly prized shellac), this was a smart move; not only could Capitol now survive, it could pass RCA and Columbia coming around the turn.

By all accounts, Mercer was an enthusiastic and attentive record executive; he liked music, he liked musicians, he liked putting them together, and he liked being there when it happened. Many songwriters were excellent interpreters of their own material—Gershwin, of course, at the piano, and Harold Arlen had a very special way with his own songs—but only Mercer, during this era at any rate, was both a first-rate songwriter and a chart-topping performer. From January 1945 to January 1946, he had four No. 1 songs that he either cowrote and/or performed: "Ac-Cent-Tchu-Ate the Positive," "Candy," "On the Atchison, Topeka and Santa Fe," and "Personality."[2]

Still, Mercer was anxious to go back east and conquer Broadway, especially now that Rodgers and Hammerstein had set a high bar for musical theater—and, not incidentally, proved that a hit song and a hit show could be mutually beneficial. In 1945, Mercer was matched up once more with Arlen to take on a tale of fast women and slow horses, set in the black milieu of turn-of-the-century East St. Louis, entitled *St. Louis Woman*. The acting company wrangled for the incipient production was to feature Lena Horne as the eponymous character who leads an infatuated jockey to rack and ruin; Pearl Bailey, a Columbia recording artist, as the comic second lead; and the Nicholas Brothers, the astonishing dance team of Chitlin' Circuit and film fame, as the jockey, Li'l Augie, and his ne'er-do-well pal. Given the postwar propensity to accept black performers in larger roles in more expansive stories, how could it lose?

St. Louis Woman was beset by problems too numerous to elaborate: cast defections, boycotts by the NAACP, a story too unwieldy for the formulaic approaches of the day. In the decade since Mercer had moved to Hollywood, storytelling priorities had changed, and he and Arlen were at the mercy of the production's chaos. Opening on March 30, 1946, *St. Louis Woman* limped along the track for a mere 113 performances; no racing tout ever tore up a losing ticket with more wistful regret. Buried under the wreckage was one of the finest scores ever written for the Broadway stage, certainly one of the finest up to 1946. Mercer knew, however, that he and Arlen had composed a masterful ballad, "Come Rain or Come Shine," and he made sure that Capitol recorded it, with his protégée, Margaret Whiting, in Los Angeles before the show went into rehearsal. (Tommy Dorsey and His Orchestra also recorded the song for RCA Victor before the show opened.) One would think that, with a hit song and with the president of a record company as its lyricist, *St. Louis Woman* would get at least priority treatment as an album set, but the Capitol release—its first, and the first cast album set of the 1940s released by any company outside of Decca—is, alas, an inferior product.

First, Mercer was somewhat hamstrung by contractual agreements beyond his control. Arlen had a previous publishing relationship with Chappell, so the sheet music went there and the publishers—under the advisement of Max Dreyfus—made sure the album set was shopped around before it came to Capitol. Also, Pearl Bailey had a contract with Columbia, so she required a special dispensation. The product graphics are extremely attractive, with a vibrant, full-color poster, and a montage of production photos on the back. The marketing copy certainly makes a viable case for what's inside:

> Although the story of Li'l Augie…can hardly be seen by the legion of music lovers unable to visit Broadway, the recorded version is appealing and delightful nonetheless. Here, in fact, is music which we think will take its place in the annals of America's most memorable musical productions. We're sure you will treasure it.

And yet the organization of the set—eleven songs on five disks—is utterly counterintuitive to understanding the context of the show: both sides of each disk contain two songs from each of the three main female characters in the show; in other words, Pearl Bailey's songs are on the second disk, sides A and B—no matter where her songs actually fall in the storyline. *St. Louis Woman* was hard enough to follow in the theater; the cast album set is so oddly arranged (and at a minimal running time of less than 30 minutes) that it's hard to get a grip on the theatrical imperative of the show. What the album set did include, perhaps as a bit of justifiable pride on behalf of the label's president, was a booklet with all of Mercer's lyrics, set off by the introduction:

> The lyrics reflect Mercer's knowledge of his subject and his genius in capturing the philosophy and descriptive vernacular of characters created in the play. Increased popularity of these songs has aroused a demand for the printed lyrics, which Capitol is privileged to present with this album.

Mercer would return to the West Coast and record two of the score's jauntier songs for a Capitol release; Bailey would record her two numbers additionally for Columbia (there was no point in being proprietary, Mercer admitted, given they had a show to market). Whiting's rendition of "Come Rain or Come Shine" would chart briefly, and the song would go on to be recorded by practically every pop singer throughout the twentieth century (and also by most jazz instrumentalists); never was there a more popular song to come out of a more unpopular musical.

At the time, however, it was all cold comfort to Mercer. His Broadway experience was never really a pleasant one. "I just don't get any kick out of spending all that time and effort, getting into backstage politics, bitching and being bitched at, when one song can make me twice the money and never say an unkind word to me," he admitted later in his career.[3] Capitol Records would transform into a commercial powerhouse within only four years; by the end of 1946, it had sold 42 million records. The need to gin up operations to support such an output bored and exhausted Mercer; he wanted to get back to doing what he did best—writing popular songs—and, when asked, recording them as well. He gave up his titular role as president in 1947. In 1952, when *Billboard* created a special "Tenth Anniversary" supplement to celebrate Capitol, the groundbreaking achievement of *St. Louis Woman*—the label's first cast album, with a score written by its own founder—wasn't even mentioned, not even in an interview with Mercer.[4]

While "Come Rain or Come Shine" was inching its way onto to pop charts in mid-1946, another Broadway score was eating up most of the oxygen. Irving Berlin's *Annie Get Your Gun* opened two months after *St. Louis Woman* and the original cast recording went to Decca. In fact, Decca recorded Bing Crosby singing "They Say It's Wonderful" as early as January 1946, five months before the opening night on Broadway, so the label must have known that not only would it release the original cast album set, but that it could get a hit single on the charts with Crosby. The Berlin score was so replete with hit songs— "Doin' What Comes Natur'lly," "I Got the Sun in the Morning," plus "They Say It's Wonderful"—that on the week of July 17, 1946, out of the top eleven recordings on the pop charts, five of them were renditions of those songs from the score of *Annie Get Your Gun*. By September, "The Girl That I Marry" joined this select group, and those four tunes occupied *Variety*'s list of twenty "Songs with Largest Radio Audiences." In the meantime, Decca's six-disk album set had sold nearly 300,000 copies.

In a way, Kapp and Decca were the victims of their own success; everyone, as Jimmy Durante would say, wanted to "get inta de act:" *Oklahoma!* alone had passed the one-million mark by mid-1947, something which very few single disks had ever done; for an album set, this was an unprecedented achievement. Given these commercial prospects, it's not surprising that Decca and Capitol's main rivals, Columbia and Victor, would soon get involved.

Columbia Records had, by and large, ceded the original cast sweepstakes to Decca, even once it was back on board with the AFM contract, but in 1946, it released a five-disk album set of *Show Boat*, based on the successful Broadway revival steered into port by Oscar Hammerstein. It was released as part of Columbia's "Masterworks" unit, which was devoted to classical music, a sign of either respect or a recognition that there wasn't a significant subdivision for theater music at the time. Hammerstein was commissioned to write a brief essay on the outside jacket: "There seems to be no way of simplifying this stubborn play. It was born big and it wants to stay that way," he wrote—and posterity has proven him right. Several important songs in the score made their American appearance on record for the first time: "Cotton Blossom," "Life Upon the Wicked Stage," and "Nobody Else But Me" (which had been written expressively for the revival), thereby adding a breadth of context for both old fans of the work and new listeners.

Columbia grabbed a more redeemable ticket to the sweepstakes in 1947, with the cast album set of Yip Harburg and Burton Lane's *Finian's Rainbow*. The label won its prize through default, the result of the kind of economic machinations that were beginning to be part and parcel of the original cast album game. *Finian's Rainbow* was Jack Kapp's to lose; he had signed up the recording for Decca, only to become furious when *Finian's Rainbow*'s producers demanded a royalty payment for themselves as part of the commercial package. Normally, Kapp would pay a small royalty to the performers, the songwriters, and perhaps the arranger, but he chafed at the idea of paying theater producers who, he felt, should be grateful for the exposure and washed his hands of the project. Columbia, under the astute guidance of its new executive vice president, Goddard Lieberson, took it on. Perhaps it was for the best, as Columbia put out one of the finest album sets to date, briskly sung by most of the original company, and with the addition of some dialogue lead-ins, which would go a long way to render Harburg's complex whimsy to listeners who had not seen the production.

After all that, Columbia was still not the first label to reach the market with music from *Finian's Rainbow*; it was beaten to the punch by RCA Victor, which, several weeks earlier in spring 1948, put out a four-disk album set of songs from the score, covered by a far inferior selection of studio singers. Victor came late, and somewhat timorously, to accessing Broadway recordings for its catalog. The company apparently was less intimidated than Decca by Leonard Bernstein's score to *On the Town*, releasing a four-disk album set of "Songs and Ballet Music from *On the Town*" back in 1945. Bernstein himself conducted the music—which included several of the ballets omitted by the Decca release (split up among several disks)—but the songs ("Lonely Town," "Lucky to Be Me") were recorded by the Victor Chorale and conducted by Robert Shaw in rather ornate arrangements that did little to convey the contemporary immediacy of the songs.

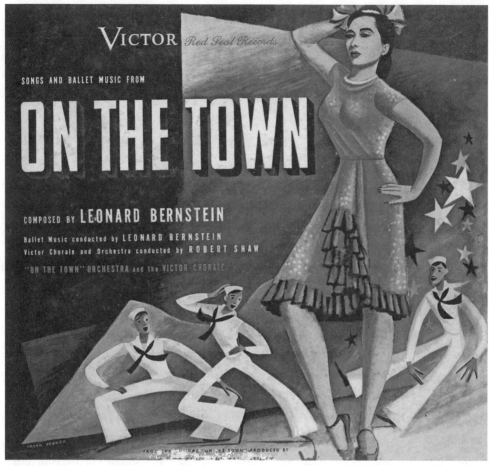

In 1945, the score to *On the Town* was carved into several recordings for different labels: this is RCA's version. Author's collection By permission of Sony Music.

The late 1940s would be the beginning of the often-intense bidding wars for Broadway scores among rival labels. Columbia made a move for the ambitious Kurt Weill and Langston Hughes *Street Scene* as well as Lerner and Loewe's upcoming *Brigadoon,* but *Brigadoon*'s strong-willed and quick-witted producer, Cheryl Crawford, brought the project to Victor instead. She got a percentage deal out of Victor and an advance against royalties that went straight to her production office (and ostensibly to keeping *Brigadoon* open). For Victor's premiere full cast recording, the five-disk *Brigadoon* is a somewhat corseted affair; it never quite breathes with the full expansiveness of its lovely score, occasionally conflating several songs on one side. In keeping with the conventions of the era, it skimps on the dance music, which on stage was particularly enlivened by Agnes de Mille's choreography.

The next project de Mille took on was the eagerly awaited next collaboration with Rodgers and Hammerstein, the highly personal and contemporary *Allegro.* Much to the

New York, New York: A helluva dancer (Sono Osato), a helluva composer (Leonard Bernstein), and a helluva mayor (Fiorello La Guardia). Credit: Photofest.

fury of Jack Kapp, who had produced the duo's first two album sets, RCA Victor snatched this score away from Decca by putting $15,000 toward the show before it had even gone into rehearsal, in order to get the exclusive recording rights. Columbia and Decca were furious, claiming that that Eli Oberstein, the RCA executive in charge of the deal, was essentially functioning as an angel; that is, investing in the show ahead of its critical reception and without any opportunity to engage in a bidding war. Max Dreyfus, who represented the Rodgers and Hammerstein music publishing interests (their own newly formed subdivision, Williamson Music, was managed by Chappell), further infuriated the recording industry by embargoing music rights to *Allegro*'s songs to any company other than Victor. Frank Sinatra, under contract to Columbia, was livid that Perry Como (a Victor artist) beat him to the punch with several ballads from the show, and Jack Kapp—a shareholder in Williamson Music—besieged Dreyfus with complaints.[5]

Eventually, Williamson Music and Victor allowed artists on other labels to record songs from the score, but the actual cast album set was a disaster—probably the first real train wreck in the original cast recording repertory. The ambitious score to *Allegro* was reduced to twelve songs shoehorned onto five disks, hardly more than 30 minutes in length; its fluid and complex choral passages were carved up or eliminated entirely, with no sense of narrative context, something that the stage version of *Allegro* wrestled with mightily and still succeeded beyond the conventions of the day. As Bruce Pomahac, director of music and music archivist for the Rodgers and Hammerstein Organization, put it, "I don't know that, back in 1947, given the limitations of recording, given what tastes Americans had in popular music, they could have recorded a more expansive, organic recording that reflected what was on stage."[6] What survived best from *Allegro*, from a recording point of view, were the commercial singles of "So Far" and "A Fella Needs a Girl" waxed by Sinatra, Como, and a few others.

What with RCA and Columbia's entrance to the field, Broadway producers' involvement in the royalty structure, and the increased competition for a commercial product, there was a lot of finger-pointing and stressful interactions in the cast recording arena as 1947 came to an end. Alas, it wouldn't end quickly or quietly in the New Year.

The AFM was on the verge of renewing its contract with the recording industry, and Petrillo threatened another walkout if broadcasters didn't raise their contributions to union pension funds. The major labels were skeptical of Petrillo's threat, particularly because they felt the federal government wouldn't support the AFM's structure for maintaining a pension fund; still, on January 1, 1948, Petrillo once again enjoined his membership from entering a recording studio.[7] The record companies had been there before and had either stockpiled material or rode out the ban. For the burgeoning original cast album market, this might have been a calamity, but as fate, or the theater gods, would have it, most of 1948 was not a particularly great year for musicals. *Look, Ma, I'm Dancin'!* would be recorded by Decca in New York before the ban struck, in advance of its out-of-town tryout; because of subsequent cuts and additions, the recording doesn't accurately reflect the score as performed on Broadway. RCA also hedged its bets by recording a version of Schwartz and Dietz's songs from *Inside U.S.A.* in advance of the ban. The album set featured Jack Haley and Beatrice Lillie, who headlined the revue, supplemented by Victor recording artists ("and the hit songs of the show sung on the album by PERRY COMO," read the cover) performing a bevy of attractive songs for the singles market; a kind of "original pre-cast" album, if you will. The main casualty was Frank Loesser's debut musical score for Broadway, *Where's Charley?*, which has never been recorded in full with an American cast. (The show's star, Ray Bolger, cut a Decca single with two songs: "Once in Love with Amy" and "Make a Miracle," and Jo Stafford and Gordon MacRae had a No. 1 single of "My Darling, My Darling" for Capitol.)

This may have been annoying, but it was business as usual. The most intense internecine warfare among the record companies during 1948, however, would come not from AFM headquarters, nor from the St. James Theatre, but from their own laboratories.

The notion of a long-playing record had been kicking around since the days of Edison. With the exception of popular songs, the format for three-minute-long 78 rpm shellac records that had been the industry standard for four decades didn't help anyone: not folks who wanted to dance, not folks who didn't want to get up every four minutes, and certainly not anyone who ever played or enjoyed listening to classical music, where the vast majority of compositions were impossible to carve up and granulate without damaging the integrity of the composers' intentions.[8] Since the early 1930s, various experiments at lengthening recording time were attempted, but the technology was usually too burdensome, inefficient, or expensive for the contemporary consumer.[9]

Still, longer recordings were the Holy Grail of the industry. Columbia Records made their implementation an internal priority around 1939, but had to suspend development because of the war. Ironically, the war—and to some degree, the 1948 strike—would work to the benefit of the research team at Columbia. Forced to reduce their use of shellac in the production of records, technicians turned to a petroleum-based polymer called vinyl. Vinyl was a more supple product and allowed for more grooves, which in turn allowed for more music and a fuller dynamic range. In addition, after the war, American companies were able to access magnetic tape that had been refined by German technicians in the 1940s; magnetic tape held a wider band of frequencies for recording and, of course, could simply be sliced and pasted together for editing purposes. This was particularly essential for long-playing recordings—otherwise, in order to make a master disk of, say, twenty minutes, the musicians would have to play twenty straight minutes, and if they made a mistake, the entire recording session would have to go back to the beginning and start over.

Columbia Records chairman Edward Wallerstein pushed his technical staff, which included engineers Peter Goldmark and Bill Bachman, to create a disk that would include up to seventeen minutes per side; Wallerstein reportedly invoked the length of Beethoven's *Eroica* symphony as the ideal duration for the majority of classical compositions. On Friday, June 21, 1948, reporters were summoned by Columbia to New York's Waldorf-Astoria Hotel (where, coincidentally, Cole Porter lived on the thirty-third floor) to hear what the innovators had concocted in their laboratories. What they produced was a shatter-resistant, twelve-inch microgroove disk made of "vinylite" that could play up to 22½ minutes of continuous music when placed on a phonograph that revolved at 33⅓ revolutions per minute.[10] It was, indeed, a revolution. Reporters were impressed and the long-playing record—the LP, as it would come to be known—was up (or sideways) and running.

Columbia also decided that it would reach out to RCA Victor and offer to share the record-pressing technology for the new format, but RCA, under the egotistical reign of David Sarnoff, who was furious at being beaten to the punch, rebuffed the offer. Columbia would go it alone, with its own technology, ultimately settling on a 7" disk that ran at 45 revolutions per minute. More portable, and more convenient for the release of singles, the 45 format still only held less than four minutes of recorded music; not much help for the commercial release of extended classical or Broadway material.

Because of the AFM ban, which was still going on throughout 1948, Columbia was kept from recording any new material for release on its new technology, but it made hay by stitching together material from its 78 rpm catalog and releasing the titles as new offerings as part of its Masterworks series in fall 1948. The 12" format would cost consumers $4.85 per LP and was packed in a flat cardboard sleeve, with an attractive graphic on the front and nominal information on the back. It was a technical challenge to repurpose multiple album sets, so most of the releases were of classical material long-awaited by fans of the "masterworks," but the 1947 *Finian's Rainbow* wound up in the catalog as one of the first Columbia LP releases.

By another stroke of good fortune, just as Columbia has mastered the craft of the LP and the AFM ban was lifted on December 13, Cole Porter's latest musical, *Kiss Me, Kate*, had opened to smash out-of-town reviews in Philadelphia. (Perhaps he was writing songs up in his apartment while the Columbia press conference was going on downstairs.) Goddard Lieberson went to Philadelphia to catch the tryout and picked up the rights to the cast recording for the label. When the show opened at the very end of 1948 to rapturous reviews, Columbia already owned the recording rights; and in early January 1949, the score to *Kiss Me, Kate* would, in fact, be the first music recorded by Columbia after the ban—it would also be the first original cast album recorded and edited expressly for the LP format.

The LP format was a savior for devotees of classical music, but it also admirably correlated with the rhythms of theatregoers everywhere. After all, one experienced a musical in, say, the Shubert Theatre (where *Kiss Me, Kate* finished out its run, three years later) as an uninterrupted experience, just the way one experienced the *Eroica* in Carnegie Hall; no one made audience members get up and go to the lobby after each musical number. Of course, even 45 minutes of the best theater score isn't enough to capture its full intentions or ambitions, but there was something about a seamless 22½ minutes of peerless Cole Porter music that felt right, or at least preferable to the massive album sets of theater music from the previous decade. There wasn't any of the counterintuitive programming one encountered on the *St. Louis Woman* album set; all the songs were in the right order, and it was infinitely easier to follow the narrative. In a felicitous turn of events, one only had to get up once—just like at intermission—to turn the record over. Sometimes, the record break occurred at the same point in the score as the musical's actual intermission. It seemed absurd even to call them albums anymore; *Kiss Me, Kate* entered consumers' lives as a lithe, jolly, red-and-yellow messenger of Broadway glamour, not a lumbering, hidebound, eight-record behemoth of musical memories, separated by ugly brown paper.

Columbia could not have asked for a better maître d' for its expansive serving of LP recordings than *Kiss Me, Kate*. Although the score was also available to consumers in a 78 rpm album set (it took a year or two to wean customers away from the 78 format), the combination of a new, acclaimed Cole Porter score with user-friendly technology seemed unbeatable. Assisted, no doubt, by the frequent airplay of singles from the show (Frank Sinatra and Dinah Washington had already released covers of "Why Can't You Behave?" and Patti Page recorded "So in Love" before *Kiss Me, Kate* even opened on Broadway), the album of *Kiss Me, Kate* sold more than 100,000 copies in its first month, making it the biggest seller in Columbia's history up to that time.

As *Kiss Me, Kate* was conquering the album charts in February 1949, becoming the No. 1 recording in the country, Richard Rodgers, Oscar Hammerstein, and Max Dreyfus convened an unusual audition for a dozen of the top record executives. Rodgers accompanied two singers—a man and a woman—as he played tunes from the upcoming Rodgers and Hammerstein show, *South Pacific*, scheduled to go into rehearsal within the week. After the debacle and the concomitant resentments following Dreyfus's exclusive arrangement for the *Allegro* songs, the *South Pacific* team put together what was, essentially, a preemptive strike. The material for the new musical would be up for grabs for any executive to record: no restrictions, no embargoes, no matter who would be contracted to do the cast album. There was one catch, however. Rodgers, ever the perfectionist, handed out recorded demo copies of the material to each of the executives; this would provide the proper method or standard by which Rodgers and Hammerstein wanted their material recorded. On a pop single or an extended album, the writers of *South Pacific* demanded little to no deviation from their musical intentions.[11]

Within a week, Columbia announced that it would get its first chance to partner with Rodgers and Hammerstein; the rights to the *South Pacific* cast album were Columbia's. Again, anticipation of a new Rodgers and Hammerstein score ran high; Frank Sinatra and Perry Como would each record "Some Enchanting Evening" and "Bali Ha'i" on single releases, and Dinah Shore would record "A Wonderful Guy" and "Younger Than Springtime" for Columbia. Each single would rank high on the pop charts, and all of these would be released before the show opened at the Majestic Theatre in New York. More impressively, albums sets covering the score were recorded by rival labels before the Columbia cast album even went into the studio. Decca put Bing Crosby, Ella Fitzgerald, and Danny Kaye singing a total of eight songs on its album set , while Capitol put out its A-listers—Margaret Whiting, Gordon MacRae, Peggy Lee—on one set covering nine songs from the score.

When, in February 1949, Richard Rodgers handed out this "standardized" recording of *South Pacific* to those dozen recording executives, it's a safe bet that Peggy Lee would have swiftly tossed the disk into the trash and sent it on its way. The same week that Mary Martin was opening as Nellie Forbush in *South Pacific* at the Majestic Theatre on 44th Street in New York, Lee was recording her two songs from the score at Capitol's studio all the way in Los Angeles. That meant that Peggy Lee would be the first professional singer—Martin, included—to record "I'm Gonna Wash That Man Right Outta My Hair."

Perhaps that gave Lee permission to let her hair down (before she washed it). Backed by her collaborator and husband, Dave Barbour, a thoroughly swinging arranger, Lee lathers and rinses her way through the song in a lively, bluesy manner, playing fast and loose with tempos, phrasing, and lyrics. She's not Nellie Forbush, but, freed of any obligation to narrative context, Lee reaches into something sassy and, well, emancipated, giving the song a kind of universality. She is so confident with the song that she's able to riff on some of the lyrics: "Rub him out of the roll call / And drum that hummm-drummmm bummm right out of your dreams…" The meticulous Rodgers would have been horrified, but on its own terms, the recording works beautifully. Better than Martin's? A matter of opinion, but Lee and her comrades on the Capitol recording—Margaret Whiting, Gordon MacRae, the obligatory male chorus making hash out of "There Is Nothin' Like a Dame"—construct a very viable parallel universe out of *South Pacific*.

> ▶ Audio Example 6.2, "I'm Gonna Wash That Man Right Outta My Hair"
> (Peggy Lee)

The real test would be the production and release of the original cast album. It would be the first Broadway LP that Goddard Lieberson would personally produce (*Kiss Me, Kate* was supervised by a house producer, Manny Saks). Lieberson knew that he had a unique opportunity to use the LP technology to tell a story. More than any other producer of previous cast albums (a job description less than a decade old), Lieberson took it upon himself to recast important elements of the stage musical for the home listener. He faced a particular challenge with the finale to *South Pacific*. To conclude an evening full of drama, discrimination, and death, Hammerstein and Joshua Logan created a very subtle ending in contrast:

> *NELLIE comes back to consciousness enough to realize that EMILE must be hungry. She leans over and hands him the large bowl of soup with an air of "nothing's-too-good-for-the-boss!" Then she passes him the soup ladle! But he doesn't use it. Instead, he thrusts his hand forward. NELLIE clasps it. Looking into each other's eyes, they hold this position as the curtain falls.*

It worked beautifully in the theater, but how could record listeners possibly grasp the sub-tlety of that ending? Lieberson went in the other direction, drafting in a section from the first act—where Mary Martin and Ezio Pinza essentially pledge their troth to one another (as a well as a brief reprise of Pinza's forte coda of "Some Enchanted Evening")—to use as a finale for the recording. To reproduce Lieberson's version in the theater would be absurd, but as a listening experience, it worked beautifully. (No doubt thousands of folks who knew only the Columbia Records version were puzzled to see what happened at the end of an actual production.)

By the time Lieberson's masterpiece was released to an eager public in spring 1949, many of the disparate strands and conflicts that defined the recording industry during the decade began to bind together into some kind of coherence. Decca embraced the LP format and got excited again about recording Broadway shows. Jack Kapp enthusiasti-cally announced that not only would he record Kurt Weill's upcoming 1949 musical *Lost in the Stars* (on both LP and on 78s) before the show went into rehearsal, he would record Weill's next show as well, even though it hadn't even been written yet. Alas, the week before *South Pacific* opened, Kapp died unexpectedly of a heart attack; Weill would suffer the same fate almost exactly a year later—neither man would live past his fifty-first birth-day. The Decca recording of *Lost in the Stars* would serve as a fitting tribute to both men. With Decca's acceptance of the LP format, the "Battle of the Speeds" was nearing an end. At the beginning of 1950, RCA also capitulated to the format, at the estimated cost of $4.5 million in lost sales over the previous eighteen months.[12] The public seemed relieved. Even Groucho Marx, writing to his good friend Goddard Lieberson, wanted the whole thing resolved: "I hope you are well and that you will some day get together with RCA and make one size records for the peasants. Your feud with them is pauperizing the nation."[13]

With Kapp's death in spring 1949, the torch would be passed to Lieberson, who would go on to become the most important producer of Broadway music in the next two de-cades. He was helped immeasurably by the success of *South Pacific*. As the 1940s evolved into the 1950s, the music from the Rodgers and Hammerstein score would dominate the musical scene across America. Sheet music sales from the show were voluminous, and "Some Enchanted Evening" became one of the most successful songs in history; seven different versions made the charts in 1949, the most successful being Perry Como's rendi-tion on RCA, which was a No. 1 hit for five weeks. Even Ezio Pinza released a single re-cording (lifted from the cast album and backed by "This Nearly Was Mine") on Columbia that charted, granting him the distinction of being one of the few performers in a Broadway musical to have their original rendition become a popular single.[14] The cast album to *South Pacific* (released on both LP and 78 formats) would reach No. 1 by

Accept no substitutes: although Capitol and Decca had already put out cover versions of the *South Pacific* score, Columbia had the real thing. By permission of Sony Music.

midsummer of 1949 and stay on the charts at No. 1 almost through the end of 1950—a total of 63 weeks, the longest run of its time, and an astounding achievement unmatched for a decade.

It was a lucky confluence of pop culture that put two highly intelligent musicals in Columbia's path at the same time. During the week of August 19, 1949, out of the top nine albums on the *Billboard* charts, five of them were cast albums: *South Pacific* was No. 1, followed by *Kiss Me, Kate*. *Variety* reported on the one-two punch of Columbia's show albums:

> Only eleven months after Columbia's introduction of the LP format—which was conceived mostly to benefit classical music buffs—ironically enough, two pop items, the LP albums of *Kiss Me, Kate* and *South Pacific,* have done more to focus the attention of record buyers on the 33⅓rpm platters than all of the longhair material Columbia has marketed via the development.... It is estimated that 35% of the overall sales of both scores are LP versions.

In 1944, only five years earlier, Decca had released an elegant, if unwieldly, album set of the latest Rodgers and Hart smash hit. Now, Columbia, which hadn't yet produced any Broadway recordings in 1944, was the undisputed leader in the field. With the most successful recording in history their fourth cast recording in only six years—the team of Rodgers and Hammerstein had also solidified their critical and commercial dominance as a Broadway songwriter team. The carefree, casual world of Rodgers and Hart seemed not a half-decade away, but, rather light years away—an admired but unrecoverable chapter in musical theater history. As the 1950s began, Goddard Lieberson would change that, too.

A star without a production: Vivienne Segal in 1950, waxing her *Pal Joey* numbers in a studio recording. By permission of Sony Music.

CHAPTER 7

Songs for Swingin' Show Fans

Hit Singles and the Catalog of Broadway

With Jack Kapp's abrupt demise, Goddard Lieberson, the executive vice president at Columbia, inherited the mantle of the most successful and thoughtful producer of the Broadway catalog of material. His path forward was, improbably, guided by a Chicago-based bandleader and pianist named Bill Snyder.

The song "Bewitched, Bothered, and Bewildered" (more commonly known as "Bewitched") from *Pal Joey* had pretty much sunk without a trace in the early 1940s.[1] Out of the blue, in 1948, composer and arranger David Rose released a very dreamy orchestral version. Snyder picked up the tune the following year and his instrumental version—very heavy on the creamy piano stylings—became an unexpected hit on the London label, reaching, as high as No. 3 on the pop charts. Several popular covers were released in short order: orchestral versions by the likes of Gordon Jenkins as well as vocal versions by Doris Day and Mel Tormé, who sang it as the ballad it was written to be—although the lyrics were slightly denatured, which tended to be the case with "Bewitched." For example, Hart's risqué original "Couldn't sleep / Wouldn't sleep / Until I could sleep where I shouldn't sleep" became "Then love came and told me I shouldn't sleep." (And "Worship the trousers that cling to him" was frequently transformed into "And long for the day when I cling to him.") In June 1950, six separate renditions of "Bewitched" made the Top 20 of songs played by disc jockeys across the country—amazingly, the songs holding the 12, 13, 14, and 15 spots on the list were each a different cover version of "Bewitched." It didn't require a genius in the recording industry to recognize a trend, but luckily there was a genius at Columbia in Lieberson.

▶   Audio Example 7.1, "Bewitched" (Bill Snyder)

As 1950 began, Lieberson brought in veteran conductor Lehman Engel to work with him on a series of albums preserving the scores to shows that had been neglected in the pre-*Oklahoma!* era. The first two releases spotlighted Mary Martin, backed up by a studio chorus, singing eight and ten songs, respectively, from *Anything Goes* and *The Band Wagon*: excellent scores, but it should be noted, not shows in which she had ever appeared. Howard Dietz, the lyricist for *The Band Wagon*, hinted at some of the limitations in his brief back cover essay on the album: "While the arrangements and tempos are not played exactly as they were heard in the New Amsterdam Theatre in 1931, they are properly modernized and keep the score as alive as anything on today's radio.... [The show] has been *slightly* abbreviated." As sprightly as these "slightly" abbreviated studio recordings were, and as vigorously conducted as they were by Engel, they, and the next entry featuring Martin, *Girl Crazy*, were a bit of a cheat, what with Martin singing every song as a solo. One could only wonder what the studio recordings would have been with the obvious inclusion of Ethel Merman or Fred Astaire, both of whom were still active, performing the material they introduced. (To be fair, Merman was a Decca artist at the time.)

Where Lieberson and Engel really got into their groove and delivered for show music enthusiasts was with *Pal Joey*. The recent interest in "Bewitched" had peaked in fall 1950, so it only made sense to record the score that surrounded the song. Lieberson brought the show's original female lead, Vivienne Segal, into the studio to reprise her legendary role as the "bewitched" socialite Vera Simpson, and matched her with Harold Lang, the young dance whiz who had a bravura supporting part in *Kiss Me, Kate,* to sing the title role originated by Gene Kelly in 1940. Engel had a full orchestra at his disposal that dove enthusiastically into Rodgers's melodies, and a full cast helped to tackle some songs that had never been recorded before: "What Is a Man?," "Do It the Hard Way," "Zip," and the delightfully risqué "Den of Iniquity." In fact, the decade-long wait for a suitable waxing of *Pal Joey* only accrued to the score's benefit in this regard; many of its more sophisticated— i.e., racy—lyrics would not have been permitted on disk in 1940, let alone on the airwaves. When the Columbia album was released at the beginning of 1951, listeners finally got nearly all of the choruses of "Bewitched," including the lyrics "Vexed again / Perplexed again / Thank God I can be oversexed again."

"Many of us have longed for a revival but wanting one we must be satisfied by a new recording," wrote the *New York Times*, but the March 19, 1951, *Billboard* review of the album took a more skeptical stance: "Admirable as it is...lacking key members of the original cast and Vivienne Segal is but a memory to many.... Some nice memory stuff and some unsuitable lyrics, too." *Billboard* was implying a subtle question: had *Pal Joey*'s time come and gone? Or was it even too corny and too sophisticated at the same time?

Broadway audiences would have a chance to decide for themselves the following year. Hollywood and Broadway composer Jule Styne had just finished composing the score to *Two on the Aisle* and was casting about for a new project. Apparently, he had been inspired to revive *Pal Joey* after seeing Bob Fosse play the lead in summer stock, although the energetically "plugged-in" Styne could not have been impervious to the immense exposure that both "Bewitched" and the Columbia LP of *Pal Joey* had received. He sought out Rodgers who was, at best, indifferent to the idea of a revival; during the Hammerstein years, Rodgers was always somewhat dismissive of the earlier collaborations with Hart, as if they were childish things that had to be put away.[2] Nevertheless, Styne persisted in raising money for a revival, although he kept being reminded by Rodgers and by Broadway wags that the fabled *New York Times* drama critic Brooks Atkinson hadn't liked the original show in 1940. Atkinson was still on deck to review the revival in 1952—should it ever make it to Broadway.

Styne further tapped into the energy of the Columbia recording by signing both Vivienne Segal and Harold Lang to play the leads, as well as adding a flinty young comedienne and singer named Elaine Stritch to perform the cameo song "Zip." Rodgers and the original book writer John O'Hara were dragged reluctantly back on board to make changes, update some lyrics (the show would be set contemporaneously), and to soften some of the rougher edges of the second act, ostensibly to make it more palatable to Atkinson and to the show's other detractors. The revival of *Pal Joey* opened three days into 1952 and became the smash hit it wasn't the first time around, running almost six months longer than the original and making it the most successful Rodgers and Hart show up to that point.

This revival of *Pal Joey* was, essentially, the stage production of a studio album. There was also a studio album of the stage production, on Capitol Records, which was something else entirely. There wouldn't seem to be an overwhelming need to record the revival production, especially as a perfectly good one was already out on the market by a highly respected label, but these were the days in popular music where there was enough interest in Broadway material that variant cover recordings and supplemental albums could be very successful. The Capitol release had a few handicaps going in; for one thing, contractually, Capitol couldn't use Segal or Lang for the recording of the actual production in which they were appearing. This was not uncommon in the 1940s and 50s when Broadway stars could get exclusive recording contracts and recording artists could become Broadway stars. Although RCA Victor spent a lot of money investing in the original cast album rights to *Call Me Madam*, they were unable to secure the rights to the show's star, Ethel Merman, because of her Decca contract and, so, counterintuitively, there were two albums of *Call Me Madam*: one with Dinah Shore, a major RCA artist ill-suited for the leading role, and one from Decca, with Merman leading a studio cast, including Dick Haymes. They cancelled each other out, and the score never received quite the legacy it deserved.

The Capitol LP of *Pal Joey* drafted the ineffectual Dick Beavers to sing the title role, but Vivienne Segal was replaced by Jane Froman for the recording. This proved to be very clever marketing, as Froman was a major recording artist and radio star. She had recovered after surviving injuries from a near-fatal plane crash during the war, and the film biography of her struggle entitled *With a Song in My Heart* was about to be released by 20th Century Fox within a month after the *Pal Joey* release. The soundtrack for the film—on Capitol Records, of course—wound up at the top the charts for almost half of 1952. On the Capitol *Pal Joey* album, "Bewitched" is subjected to a lot of alterations and elisions from the original; Froman sings, "Dumb am I / Half numb am I / A rich little ripe little plum am I." Still, the Capitol version captures a bit more of *Pal Joey*'s antic energy than the Columbia studio album; "Chicago" and "That Terrific Rainbow"—the tawdry nightclub tunes brilliantly pastiched by Rodgers and Hart—are included for the first time, as is Elaine Stritch's wonderfully acerbic rendition of "Zip." In the 1920s and 30s, folks in the media used to quote Paul Whiteman's hoary comment about Gershwin, that "he made a lady out of jazz." Columbia made a lady out of *Pal Joey* but the Capitol recording reminds one that, in Rodgers and Hart's original intention, that lady is a tramp.

Variety opined that Rodgers had now become a "colossal" composer, with an unprecedented reach in popular music: "With the click opening of the *Pal Joey* revival in NY last week, composer Richard Rodgers hit an all-time high in being represented with three musicals running on Broadway, and carbons of his work being offered on tour, on records, and in books. . . . Some of the single disks of Rodgers' tunes (with Hart or Hammerstein collaborations) which have been recorded by orchs or vocalists are standard sellers."[3] As the 1950s began, the ubiquity of a hit song from Broadway was at its zenith; Richard Rodgers may have been the greatest beneficiary of this confluence of popular tastes and a multiplicity of recording formats, but he was by no means the only one.

Only seven years earlier, before *Oklahoma!,* when consumers bought a recording of a song from a Broadway musical, or heard one on the radio, they were sampling material from a level playing field; in other words, it was either this popular rendition of "This Can't Be Love" or that popular rendition of "This Can't Be Love." Now, there was a more nuanced selection to be made: if you enjoyed the tunes from Rodgers and Hammerstein's *The King and I,* you could sample Dinah Shore singing "Hello Young Lovers" on an extended play recording on RCA Victor; or Frank Sinatra singing "We Kiss in a Shadow" on a Columbia 78 single; or Gertrude Lawrence singing "Getting to Know You" on the Decca LP release of the Broadway cast album, bracketed by all the other original songs she (and her fellow cast members) sang in the show. Consumers now had a choice: all recordings supplied content, but only the cast album supplied content *and* context. Far from one detracting from the other, the two versions helped promote each other, in terms of sales and visibility, just as *Billboard* had predicted in 1943, when it opined that, with a hit song and a successful Broadway show, "the gravy will be thick everywhere."

One could never predict what might emerge as a hit song or from which show it would come. To say it was all a crapshoot is putting it mildly. Speaking of crapshoots, the cast album of *Guys and Dolls* was a big hit for Decca in 1951 (the show itself opened in late 1950), hitting No. 1; it contained such eventual standards as "If I Were a Bell," "I've Never Been in Love Before," and "Luck Be a Lady." What was the big breakout hit from that show? No contest: "A Bushel and a Peck," sung as duet by Perry Como and Betty Hutton on RCA and, again, released before the show opened. It would stay on the charts for eighteen weeks and go as high as No. 6. In addition, Doris Day had a single version that charted for Columbia; Margaret Whiting had one for Capitol. Decca's single release of the tune, however, came up snake eyes. (The song would wind up being cut out of the film version of *Guys and Dolls* in 1955, if that makes any sense.)

A hit show was no guarantee of a hit song. The cast album of *Wonderful Town* made money for Decca, but nothing from it charted. *Can-Can*, Cole Porter's return to success after a stumble with *Out of This World*, was a moneymaking cast album for Capitol; but only a single release of "Allez-Vous En" made a little noise for Kay Starr. Rodgers and Hammerstein's *Me and Juliet*, a rare contemporary musical for the team, set backstage during the run of a Broadway show, had a financial injection of $185,000 from RCA Victor, and the cast album was a comparative bust. Yet, for a musical that has never been revived and was Rodgers and Hammerstein's first big failure, one ballad from the show managed to sneak out unscathed. It was "No Other Love" (repurposed from Rodgers's film score to *Victory at Sea*); luckily, it was recorded as a single by RCA Victor artist extraordinaire Perry Como and skyrocketed up the charts, landing at the No. 1 spot for the entire month of August 1953. RCA made back its investment in *Me and Juliet*, based on its ability to assign a potential hit song to one of its artists.

The score to a new Broadway property was a unique entity that was tightly controlled by its music publisher and its producers, and promotion of that music commercially had to be carefully managed. It made no sense for Columbia to spend the money on, say, *South Pacific*, then sit back and watch Peggy Lee release songs from the property on another label first. Columbia had mostly stayed away from the cast album acquisition game in the early 1950s, but bounced back in 1953 by purchasing the rights to *Kismet*, *The Girl in Pink Tights*, and *The Pajama Game*. To ensure the maximum exploitation of those scores, the label turned to an increasingly important employee in the record industry: the A&R man (for artists and repertory). In the 1964 book, *Anything Goes: The World of Popular Music*, author David Dachs writes: "Records are king in the popular music business and it is the A&R men who are the uneasy rulers of the vinylite monarchy that uses a record spindle for a scepter and a glass-enclosed booth for a throne room."[4] In 1950,

Columbia crowned a classically trained oboist as its reigning monarch for matching singing artists to the repertory of new material: Mitch Miller.

The goateed Miller, about whom writer Elijah Wald commented, "[he] had the air of a Renaissance count or mountebank,"[5] had a healthy respect for his own aesthetic choices in the studio—however bizarre or corny they might be perceived. He was famous for adding a harpsichord to the eccentric pop song "Come on-a My House" that he chose for Rosemary Clooney in 1951. Clooney supposedly hated the song and found it unbearably contrived; however, listeners found it fascinating and it became a No. 1 hit for Clooney.[6] One of Miller's next challenges was to match the hot new singer in the Columbia stable, Tony Bennett, with a rhapsodic piece of material from *Kismet*, "Stranger in Paradise." It became a substantial hit across the country and, unpredictably, sat at the No. 1 spot in the United Kingdom for weeks, even though *Kismet*'s West End production hadn't opened yet. Bennett had a huge success for Columbia the previous year with "Rags to Riches," a pop song written by a new duo, Richard Adler and Jerry Ross, who were published by Frank Loesser's company. Loesser recommended them for a new Broadway-bound musical directed by George Abbott, *The Pajama Game*. Although the musical, scheduled to open in late spring 1954, had little buzz around it, the songs were jukebox ready, primed by Adler and Ross's uncanny skill at matching accessible and witty lyrics with a contemporary, hip musical style. Once Columbia signed on for the cast album, Miller immediately placed four of its songs with Columbia artists before the show even opened: "Hey There" and "Hernando's Hideaway" for Johnnie Ray, as well as "Steam Heat" and "There Once Was a Man" with other house singers. A hyper-caffeinated bandleader named Archie Bleyer had a castanet-heavy hit with "Hernando's Hideaway" on his Cadence label that reached No. 2 on the charts.

As pleased as he was with Johnnie Ray's version, Miller knew the perfect singer for "Hey There" was Rosemary Clooney. By 1954, Clooney had married José Ferrer, moved to Los Angeles, and was expecting their first child. Miller flew out to California and recorded Clooney in the Los Angeles Columbia studio in mid-June. The ballad fit Clooney's style and Miller's predilections for effects perfectly; it required her to overdub her own voice (in the show, John Raitt sang to his own voice, played back on a Dictaphone), thereby singing a duet with herself. With some small changes in the lyrics ("Won't you take this advice I hand you like a brother" becomes, felicitously, "like a mother") and the addition of a verse created just for Clooney, it was quickly released and rapturously reviewed: "One of the loveliest waxings by the warm-voiced thrush in a long time," cooed *Billboard*. "Could put her back on top again." By the fall, the single shot to the top of charts, holding the No. 1 spot for six weeks. "Hey There" went on to sell more than two million copies for Columbia, making it the most successful show tune since "Some Enchanted Evening." *The Pajama Game*'s original co-producer, Harold

Prince, credits the hit single with generating the interest that turned an outlier musical with no advance sales into a long-running hit: "I recall that when we debuted *The Pajama Game* in Boston, Johnnie Ray's recording was already on the charts. The show had three hits: 'Hey There,' 'Hernando's Hideaway,' and 'Steam Heat.' They had enormous impact on the show." [7]

(▶)   Audio Example 7.2, "Hey There" (Rosemary Clooney)

Mitch Miller could justifiably take credit for Clooney's and Bennett's success; he also has to take some of the responsibility for Frank Sinatra's exit from Columbia in 1952. Sinatra was no longer the hit-making machine he had been in the 1940s. It didn't help that he and Miller were both temperamentally and aesthetically at odds with one another. Sinatra needed the right material to score a commercial hit; from Miller's point of view, since novelty numbers and country numbers were scoring big, these might give Sinatra's career a boost. Sinatra recorded a few of them, glumly, in between screaming matches with Miller in the recording studio. At the end of 1952, he was released from his Columbia contract. [8]

The following year, Capitol signed him up; the Los Angeles location was convenient to Sinatra's Hollywood ambitions, and Capitol's blend of artist and material—Jo Stafford, Peggy Lee, Nat King Cole, and their respective ballads—was more suited to Sinatra's style. He slowly made his way back up the charts, first with a few singles, then, historically, with a 10-inch LP entitled *Songs for Young Lovers,* arranged and conducted by his talented collaborator Nelson Riddle. Among the eight songs were two Gershwin film songs, Porter's "I Get a Kick Out of You," and two Rodgers and Hart songs, "My Funny Valentine" and "Little Girl Blue"—the first time they were sung by an important male singer. Excellent songs from the Broadway canon were essential to Sinatra's reimagining of himself in the 1950s, and his curiosity about little-known songs by major Broadway composers helped to transform him into an icon.

For Sinatra, the LP format was the canvas that allowed him to paint the first recording masterpieces in popular music. Certainly, his 1955 LP release on Capitol, *In the Wee Small Hours,* is considered to be one of the very first non-original cast album recordings to use its extended 49 minutes to stitch together a tapestry of great songs into something larger than the sum of its parts. A collaboration between Sinatra and Riddle, *In the Wee Small Hours* is a symphony of melancholy, using six Broadway songs out of sixteen to weave its woeful tale. The extended form also allowed Sinatra to record the introductory verses to many of the songs. Useful on Broadway to smooth the transition from dialogue to song, verses were more often regarded as unnecessary padding in commercial recordings and frequently omitted. Sinatra's project of reclamation on the album would also include such Rodgers and Hart classics as "Glad to Be Unhappy," "It Never Entered My Mind," and

"Dancing on the Ceiling," as well as "I See Your Face Before Me," an uncelebrated Schwartz-Dietz gem from their 1937 musical *Between the Devil*.

▶   Audio Example 7.3, "Glad to Be Unhappy" (Frank Sinatra)

Sinatra had been one of the inheritors of a substantial shift in the role of the singer in popular music. After the war, due to the decline of the popular (and expensive) swing orchestras of the early 1940s, the singer claimed supremacy in the recording studio. Some of this shift came, no doubt, from the interesting personalities of the postwar singers—Jo Stafford, Perry Como, Nat King Cole, Clooney. Perhaps listeners simply wanted to hear words again; they wanted their feelings expressed in a literate, poetic way, after the somewhat incessant rah-rah boosterism and overt sentimentality of the war years.

What the late 1940s also gave to singers, of course, was the new technology of the LP. Initially, many LP recordings were simply repurposed versions of 78s tacked on, one after the other, but gradually, listeners and singers wanted to take on the challenge of an organically related twenty-five minutes of continued listening. It would also be a challenge to create twelve to sixteen tracks of brand-new material—or at least twelve to sixteen tracks of *good* brand-new material. The catalog of standards from the 1920s, 30s, and 40s could be artfully rearranged and, depending on the song, a talented singer could provide an innovative approach to the material, which is exactly what happened to "Bewitched." In addition, the imprimatur of a classic song could help to sell LPs, which were more likely to be bought by adult listeners with more disposable incomes. And perhaps, best of all, a singer didn't have to put up with demo recordings from pushy publishers or novelty notions from A&R men: the songs of Gershwin, Porter, and Rodgers and Hart didn't have to prove a thing.

The notion of reclaiming Broadway songs from an earlier era began quietly as the 1930s drew to a close in a tiny record store on Madison and 50th called the Liberty Music Shop. Liberty, which also functioned as a kind of boutique record label, recorded Broadway material that was shunned by the more commercially oriented big three of the day: Decca, Victor, and Columbia. Often, Broadway stars such as Ethel Merman, Mary Jane Walsh (the lead in several Rodgers and Hart shows), Beatrice Lillie, and Ethel Waters would head to the east side and lay down some tracks when they had time to spare. These records were bought by fans and aficionados for almost twice the price of a commercial album, but they became cherished artifacts because they were never released to a wide market.

Lee Wiley had been a singer with Leo Reisman and Paul Whiteman in the 1930s and had a career as radio actress. In 1939, she recorded some Gershwin tunes with a small jazz combo—something relatively unheard of—and Liberty pressed some copies; the songs included "My One and Only" and "Sam and Delilah," tunes no one had heard for years.

She then recorded eight Rodgers and Hart songs in 1940 for a friendly competitor of Liberty Music Shop, Rabson's; these were songs that never had much, if any, airplay in the previous decade. Music archivist Bruce Pomahac recalled that director Joshua Logan told him: "At the time they were running on Broadway, the Rodgers and Hart shows were thrilling to the audiences because of all the comedy songs—everybody was knocked out by 'I Wish I Were in Love Again' and those songs what Rodgers referred to as 'the mechanicals.' Nobody listened to 'My Funny Valentine' or 'Where Or When' when *Babes in Arms* opened in 1937."[9]

Wiley's songbook collections (there was another with songs by Harold Arlen) were known by the "in crowd" and circulated among musicians and arrangers; Sinatra, too, was apparently a fan. The first "songbook" from a major singer on a major label occurred in 1947; Margaret Whiting, who had a successful recording contract with Capitol, released her own set of eight Rodgers and Hart songs, including "My Funny Valentine," the first time that song had been recorded—a decade after it appeared on Broadway. Songbook compilations of Broadway composers on LP continued to be commercially attractive prestige items throughout the 1950s, with such honorable projects as *Sarah Vaughan Sings George Gershwin*; *Chris Connor Sings the George Gershwin Almanac*; and Ella Fitzgerald's mammoth achievement, the songbooks for Verve Records, a seminal contribution to the legitimization of the classic Broadway catalog.

Fitzgerald had a recording contract with Decca that dated back to 1938 and, with the exception of a lovely and subtle album of eight Gershwin tunes, accompanied by Ellis Larkins at the piano in 1951, most of the material she covered was transient at best, trivial at worst. Jazz producer Norman Granz had worked with Ella and felt that her bright light of sensitive interpretation was being buried under the bushel of Decca's lack of inspiration. Pulling several different contractual levers, Granz signed her in 1956 to a new label of his called Verve Records; the first collaboration with Fitzgerald would be *The Cole Porter Songbook*.

Porter was still very much alive and lively, having just concocted his highball of a score for the film *High Society*. Granz hired arranger Buddy Bregman to work with Fitzgerald and select the offerings for what would constitute a two-record set, something very unusual for a collection of popular music vocals on a jazz label. Eventually, a total of 32 of Porter's most glorious offerings was selected—songs of the 1930s such as "Night and Day" to his more recent compositions, such as "I Love Paris" from *Can-Can* and "All of You" from *Silk Stockings*, which was still playing on Broadway when Ella recorded the Porter material in Los Angeles. In addition to being an elegant way to honor Cole Porter's oeuvre, the two-LP set provided another milestone in preserving the composer's intentions. As Granz put it, in an interview for the 1993 release of the songbooks on CD:

"[I] insisted we do the verse. That was rarely done in those days—on a three-minute single, no singer could give up a chorus for a verse. But this was an LP, so I didn't care about time."[10]

The critical and commercial success of *The Cole Porter Songbook* inspired a follow-up series of classic Broadway songs, courtesy of two other first-rate songwriters: Rodgers and Hart. Granz thought that the obvious commercial choice would have been to go with Rodgers and Hammerstein, but "there was a certain leanness and edge in [Rodgers's] work with Hart. With Hammerstein, the lyrics were a little schmaltzy—not the best for Ella, I thought."[11] Bregman conducted his arrangements for an epic thirty-four songs over two disks, which ranged from Rodgers and Hart's first hit, "Manhattan" (1925), to their last song, "To Keep My Love Alive" (1943). (In "Manhattan," Fitzgerald alters a famous lyric from the original—"Our future babies / We'll take to *Abie's Irish Rose* / Someday, we'll live to see it close"—to wink at a current long-running Broadway smash: "And *My Fair Lady* / Is a terrific show, they say / We both may see it close / Some day.") Songs that had been mislaid since the 1920s and 30s—"Give It Back to the Indians," "I've Got Five Dollars," "Have You Met Miss Jones?"—were rediscovered by Fitzgerald. "Bewitched" would have been obligatory on her album; Fitzgerald's rendition was the longest recorded version to date, clocking in at seven minutes, which allowed her to sing the more popular bowdlerized lyrics before circling back to sing some additional risqué Hart choruses as heard originally on stage in 1940.

Granz and Fitzgerald followed up with a *Duke Ellington Songbook* of thirty-eight selections (with the composer and his orchestra backing Fitzgerald), and the reputation of the project was growing. Irving Berlin, now seventy years years old, had heard about the songbook project and wondered why he wasn't being considered; he was. Several songs from *As Thousands Cheer* were recorded in Fitzgerald's two-disk songbook devoted to Berlin, arranged by Paul Weston, including "Supper Time" and "How's Chances?," one of the few, if only, renditions of that number in nearly twenty-five years. That was followed by a monumental five-disk, two-part *George and Ira Gershwin Songbook*, which blended the best of their stage songs (many long-neglected) with their movie songs.

The *Songbook* series was a costly labor of love. There would be a two-volume Harold Arlen songbook (mostly film and Cotton Club songs); a one-volume Jerome Kern; and a one-volume Johnny Mercer (with none of his theater material) before the series petered out eight years after its initiation. Cumulatively, the series contains nearly 250 classics, most of which had debuted on Broadway, bound in elegant LP volumes (the cover of the Arlen songbook was a Matisse), enshrined by the one of the most sensitive and lyric-friendly singers of the twentieth century. In later decades, it has not been uncommon that associating with the Great American Songbook can cloak a performer in reflected glory (Linda Ronstadt, Rod Stewart, even Seth McFarlane, meagerly), but Ella Fitzgerald came by this kind of glory honestly, creating a sonic encyclopedia of American popular music between the wars.

Still, for all their considerable achievements, the Fitzgerald songbooks were prestige items that only occasionally cracked the charts in the jazz category. Frank Sinatra's work at rehabilitating the Broadway songbook relied on the bully pulpit of Capitol Records, and his albums reached a far wider audience. Sinatra had always been eager to bring current songs from Broadway scores to the recording studio—witness "People Will Say We're in Love" and "Some Enchanted Evening"—but, he was also a fanatical listener of every recording of pop music and rare gem he could find, and armed with a staff of arrangers and music professionals to help him find even more. He also had another venue for bringing Broadway to Main Street that eluded Fitzgerald and Tony Bennett, his only other rivals in devotion to Broadway tunes: the movies.

One of his very first appearances was in a 1943 film adaptation of Rodgers and Hart's musical, *Higher and Higher*—although practically the only thing the movie shared with the Broadway production was its title. But throughout Sinatra's fluctuating film career, he was hired to play the lead in several adaptations of Broadway musicals: *On the Town* (which preceded *From Here to Eternity*), *Guys and Dolls*, and *Carousel* (Sinatra stomped off the set on the first day of location shooting, never to return; he was reportedly ticked off over some onerous film setups for CinemaScope 55). By 1956, he had regained enough clout in Hollywood to sew up the lead in a new musical film on his own terms, which included co-producing the movie while earning a tremendous salary, plus 25 percent of the box office receipts; the new project was Columbia Pictures' version of Rodgers and Hart's *Pal Joey*.[12]

Pal Joey had been optioned by Columbia's Harry Cohn in the mid-1940s, as a possible follow-up to *Cover Girl*, which starred Rita Hayworth and Gene Kelly (who originated the role of Joey on stage). The project languished until Sinatra's involvement; now, more than a decade later, Hayworth would be cast as the mature Mrs. Vera Simpson, not the ingénue. Typically for the period, when studios still operated under the Production Code, the musical's racy storyline was toned down; additionally, Sinatra's Joey was transformed into a nightclub singer, not a dancer. The original Rodgers and Hart score was cherry-picked for its highlights (several songs were reassigned with bowdlerized lyrics), and four other songs from different 1930s Rodgers and Hart stage musicals were incorporated.

But for audiences in the late 1950s, this was not necessarily a problem. "The purist might also note that several songs from the original score have been dropped in favor of tunes from other Rodgers-Hart hit musicals," wrote A. H. Weiler in his *New York Times* review. "This frankly biased observer contends that this does not constitute short-changing the public."[13] The public had already been embracing Frank Sinatra's renditions of classic Rodgers and Hart songs for most of the 1950s. In fact, for the film, Sinatra recorded

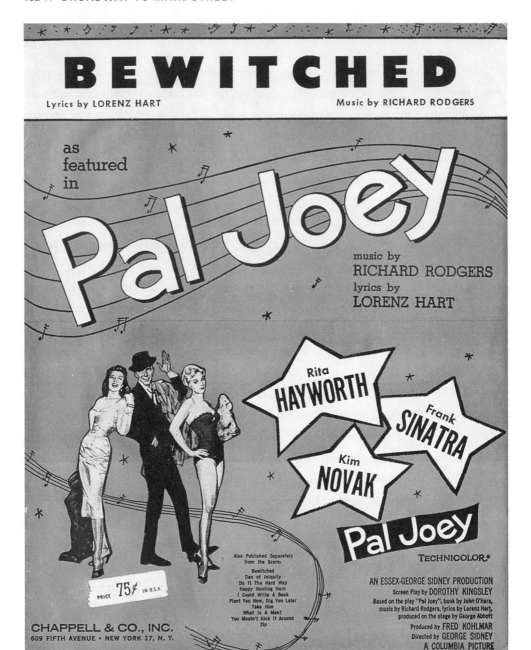

"Bewitched" gets rescued from obscurity and reunited with *Pal Joey*, courtesy of the Frank Sinatra film version, 1957. Author's collection.

"There's a Small Hotel," "I Didn't Know What Time It Was," and "The Lady Is a Tramp," each rendered for the first time in his career. The latter, one with which he would be associated for the rest of his life, was one of the first recordings of the number (from *Babes in Arms*) by a male vocalist; the shift in gender meant a shift from first-person, in the original show, to the third-person and completely alters the tone of the song.

And, by 1957, it was now inevitable that "Bewitched" would make an appearance in the film of *Pal Joey*. Sung initially by Rita Hayworth (dubbed, and in a slightly less egregiously altered version than the popular renditions of the time) and then reprised by Sinatra, singing the lyrics solo, "Bewitched" becomes a central theme of the film. It was rare for a man to perform the song (it was written only to be sung by Vera Simpson in both the original and revival productions on Broadway), but Sinatra made it his own. He continued to sing it throughout his career and passed the torch to dozens of vocalists, female and male, transforming "Bewitched" into one of the great American standards.

An instrumental version of a Broadway song, its subsequent studio recording, a cast album, a songbook LP, a film soundtrack—all of these conspired within less than a decade to make the American listening public bewitched, bothered, and bewildered once more.

Julie Andrews dreams of someone's head restin' on her knee at the recording session for the original cast album of *My Fair Lady* in March of 1956. By permission of Sony Music.

CHAPTER 8

"And *My Fair Lady* Is a Terrific Show, They Say"

The Record Producer and the Blockbuster of Broadway

Goddard Lieberson was having a hell of a time getting either Richard Rodgers or Oscar Hammerstein to return his phone calls.

Surprising, as under Lieberson's aegis as executive vice president at Columbia, in charge of the Masterworks catalog, the *South Pacific* cast album had become the most successful LP of its time. On top of which, Lieberson's producing of the *South Pacific* album was the finest work of transforming a Broadway musical in a studio up to that point, yielding a recording that, had it not even sold one copy, would have still set the gold standard for narrative story-telling and skilled performance. But, in the six years after *South Pacific*'s release, the potential cash bonanza of an original cast album—along with the concomitant attraction of single releases—turned a previously benign market into a feeding frenzy among the major labels: RCA Victor, Decca, Capitol, and, of course, Columbia. Record companies have always been reactive, rather than proactive—so, when Columbia had the, well, kismet of financial success with its cast albums, the other labels charged into the arena.

A successful Broadway show was the gift that kept on giving, its music parceled out any number of ways. Record companies would parry and thrust their way into the melee every time some major producer or songwriting team would announce a new show. Inducements of all kinds were offered to theatrical producers in order to procure their scores. As RCA did with *Allegro*, a company might advance the production tens of thousands of dollars (by 1955, a big musical would cost around $300,000 to bring to Broadway) in order to get the recording rights. It might offer to embargo songs from other labels or radio, or make available its stable of recording artists; or it might offer sweepstakes, publicity, and an onslaught of promotional incentives to disc jockeys, who were becoming increasingly influential. RCA and Columbia even had television networks behind them (NBC was RCA's parent company and Columbia was obviously owned by CBS) that could offer extraordinary exposure via special programming and pressuring their television hosts to present new Broadway songs on their show.

Of course, it was all guesswork, too. Labels rarely had the "look-and-see" luxury of signing a show after it opened, or even waiting until a new musical was trying out in Boston or Philadelphia. Record executives wouldn't know if the show was a hit or a flop until the dozen or so reviewers of daily newspapers weighed in the next morning. *Carnival in Flanders* sounded like a sure thing to Decca Records. The show was the first big musical to open the 1953-54 season; it had a score by Johnny Burke and Jimmy Van Heusen, two of Hollywood's most successful songwriters; what's more, the two leads—Dolores Gray and John Raitt—were Decca recording artists, so there'd be none of that pesky contractual business. Decca nudged ahead of its competitors to get the rights to the cast album for the musical—which closed after six performances. Rather than incur the expense of what would have been a curiosity for collectors, Decca took the financial loss and ate the contract. This made Decca, the premiere label for cast recordings in the 1940s, intermittently gun-shy in the 1950s. Columbia had lost its entire $100,000 investment in *A Tree Grows in Brooklyn* in 1951 and stayed out of the game until 1954, when it went all in for *Kismet, The Pajama Game*, and *The Girl in Pink Tights* (Sigmund Romberg's last show, and a flop).[1]

Once Columbia became more competitive, the idea of losing a third Rodgers and Hammerstein show to RCA, after *Allegro* and *Me and Juliet*, was apparently unthinkable to Goddard Lieberson, who doubled down in a letter dated May 22, 1955, to Rodgers, copies of which were sent to Hammerstein, Max Dreyfus, and their lawyer, Howard Reinheimer:

> Dear Dick:
> Filled with determination that there should be no misunderstanding, slip-up, or malfeasance, I want to definitely, unalterably, and irrevocably say to all persons concerned that I and Columbia Records are desirous of obtaining the recording rights (or any other rights the authors are willing to give up) for the new Rodgers & Hammerstein opus entitled "Pipe Dream."
> 1) Please don't forget.
> 2) The writer of this letter is available at any time for discussion, lunch, cocktails, dinner, tennis, swimming.[2]

Characteristically, Lieberson polished off any rough edges to his hard sell by including (as a gag) the following names under "blind copy:" President Eisenhower, Adlai Stevenson, Billy Graham, David Sarnoff, and Irving Berlin.

Within the Rodgers and Hammerstein team, Rodgers was often curt, but Hammerstein was always courteous. His response to Lieberson was polite, but offered little hope:

> I have talked the whole thing over with Billy Graham and Irving Berlin and the other recipients of your letter, and we all think that we must wait a little time before we shall be able to make a positive decision on this matter. We nevertheless deeply appreciate your interest in us and your forthright way of expressing it.[3]

Well, there it was. However, Lieberson was never one to sit on his hands and wait. While Rodgers, Hammerstein, and Reinheimer (their hard-nosed lawyer) were making a decision, Lieberson would find another project to record, worthy of Columbia's care, attention, and resources. After all, the 1955–56 Broadway season hadn't yet begun—there had to be something waiting around the corner.

If Jack Kapp was the Giotto of the original cast album, Goddard Lieberson was its Michelangelo. He not only filled all the qualifications of being a great producer of cast albums, he practically wrote the job description himself. Lieberson was born in Staffordshire, England, in 1911, the son of a Russian manufacturer of bootwear, who brought his family to Seattle. As the Depression began, Lieberson enrolled at the Eastman School of Music in Rochester, where he was trained in composition and, while gaining experience as an amateur essayist and music critic, he took a job in a private school in Rochester, teaching music and directing concerts and plays. His considerable ambition took him to Manhattan in 1939, where he rubbed elbows with all sorts of musical, literary, and social types. An introduction got him hired that same year as an assistant in Columbia's Masterworks division; he would never work for any company other than Columbia—in one post or another—for the next thirty-six years.

Six years after his start at Columbia, he was promoted to head the Masterworks division, where he oversaw the Modern Music Series. In appreciation of his support for Columbia's development and promotion of the LP, as well as for his personal skill and acumen, he was made executive vice president in 1949, where he oversaw all the artists and repertory staff. By the end of 1955, the Columbia stable included such diverse performers as Doris Day, Johnnie Ray, Tony Bennett, Rosemary Clooney, Johnny Mathis, Duke Ellington, Louis Armstrong, arranger Percy Faith, the New York Philharmonic, the Philadelphia Orchestra, and the Cleveland Orchestra. Orchestrating, as it were, all those personalities and all those performance styles would require considerable business acumen, but, as good as Lieberson was behind a desk, he may have been even better after quitting time. He loved being socially well-connected and managed to strike a uniquely judicious balance between his personal and professional relationships. In 1946, he married the ballerina and actress Vera Zorina (who had previously been married to George Balanchine), who was one of the most effervescently charming women of her day. In fact, not only did she appear in several Rodgers and Hart shows in London and on Broadway, they immortalized her in a lyric from "Zip" in *Pal Joey*: "I don't want to see Zorina / I don't want to meet Cobina / Zip! I'm an intellectual." Perhaps that's why Lieberson was so keen to record *Pal Joey* in 1950.

A compelling presence—a sort of Jewish Sherlock Holmes with buckets of charm—Lieberson had a unique command of business contacts, diplomacy, and grace; an appreciation of historical tradition, persistence, and musical and theatrical training; kindness toward performers and writers; and, ultimately, a gift in the studio for transforming a theatrical event into a musical one. The Columbia initiative to record neglected scores from the 1920s, 30s, and 40s was a mission for Lieberson, who saw it as a way of reclaiming a national musical heritage. As he wrote for the *New York Times* in 1956, comparing the American musical canon with that of great Italian lyric opera, "I would say that we have produced many works which deserve re-listening and re-seeing, which is perhaps the true measure of the entertainment value of a work of art." With his sterling comrade, conductor and arranger Lehman Engel, at his side, Lieberson recorded a dozen classic scores throughout the 1950s, including *On Your Toes, The Merry Widow, The Desert Song, The Boys from Syracuse, Roberta, Oh, Kay!,* and *Babes in Arms*. They assembled an informal repertory company, which included such up-and-coming talents as Jack Cassidy and Kaye Ballard. Lieberson and Engel were also cheeky enough to record new renditions of *Brigadoon* and *Oklahoma!,* allowing Columbia to offer consumers expanded versions of those scores.[4]

Perhaps the most enduring of these studio recordings was *On the Town*, recorded in 1960 and released the following year—only fifteen years after the original production closed. Banking on Leonard Bernstein's enhanced reputation over that time, Lieberson brought the composer into the recording studio to conduct the orchestra. Because of Bernstein's involvement (he was also a Columbia Masterworks artist), the show's extraordinary ballet music was also copiously recorded, something unusual for a cast album at the time (although four of the dances had appeared earlier on the 1945 Victor album set release). The Columbia *On the Town* featured Nancy Walker, Cris Alexander, Betty Comden, and Adolph Green of the original cast, supplemented by John Reardon, taking on the rhapsodic ballads originally sung by John Battles. Comden, Green, and Walker no longer had the same youthful enthusiasm as their 1945 waxings for Decca, but it was an important step for Lieberson to recognize that this score deserved a proper archival recording—it's hard to know if *On the Town*'s canonical reputation would have occurred without it, especially given the evisceration of its score in the 1949 MGM film version.

Lieberson also knew that he was between a rock and a hard place when it came to preserving the scores of the past in studio recordings. He sensitively and eloquently described the challenges of reviving material in any venue, raising issues that would nettle record and theater producers for decades:

> And there were difficult decisions to make when it came time to record: the kind of voices, the size of the chorus, and most important, the great question as to whether we should try to reproduce the musical style contemporary with the show, or add later musical developments, for better or for worse. This was an important consideration because, curiously enough, the concepts of some well-known songs had so radically changed that had they been done in the original tempo and style, they would be found grotesque, or we would have been accused of burlesquing the music.[5]

Among the other orphaned scores that Lieberson and Engel wanted to adopt in the recording studio were Cole Porter's *Jubilee*; *Where's Charley?*; and Berlin's *As Thousands Cheer*. Berlin himself volunteered to find the score and orchestrations in his office at the Music Box Theatre; alas, he came up with nothing. Still, the decade of Columbia studio recordings inspired several requests from various show folk, hoping to get an album done of a neglected work. Lieberson had to turn down Burton Lane's inquiry about finally making a recording of *Hold on to Your Hats*: "There are so many great shows that have not yet been recorded and that should be done, that it would be some time before we get to the more obscure—if, nevertheless, no less deserving—shows."[6] In 1958, Moss Hart asked Lieberson to consider a decent studio version of his ambitious *Lady in the Dark* (for which he wrote the book), which had never had a full cast recording. What's more, he suggested that his wife, the talented singer Kitty Carlisle Hart, should sing the title role. Lieberson phrased his rejection diplomatically:

> Now I have another sad story to tell you. As you probably know, I have, in the past, mostly for the amusement of friends, recreated on records certain shows which were done before the time of recording complete shows. They have been very well received by the cognoscenti, reviewed brilliantly, et cetera, et cetera. The peculiar truth is that with very few exceptions, these do not sell well. Don't ask me why. I can't possibly tell you.[7]

Lieberson became an epistolary master at conducting business and kept up a vigorous round of correspondence, collaboration, and social contact with Broadway royalty, often priming the pump of professional pleasantries with complimentary releases, fresh off the presses. Lieberson parried and thrust, capable of deflecting some grudging Rodgers criticism about the "hot" arrangements of "This Can't Be Love" on *The Boys from Syracuse* studio album; embracing suggestions from Ira Gershwin for the use of additional, more obscure, lyrics on the *Girl Crazy* album; and receiving heartfelt aperçus from Cole Porter on the morning after the mixed notices for the composer's *Can-Can* had just appeared in the dozen or so New York newspapers: "It is very strange, but always throughout my life I have nearly always received notices saying 'not up to his usual standard.' One time Linda and I looked through all of the press clippings which she had saved in scrap books, through the years, and as far back as we went we could never find a place where I was up to my usual standard."[8]

But being a good listener didn't always lead to winning the game (in fact, Columbia lost the cast recording of *Can-Can* to Capitol); many of his entreaties to music publishers, who still held the keys to the kingdom of ongoing recording and performance rights, fell on deaf ears. A letter to Frank Loesser (who published Richard Adler and Jerry Ross's *The Pajama Game*) ran: "Boys just played me some of the songs from *Damned Yankee*. [*sic*] Please make damned sure we get this show. How else can we give you two million sales on singles?" ("Hey There" had earned exactly that.) Loesser went with RCA instead and had a lackluster recording of *Damn Yankees* to show for it. (Mitch Miller, from the Columbia A&R, who did so much to produce and promote "Hey There," told *Variety* that he was "penalized for success:" "What was on Frank Loesser's mind?" The short answer: Dinah Shore.)[9]

"I like creative people," Lieberson told a reporter, and they liked him as well. "Goddard and his people make you feel a little more appreciated," Rodgers told the same reporter.[10] Betty Comden, who wrote *Bells Are Ringing* with Adolph Green and Jule Styne, recalled how Lieberson treated her dear friend (and star) during the recording session in 1956: "I was always struck by his sensitivity in working with creative people, and his deep understanding of the special problems of performing artists. While making the recording of *Bells Are Ringing*, I remember an uncertain and scared Judy Holliday, and how Goddard, with kindness, and patience, and a light but caring touch, soothed her terrors and elicited a glowing performance."[11] Ted Chapin, president of the Rodgers and Hammerstein Organization, assessed Lieberson's gift for eliciting performances from a listener's perspective: "Listen to the performances on his cast albums of people like Mary Martin on the original cast album of *The Sound of Music*. At first she has no voice left—and you don't care. The performance is of such confidence that you never wince because she's comfortable and has such charm and she's delivering a wonderful performance."[12] Harold Prince, who worked with Lieberson on recordings of five musicals that he produced, put it best: "Goddard represents the gold standard. He was the guiding force in masterminding cast albums and produced brilliant recordings. He knew everything about show scores and how to present them at their best. He was of another time insofar as he was a true gent—honest, with extraordinary taste, and with a great enthusiasm for Broadway scores."[13]

Lieberson was also lucky in that he had come along at the right moment—when narrative musicals intersected with the technology that could best exploit them at the time—and because he intuited that narrative in the musical theater could be attractive to the consumer:

> If there were those in the beginning [1943] who doubted the public's interest in these albums [referring to the Decca recordings, beginning with *Oklahoma!*], *South Pacific* six years later quickly changed their minds. Both shows are by the same authors, and this is not a coincidence. But their success is not based solely on the high quality of their music and lyrics, but on the fact that both scores... are brilliant examples of the integration of music, words and story; and each song of the score relates, to some extent, to what has happened before and what is yet to happen. It is true that many thousands of people like "Some Enchanted Evening," but even more like *South Pacific* in the aggregate, which, after all, was the authors' main intention.[14]

Lieberson would immerse himself in the "authors' main intention" by learning the score (he was, of course, a skilled musician) and following its peregrinations during the rehearsal and production process. He attended *South Pacific* fourteen times, by his own count, before it was recorded: rehearsals, tryouts, previews, and so on. He knew what was important in the show, and he understood the limited technology with which he had to work; in order to bridge the gap between the two, he often had to make cuts, compressions, and elisions.

Usually, extended dance music was the first to go, because shy of the actual choreography, the dance music could rarely be counted on to move the narrative forward. While not averse to dance or dance music (he had married one of the great ballerinas of the twentieth century, after all), Lieberson would leave out as much dance music as he thought the narrative could bear in his recordings, or speed up the tempos of what dance music he did include, in order to whip up additional excitement for the listener. John Kander recalled a rather listless section of dance music during the recording of *Cabaret*, when Lieberson made the decision to double the tempo: "All of a sudden, it sounded like what you remembered seeing in the theater. But God help the person who was doing the show and taking on the tempo on that recording—because nobody could have danced it."[15] Lieberson might add a small dance floor in the studio for certain numbers; he was able, at any rate, to create an atmosphere for a dancer to transform his or her talent from one medium to another. Chita Rivera worked with Lieberson on the cast recordings of *West Side Story* and *Bye Bye Birdie,* and credits him for capturing kinetics on tape: "Dance energy is different on a recording. If I did a cartwheel and then I sang something afterward, I would know, in my mind, that I had done that cartwheel; your physical body is used to it. You can absolutely make a lyric visible by putting in an internal energy that you can pull right down to that microphone—and Goddard helped us find that."[16]

In addition to reducing dance music, Lieberson loathed the application of dialogue to a musical recording, and only used it to point the listener in the right direction: "The nature of the phonograph record, which, if it is to be successful—as a record, not in sales, necessarily—is something to be played over and over again. What is poignant and moving in the theater, when removed from that context and put down on a record and played over and over, deteriorates in its emotional appeal and can even become an embarrassment."[17]

For example, in *The Pajama Game*, the show opens with a monologue by a supporting character, Hines, who tells the audience what they're going to see and why: "This is a very serious drama. It's kind of a problem play. It's about Capital and Labor. I wouldn't bother to make such a point of all this except later on, if you happen to see a lot of naked women being chased through the woods, I don't want you to get the wrong impression." Well, as amusing as that is, there was no way Lieberson was going to record all that when he produced the cast album in 1954. After the overture, he segues into the jaunty fanfare of the title number. After singing the first chorus of the song ("I can hardly wait / to wake and get to work at eight / Nothing's quite the same as the pajama game!"), Hines speaks for the first time, saying, "I'm an executive. I'm a time study man. I can tell you per second exactly how many stitches go into a pair of pajamas. I can time anything. You'll see when we get down to the factory. Let her go!" Then comes the busy factory music and we're off and running (or "racing with the clock," as the song goes). Lieberson trusts the dynamism and the purpose of the lyrics to tell the story of the beleaguered pajama factory workers: "When will Hasler give us our seven-and-a-half-cent raise?" sings one of the laborers. Who's Hasler? Who cares? He's the boss and he's oppressing his workers—that's perfectly clear from the song itself.

▶   Audio Example 8.1, "The Pajama Game / Racing with the Clock" (*The Pajama Game* original cast)

There were many other tricks that Lieberson had up his Turnbull & Asser sleeve. In producing more than 70 original cast albums, he would supplement orchestration (and occasionally scale it back) and flip material around. Like a good theater director, he liked Act Two (that is, side two of an LP) to open with a bang, to re-engage the listener who had gotten out of his or her easy chair to turn the record over, perhaps going to the refrigerator to get a can of soda or something in the meantime. He would occasionally move songs around to achieve this effect; for example, in *Camelot*, he switched the show's order of "Before I Gaze at You Again" and "If Ever I Would Leave You," so that the latter song— Lancelot's big ballad, which was not-so-coincidentally released in advance of the cast album as a Columbia single featuring Vic Damone—would be heard the minute the tone arm hit the beginning of side two.

Lieberson expressed his philosophy in the liner notes to a 1961 Columbia anthology called "This Is Broadway's Best." His cogent reasoning bears repeating:

> The microphone must be subservient to the dramatic idea and not the other way around as, I fear, is often the case.... As with a director or a scene designer, a record producer of taste can only enhance the qualities of a show: conversely, a record producer without taste can destroy the qualities of the original production. All of this, perhaps, sounds simple-minded; yet it should be stated since the wide currency given recordings of original cast albums is assuming proportions which make the record, in many cases, not only the most widely distributed representation of a musical show, but in addition, its most permanent representation.

In spring 1955, still cooling over Rodgers and Hammerstein's procrastination over *Pipe Dream*, Goddard Lieberson would make a decision that would propel the original cast album into assuming proportions beyond the wildest dreams of distribution.

Lieberson had been friendly with librettist and lyricist Alan Jay Lerner for years (they had country homes near each other in Rockland County). Lerner had been working on a musical adaptation of George Bernard Shaw's social critique from 1912, *Pygmalion*, off and on, for several years with his composer/collaborator Frederick Loewe and producer Herman Levin, trying to put the disparate pieces of this peculiar puzzle together. As one of the great Broadway legends has it, a musical adaptation of *Pygmalion* was viewed by the theatrical community as a nonstarter from the very beginning; a dramatic play so devoid of the conventions of traditional musical comedy that it could never be successfully musicalized, cast, or staged. However, by late spring 1955, the casting of the musical was coming tantalizingly close to completion: the young British actress Julie Andrews had agreed to keep her schedule clear and the British star Rex Harrison had committed to playing Henry Higgins.

This was a good time to wrap it all up by getting a financial backer. Lerner, according to his autobiography, was mindful that both the NBC and CBS networks were major players in the Broadway musical investment game and that, as *Variety* put it, "the intense rivalry between CBS and RCA-NBC means that tv rights will be the crux of any [recording] deal."[18] Lerner's entreaties to David Sarnoff at NBC were met with silence, but a call to Goddard Lieberson elicited considerable interest. Within a few weeks, Lieberson sat down with William Paley, the chief executive of CBS, over lunch at Manhattan's tony 21 Club and suggested that CBS invest in the new project. "At that time," Lieberson recalled in an interview some years later, "it was known as *London Bridge*. We weren't all that confident about any of it. I remember saying to Paley, 'If worse comes to worst, let's get a commitment from Rex Harrison to do *Pygmalion* on television, as a backup.'"[19] Paley set up a meeting with producer Levin for the first week of July and, for a reported $400,000, CBS quickly sewed up the entire rights to show, cast recording, and any possible ancillary television or film income.[20]

For a media company to go all in for a Broadway show was not unprecedented (RCA had backed *Call Me Madam* in 1950 for its entire budget of $275,000), but the sum was still a large one. Ironically, the Shavian provenance of the material, which had put off so many theatrical backers, worked to the advantage of the network's interest, as a television version of *Pygmalion* starring Rex Harrison would have been a prestigious and anticipated broadcast back in the day. But, with Moss Hart signed to direct, the musical version was now off and running, and Columbia got its ducks in a row to make the most out of its investment. In an April 1956 newsletter addressed to the company employees, Columbia president John Conkling recounted the company's history with *My Fair Lady*: "Mitch Miller and Marv Holtzman were shown the score and they started at once to create popular single records of some of the songs, because if they could make a top-selling single from one or more of the songs, it would greatly enhance the potential of the show and the success of our original cast album." As the show began its out-of-town tryouts in February 1956, accordingly to Conkling, "Our sales department immediately started teaser campaigns and arranged for the disc jockeys, dealers, and distributors to see the show while it was still playing out of town in New Haven and Philadelphia."

Of course, when *My Fair Lady* opened at the Mark Hellinger Theatre in New York on March 15, it was an immediate smash: the *Times* called it the "show of the century," which—with forty-four years left to go—was a pretty impressive statement. Ten days later, the cast album was recorded at Columbia's voluminous 30th Street studio in a fourteen-hour session. Lieberson had already scoped out every aspect of the score and had made some important decisions. According to Lerner, "The climax of the play, when Eliza returns, happens to be a line of dialogue ['Eliza, where the devil are my slippers?'].

Goddard's solution was to go directly from 'I've Grown Accustomed to Her Face' into a dramatic and emotional orchestral reprise of 'I Could Have Danced All Night'—Eliza's theme—which then built to a climax."[21]

In a promotional post-recording interview (at past midnight), Lieberson interviewed the principals, who were giddily incoherent with exhaustion. "Wonderful fun," admitted the usually cranky Harrison, "after a gruelingly long day;" Andrews owned up that "you hear the orchestrations for the first time—you're so close—all the bits and pieces." When Lieberson asked Lerner (who had hung in there for the entire fourteen hours) what was his favorite song of the session, he replied, "Oh, What a Beautiful Mornin.'" It had been that kind of day.[22]

The rest of the company had been released hours earlier, following the tradition of recording the largest number of folks first, then peeling them off, group by group, but by the time Harrison, Andrews, and Lerner stumbled into the cold Monday morning after, musical editors were already arranging the tapes, and the engineering department started work on the masters. The masters would be assembled and sent to the Columbia factory in Bridgeport, Connecticut, almost sixty miles northwest of the city. Cardboard record jackets had been printed and assembled weeks before, with the iconic Hirschfeld poster design of Shaw, Harrison, and Andrews (although the colors of the show's poster—blue and yellow—were curiously leeched out). By late Tuesday afternoon, less than two days after the recording was done, the final product was beginning to come out of the factory, and delivered to executives, promoters, disc jockey, and eventually an eager public.

There was an advance order of 100,000 copies, and, by April 3 (Tuesday being a typical release day), consumers could purchase their very own copy. (That same night, Elvis Presley made his television debut on Milton Berle's program.) The album was already being heralded as "Fort Knox on wax... it could be one of the alltime best sellers, it's that hot a property," according to a *Variety* piece on April 4. Later in the week, *Billboard* concurred, but offered an insightful cavil: "Many of the show's best tunes are so closely integrated with the show's great book that the impact of their clever lyrics are considerably diminished on wax."[23]

In a post-release letter to the Columbia staff, President Conkling concluded, "I would guess that almost everyone who reads this article has, at some place, along the line had something to do with 'My Fair Lady.' The nicest part about this is that it will probably become one of the biggest LP sellers of all times, and we should all feel the benefits." In fact, it zoomed to No. 1 by the end of April, spending eight consecutive weeks there (and hitting No. 1 seven more times over the next four years), and became the fastest album to sell one million copies. By 1965, it was the most successful album of all time; by 1976, it had sold eight million copies and was certified as triple platinum. It would stay on the

Billboard Top 10 chart (which was, initially, limited to only the top fifty albums until 1959) for 173 weeks (a record by 57 weeks); in the Top 40 for 292 weeks (another record, and double the next runner-up); and charted for a total 480 weeks—more than nine *years*, surpassed by only two other albums since: Pink Floyd's *The Dark Side of the Moon* and Johnny Mathis's *Greatest Hits*.[24]

There was also a cover of "On the Street Where You Live" by Vic Damone on Columbia (restructured by Mitch Miller, who moved the bridge to the top of the song), which was on the Top 10 Singles chart for six weeks, as well as untold cover albums devoted to the entire score by a variety of performers—singers (Andy Williams, Nat King Cole), easy listening orchestras (Robert Farnon, Percy Faith), jazz musicians (André Previn, Shelly Manne)—not to mention a half dozen international cast albums from companies all around the world.

Would it be churlish, at this point, to remark that *Pipe Dream*—the Rodgers and Hammerstein musical for which Lieberson had abased himself—was acquired by RCA and didn't run past the 1955–56 season and closed as Rodgers and Hammerstein's biggest flop? (It didn't even yield a good Top 10 number, like *Me and Juliet*.)

For Goddard Lieberson, this embarrassment of riches only accrued to his professional success; he was promoted to president of Columbia Records two months after *My Fair Lady* hit No. 1.[25] This gave him a bully pulpit, and he acquired eight cast albums in 1956, including Johnny Mercer's *L'il Abner*; *Bells Are Ringing*; Leonard Bernstein's *Candide* (a financial failure as a show, but a successful recording, to which Lieberson committed because of Columbia's relationship with Bernstein); and Frank Loesser's *The Most Happy Fella*. The last three shows, in addition to *My Fair Lady*, comprised all four Tony-nominated musicals for the 1957 awards. Whatever ill will Lieberson had toward Loesser with the kerfuffle over *Damn Yankees* must have been quickly forgotten with *The Most Happy Fella* as Lieberson, setting his normal aversion to dialogue aside, gave Loesser's masterpiece the full operatic treatment: a three-LP release in a boxed set—something unprecedented for a contemporary musical. (Apparently, Lieberson was so taken with the performances in the studio that he made the decision to expand the release from two disks to three in the middle of the recording session.)

Several other commercial initiatives at Columbia Records had an impact on its production of the cast album and its dominance of the field: the introduction of the Columbia Record Club in 1955 and the commercial application of stereophonic sound in 1958. The Columbia Record Club was a subscription-based way of maintaining a steady income stream for Columbia products. Inspired by the Book-of-the-Month Club and other such media subscription distribution plans, the Record Club had long been a dream of

Lieberson's and, with the advent of LPs, the product was now light and durable enough to be shipped through the mail. Customers could sign up for four categories: classical; "easy listening"; jazz; and cast albums and soundtracks. The advent of stereo recording—another initiative long in development—had a substantial impact, too. The more sophisticated grooves in a stereo LP allowed the record player stylus to separate the sound into two different, and often complementary, channels. Studio engineers used the technology to achieve more ambient, realistic sound, but it soon became apparent that stereo could be used to create movement, tension, depth, and other effects on a recording. For a medium that used song, voice, speech, and (often) dance, such as the Broadway cast album, the stereo LP was a natural platform for experimentation.[26]

Consumers with fancy new stereo hi-fis wanted something to play on them that would show off the technology, so the original mono LP recordings on Columbia—which comprised Columbia's catalog—were put on the back burner. Lieberson asked staff producer James Foglesong (who produced an excellent new recording of an off-Broadway *Anything Goes* on the subsidiary label, Epic) to start an informal series of stereo studio versions of classics with first-class Broadway and pop talent. Foglesong brought a recent hire onto the project, a young musician named Thomas Z. Shepard, to help him produce, and Columbia stole the thunder from three Decca classics: *Oklahoma!* (now with John Raitt and Florence Henderson); *The King and I* (Barbara Cook); and *Annie Get Your Gun* with Doris Day and Robert Goulet, which was produced by Schuyler Chapin, one of Lieberson's producers from the Masterworks division. All of this was well and good because it would supply consumers with crisp stereo versions of cherished favorite scores from the canon.

But how to get a new version of a new favorite? That was Lieberson's major challenge when it came to *My Fair Lady,* an album only months into its release and still a powerhouse on the charts. Existing only in mono-land, the momentum of *My Fair Lady* could be stopped dead in its tracks by the increasingly large cadre of consumers purchasing stereo equipment. So, if Lieberson couldn't bring *My Fair Lady* to stereo, he decided to bring stereo to *My Fair Lady.*

As fate would have it, in 1958, *My Fair Lady* was still running with its original cast—no longer on Broadway, but on the West End at the fabled Drury Lane, where it had opened after an overwhelming welter of anticipation in April. The New York cast album had been embargoed prior to the British opening and could only be found on the black market—or smuggled in by the crew of transatlantic liners—for an asking price of up to four times the retail price of $5.98. On February 1, 1959, Lieberson reassembled the cast in a London studio to take on another twelve-plus-hour session. As he wrote in the liner notes: "How is it that [after three years], Rex Harrison is giving what is by far his best, his most touching, his most sensitive performance of 'I've Grown Accustomed to Her Face?' If you think you have previously experienced fully an attachment to this remarkable score, be prepared, in listening to this record, for a second honeymoon."[27]

▶ Audio Example 8.2, "I've Grown Accustomed to Her Face" (Rex Harrison)

Lieberson effectively married the novelty of stereo with the prestige of the Lerner and Loewe score; the new stereo album was released early in 1959 in a golden cover and a new presentation: the gatefold, which opened up (like a book) to provide two pages of liner notes, along with a full-color photograph on the back cover. This format was known as the "K-series" and would expand, with additional pages and color photographs, into the early 1960s, making the Columbia (stereo) cast albums the most attractive product of its kind and the best at capturing the glamour of Broadway. The "K" gatefolds would be cherished by a generation of cast recording fans. Capitol Records would also add gatefolds in the early 1960s, but the packaging—including only black-and-white photos variably reproduced—wasn't nearly as attractive as Columbia's, although occasionally it would slip in a souvenir program.

Lieberson was able to work a similar marital magic with Rodgers and Hammerstein, bonding with them over their final three projects, despite the producer's disappointment about *Pipe Dream*. On January, 22, 1957, he wrote to Rodgers after listening to a demo of a score to their upcoming original primetime CBS special, a musical written by the team for Julie Andrews and based on the *Cinderella* story: "I am so enchanted and thrilled and overcome by your newest creative efforts. In this era of 'Hound Dogs,' I don't know what the public is going to say, but I, for the first time, am saying 'The public be damned.' If they don't recognize these melodies and liltings for what they are, it's their loss." The CBS broadcast had the kind of corporate synergy that networks had been angling for since they got into the cast album business. The special itself aired on the evening of March 31 and was watched by more than 107 million people. A complementary studio recording did very well for Columbia; perhaps more importantly, the project appears to have patched up Lieberson's relationship with Rodgers and Hammerstein.

For their next show, *Flower Drum Song*, in 1958, Rodgers and Hammerstein formed their own record company to co-produce the album with Columbia, and it was the team's first original cast album to be recorded on "stereo fidelity." *Flower Drum Song* was a decent-sized hit on stage, but a phenomenal success for Columbia on record, hitting No. 1 for three weeks and staying on the charts for an impressive 151 weeks. The musical's opening date, December 1, made it difficult to get the recording of *Flower Drum Song* under the Christmas tree, so thousands of gift certificates for the album were supplied to dealers by Columbia.

The next collaboration between Columbia and Rodgers and Hammerstein, a year later, was *The Sound of Music*. The album was also a rush job—it was primed to hit the shelves in early December, a few weeks after the show's opening—and the in-house design team was feeling a lot of pressure, especially about the cover, for which an immense number of credits were contractually required. "It is very difficult to get any kind of design when you have to print the telephone book on the front page," complained the lead designer. After considering printing the album with a green velour border—"for the Tyrolean appearance"—the cover succumbed to the huge amount of typography needed to make everyone happy.[28] Everyone who had a royalty participation was happy, too: after Christmas 1959, the album settled in at No. 1 for sixteen weeks, a record for its time. Max Dreyfus, who was still looking after Rodgers and Hammerstein's publishing interests at Chappell—and had been responsible for the decisions that kept quite a few Rodgers and Hammerstein cast albums and soundtracks out of Lieberson's hands—wrote a gracious note to the record producer: "We like it very much, in fact, we could say it is outstanding, but how could it be otherwise, since it is produced by our friend Goddard."

If the advent of the 1960s and the increasing popularity of rock and roll suggested that original cast albums would be consigned to a quaint 1950s fad, like Davy Crockett hats, hula hoops, and Patti Page singing "(How Much Is) That Doggie in the Window?," it didn't work out that way. In fact, with the addition of the Capitol blockbuster recording of *The Music Man* (as a label, it had hung back in the early 1950s on original cast albums, but did phenomenal business in 1958 with this Meredith Willson celebration of Americana; it was No. 1 on the charts for twelve weeks), companies were scrambling more than ever to sign up an incoming show. The composers and publishers were getting a bigger piece of the action, too; just as Rodgers and Hammerstein formed their own record company, so did Lerner and Loewe. An article in *Billboard* observed the frenzied financial scrum and commented, "Although you might latch onto a flop, with the right show, the money is as good as gold for a long, long time; and from a prestige point of view, a successful cast album is the ne plus ultra of packaged goods." And, yet, the article honed in on a trend that had been developing since *My Fair Lady*: "The past few years have emerged with fewer and fewer hit singles, due to the specialized nature of the material."[29]

Lieberson rode out the 1950s having seemingly secured a much more confident relationship with Richard Rodgers (Oscar Hammerstein would pass away of stomach cancer in 1960), but it was the cast album of *My Fair Lady* that had defined his success at Columbia and certified Columbia as an industry leader. Alan Jay Lerner recounted in his memoir that "when I heard the completed album [of *My Fair Lady*], I phoned Goddard and thanked him. I said to him, and I remember this very clearly: 'Goddard, it's terrific. If it sells fifty thousand albums I'll be satisfied.'" It would become a cultural phenomenon

April 1956

COLUMBIA

On the cover of an in-house marketing magazine, a Columbia worker demonstrates how quickly the *My Fair Lady* album was packaged, literally hot off the presses. By permission of Sony Music.

and wind up selling millions. Lieberson knew that success had its own concomitant challenges and that his job at Columbia was only going to get harder to sustain. "Our business is to make records, not invest in shows. We were forced into this nutty competition mainly by of our own success with *My Fair Lady*," he told the *New York Times*. "Other companies are investing large amounts to obtain recording rights and we have to keep on doing the same. We are the victims of our own Frankenstein monster."[30]

Three American institutions of the 1950s: (l. to r.) Oscar Hammerstein II, Richard Rodgers, and America's favorite host, Ed Sullivan. By permission of SOFA Entertainment.

CHAPTER 9

Hymn for a Sunday Evening

Television and the Mythology of Broadway

On the evening of Sunday, February 9, 1964, the 54th Street Theatre was, in the old showbiz phrase, packed to the gunnels. There wasn't a spare ticket to be had; luminaries such as Leonard Bernstein and Jack Paar were among the 50,000 citizens who begged for seats, hoping to be covered in glory in their children's eyes by snagging entry to the exalted event: the live broadcast of *The Ed Sullivan Show*. Sullivan, executive producer and host of his eponymous television program, was about to present a group of talented youngsters who would be performing a few songs that had been captivating British audiences for months. Their music had just recently been introduced to an American audience, but this night would be the first major exposure of the songs to a wide national demographic in the States. A house full of screaming teenagers (and the occasional bewildered adult) would be eagerly watching these animated youngsters perform live.

The group on stage was the juvenile cast of Lionel Bart's West End musical *Oliver!*, then in its thirteenth month on Broadway at the Imperial Theatre.

Posterity, of course, records the reception of a far more celebrated group that night: the Beatles performing live on American television for the first time. Indeed, the exceptional interest in the Beatles gave *The Ed Sullivan Show* that night a national audience of nearly 74 million viewers, a record that would stand for the next fifteen years as a rare moment of national consensus. But the singular triumph of Sullivan's "scoop" of the Beatles shouldn't obscure the fact that, for viewers of Sullivan's program, the February 9 broadcast was, from a programming standpoint, business as usual. And business as usual for Sullivan always meant delivering a generous glimpse of Broadway on nearly every program, nearly every Sunday for twenty-three years. Ed Sullivan may have been unlikely casting for the role of intrepid pioneer but, through the medium of television, he led the music of Broadway into new territory, providing a transition from the waning days of radio into a burgeoning cultural landscape.

The *Oliver!* portion of the February 9 broadcast was also not remarkably different from Sullivan's usual presentation of Broadway fare. He introduced the segment himself ("And now, from the Imperial Theatre, where *Oliver!* is continuing to delight audiences...") and turned it over to the cast, in costume, gamboling on an abstracted adaptation of Sean Kenny's Tony-Award-winning set for a couple of energetically performed numbers. It was a generous and attractive advertisement for a Broadway musical of obvious appeal to families in the metropolitan area and beyond—and it had nothing whatsoever to do with the Beatles or their promotional machine. In fact, when one adds in the medley of Gershwin tunes performed that evening by Welsh entertainer Tessie O'Shea ("currently featured in the hit musical, Noel Coward's *The Girl Who Came to Supper*"—which wasn't really a hit), Sullivan had devoted nearly as much time on this epoch-making broadcast to the music of Broadway as he had for the Beatles—possibly more, as the Beatles (who performed in two separate sets, one at the beginning of the program, the other toward the end) sang "Till There Was You," a ballad from Meredith Willson's *The Music Man*.[1]

Make no mistake: this kind of artistic decision making was almost entirely in Ed Sullivan's hands. He wasn't simply the host of the show, he was its progenitor and its executive producer; every creative decision—from guest entertainers to their material to their presentation, even to costume and make-up—came straight from Sullivan. Although as a host he was legendarily awkward and stiff, prone to mortifying gaffes, and hopeless at the genial banter that was the lingua franca of variety programming, Sullivan was in full control of his own show. Comedienne Joan Rivers, who appeared on his program dozens of times in the 1960s, said, "Ed Sullivan was the taste of America for thirty years. He knew what they would like and he had no other talent, but, boy, he called those shots."[2]

Critics of American popular culture and American history have given Sullivan his proper credit for shaping and managing the tastes of the public in the postwar years. He not only exposed America to rock and roll, he opened the door for African American performers and cultivated the careers of dozens of performers who would become national mainstays. Yet, Sullivan is never given full credit for what he did for Broadway, and for the dissemination of its music in popular culture. Over the course of his twenty-three-year-long program, Sullivan would present to the American public thousands of songs that had originated on Broadway's stages, but Sullivan was more than a televisual disc jockey; those thousands of songs were frequently showcased in extensive clips from a show currently running on Broadway, featuring the cast members who were performing it eight times a week. When Sullivan became a video impresario in the late 1940s, Americans had already been enchanted by show music in their living rooms for decades—around the piano, by the radio, from the phonograph--but they hadn't yet been treated to the visual spectacle of Broadway in so intimate a private space. Sullivan was a Ziegfeld of the television console, and he yielded a tremendous influence on attentive consumers throughout the land by boosting careers, promoting records, and showcasing theatrical productions.

In addition, he would constantly and consistently enshrine Broadway's greatest creators and performers with tributes, encomiums, and hour-long specials dedicated to their work, venerating their trials and triumphs to viewers in Walla Walla and Wichita and Westchester, thousands of miles or forty-five minutes from the Theater District. Unifying all these spectacular moments was Sullivan's deep and abiding love for Broadway and its "broken heart for every light" mythology. Perhaps more than any other individual of the postwar years, as Broadway's most enthusiastic and effective curator, Sullivan brought Broadway to Main Street.

Of course, Sullivan wasn't the only theatrical ringmaster for the circus of television's early days. Producer Max Liebman brought his impeccable skills at crafting lively revues from his Broadway and Camp Tamiment days to NBC, where he engineered the breathtaking *Admiral Broadway Revue*, which morphed into *Your Show of Shows*, the incomparable showcase for Sid Caesar and Imogene Coca and others from 1949 to 1954. Liebman would go on to produce nearly a dozen streamlined versions of classic Broadway operettas and musicals—*The Desert Song, Lady in the Dark*—for primetime consumption into the 1950s. An early program out of New York, *Musical Comedy Time*, also apparently broadcast "tab" (condensed and abridged) versions of Broadway revivals such as *Hit the Deck* in 1950 (the recordings of these programs are lost). *The Colgate Comedy Hour* might resurrect *Anything Goes* as a primetime vehicle for Frank Sinatra and Ethel Merman; *Hallmark Hall of Fame* might reunite Alfred Drake and Patricia Morison in *Kiss Me, Kate,* a decade after their indelible Broadway performances. But these were largely one-shot efforts; effective, but by no means as extensive as *The Ed Sullivan Show* was in creating a viable and vibrant bridge between television and Broadway.[3]

From its very beginning, television had a tangled relationship with Broadway. As an industry, it came of age in the late 1940s in Manhattan, so it had easy access to Broadway artists and to the theaters in which they performed. Television was not only dependent on Broadway for talent, it drew on the Great White Way for a kind of cultural imprimatur. As a way of bolstering its own derided integrity, TV invoked the glamour of the legitimate stage for many of its programs. A quick survey of variety show titles of the early days reveals *Texaco Star Theater, All-Star Revue, Broadway Jamboree, Broadway Spotlight, Broadway Open House, Showtime, USA,* even *Stage Show,* a variety series produced by Jackie Gleason, in which the show opened with a camera-eye view of a spectator getting out of a limo, entering a theater, walking down the aisle, grabbing a program, and sitting in a fifth-row aisle seat.[4]

But where many producers and productions had only a tenuous relationship to Broadway and its traditions, Sullivan had a long history with the Great White Way. By the late 1920s, he had become a recognized and respected sports writer for the *New York Evening Graphic,* perhaps the tawdriest tabloid of the glory days of metropolitan journalism. Across the proverbial city desk was Walter Winchell, who was the master of the vast Theater District that he surveyed from his "Your Broadway and Mine" column. In 1931, Winchell was hired away from the *Graphic* and hung his fabled fedora at the *Daily Mirror.* The *Graphic* was stuck without a Broadway gossip columnist. Sullivan became the natural substitute for the Broadway beat. He was a night owl; he knew the beat; and he knew everyone there was to know. "I didn't want the job," Sullivan later claimed, "but it was either take it or be fired."[5]

Within weeks of Sullivan's new assignment, the *Graphic* folded. Luckily, the *Daily News* hired Sullivan almost immediately to cover the Broadway beat. He would continue a daily theater column at the *News* called "Little Old New York" for the next four decades, until 1973. Sullivan quickly fell under the thrall of Broadway royalty; the 1932–33 season— though diminished from the pre-Depression bonanza of the late 1920s—still had much for Sullivan to report, not the least of which was the exodus to Hollywood: "Before Larry Hart and Dick Rodgers left for the Pacific Coast to write songs for Maurice Chevalier's latest picture, I had lunch with them and George Gershwin on Broadway." His boosterism for the major celebrities of musical theater could verge on obsequiousness, but it made Ed Sullivan a minister without portfolio for Broadway.[6]

The years wore on, and after the war Sullivan increasingly felt the need to diversify his media portfolio, as it were. The columnist, who was surprisingly ambitious beneath his dour demeanor and accommodating profile, saw in the new medium of television a way to reach a wider audience, a way to elbow past more widely read (and better paid) entertainment reporters and columnists such as Walter Winchell and Louella Parsons. By the end of 1947, there were fewer than 50,000 television sets in all of America—most of them in living rooms in the northeast. A year later, there were ten times more consoles in homes across the country. All the young industry needed to spur sales was a new superstar, which it found in spring 1948, when Milton Berle burst upon the scene, a ratings triumph for NBC. CBS, the other major player in the broadcast industry, wanted to get some new programming on its television network as soon as possible. Among the first mandates would be a variety show.

Knowing of the network's desire to jump on the variety show band wagon, Sullivan made some initial overtures to CBS, through an ad executive colleague named Marlo Lewis. He was able to bring something to the table that few other producers had when it came to wrangling on-air talent for the nascent medium of television: a thickly stocked

Rolodex. So, in spring 1948, to everyone's surprise—except perhaps to Sullivan's—the forty-six-year-old columnist became a television host. To his ongoing vexation, his vehicle would be known as *The Toast of the Town*; he didn't get his name in lights until 1956, when the program was redubbed *The Ed Sullivan Show*.

CBS had owned a converted radio studio on Broadway and West 39th Street; it had once been the Maxine Elliott Theatre, a Broadway house with a lamentable career for box office success (this was the theater padlocked on the scheduled opening night for *The Cradle Will Rock* in 1937). Vacant as a theatrical space since 1940, the Maxine Elliott was hastily transformed by CBS into a television studio (with famously cramped wing space) for *The Toast of the Town*'s debut on Sunday, June 20, 1948. With a talent budget of $375, Sullivan delivered the up-and-coming comedy act of Martin and Lewis; a classical pianist; a ballerina; a singing group composed of New York City firemen—and the songwriting kings of Broadway, Richard Rodgers and Oscar Hammerstein II, discussing their upcoming production of something called *South Pacific*. (Alas, the kinescopes of Sullivan's first five months of broadcasts are lost.)

Thus, from the moment he first appeared in front of the viewing public, Sullivan identified himself with the music of Broadway. In addition to his personal connection with Broadway, Sullivan was unusually lucky in the scheduling of his new program: Sunday nights. Broadway shows were dark on Sundays and, hence, its performers were available. This would also be particularly helpful because Sunday afternoons were Sullivan's all-important dress rehearsals—this was the crucible wherein material was cut, reshaped, and reorganized by Sullivan himself. Sunday matinees on Broadway were not common until the 1970s; if CBS had scheduled *The Toast of the Town* on Saturday or Wednesday nights, it might have proved an infinitely less felicitous venue for Sullivan's interest in procuring Broadway talent.

All variety programs have songs—that's their bread and butter—but Sullivan's brief included not songs, but stars. Not only stars, but shows—each exponentially more difficult "gets." Frequently Broadway songs would be covered by a member of Sullivan's informal repertory company—telegenic and earnest stage and/or recording stars to whom he returned time after time to deliver the Broadway goods: Lisa Kirk, John Raitt, Florence Henderson, Dolores Gray, Helen Gallagher, Carol Haney; then later, Nancy Dussault, Sergio Franchi, Robert Goulet, Steve Lawrence, and Eydie Gormé. Some of their performances were simply incongruous—Sergio Franchi singing "If I Were a Rich Man" in Italian—but others could be thrilling, insightful, or tantalizing. For example, in a 1962 tribute to Richard Rodgers, broadcast from Carnegie Hall, Peggy Lee and Steve Lawrence duetted in his first hit, "Manhattan"—a song rarely performed by two people (as originally written) and rarely as charmingly as Lee and Lawrence's performance.

Not that Sullivan relied simply on nightclub entertainers and pop singers; he was able to deliver Broadway Hall of Famers. His tastes stretched all the way back to vaudeville and operetta, and, late into the 1950s, he showcased performers such as George White, Harry Richman, and Sophie Tucker, venerated performers who hadn't starred in a successful Broadway show since Roosevelt introduced the New Deal. Sullivan could corral Victor Moore and William Gaxton to deliver comedy material from *Of Thee I Sing*—a musical they opened in back in 1931—and he would consistently feature Bert Lahr and Beatrice Lillie in sketches or songs they had made famous decades earlier and even devoted (separate) full-hour tributes to the breadth of their careers.

It wasn't all nostalgia, however; Sullivan would consistently get Broadway stars to reprise their greatest hits, usually in one-off numbers, often staged outside their original context. Yul Brynner might render "A Puzzlement" in a suit and tie, just as John Raitt might belt out "Soliloquy" in a striped polo shirt. In 1967, nearly a decade after her career triumph as Mama Rose, Ethel Merman appeared on *Sullivan* to sing her opening number from *Gypsy,* "Some People"—but oddly dressed in a beaded gown, loaded down with heaps of mascara. It would be her only known television rendition of the song.

All of these were either thrilling (to savvy theatergoers) or curiosities (to general audiences) or, perhaps both, but there was one element of magical alchemy that Sullivan brought to bear on his program that no other producer could match. On Sunday night, July 6, 1952, nearly four years to the day that *Toast of the Town* premiered, Sullivan stepped in front of the sequined curtain and made a solemn, if syntactically challenged, announcement:

> Leland Heyward and Josh Logan have done magnificent things for the New York stage and for the national theater; their latest adventure in entertaining the national appetite is *Wish You Were Here*, now at the Imperial Theatre. I'm very proud for the first time that excerpts of a Broadway musical have ever been put on stage, before television cameras, are on our show.

Heyward and Logan had known Sullivan as a Broadway columnist for years. Heyward had produced *Mister Roberts,* a Logan smash, and co-produced *South Pacific*—co-written and directed by Logan, which was still running in summer 1952. To say that *Wish You Were Here* was slight by comparison is not quite accurate: it was emaciated. Because of a scenic innovation concocted by designer Jo Mielziner—an actual swimming pool downstage center—*Wish You Were Here* eschewed a traditional out-of-town tryout. Director Logan apparently tinkered with the show relentlessly during its three-and-a-half weeks of previews on Broadway. "It's a doubtful box office bet," opined *Variety* before the opening.[7]

The dire predictions largely came true. Opening on June 25, 1952, the show received reviews that were, in the words of *Times* critic Brooks Atkinson, "filled with regrets:" one positive notice, one mixed, six pans. Atkinson himself was wearied by the proceedings, proclaiming that "[The show] lacks variety and subtlety. For all its friskiness, it is joyless; and it gives the impression of saying the same thing over and over again."[8]

One would never have known that from Sullivan's relative enthusiasm (that is to say, Sullivan at his most enthusiastic read like an audit by the IRS) in his introduction:

> The show is a musical version of Arthur Kober's story, "Having Wonderful Time," set at Camp Karefree. There for a few weeks, the girls are looking for the young boys to get married and the boys are looking for the girls to get married to. On stage at the Imperial Theatre is an actual swimming pool—we haven't got room for it—it's an amazing thing.

For the next fifteen minutes, *The Toast of the Town* devotes its airtime to three numbers performed by the original cast—which includes Jack Cassidy and Patricia Marand: "Wish You Were Here," "Where Did the Night Go?," and "Shopping Around." Sullivan then asks Logan to take an obligatory bow from the audience. Perhaps the most revealing moment about the broadcast was Sullivan's closing speech for the segment (again, syntax carefully preserved):

> I really must go and see *Wish You Were Here*. It's just as young and attractive and interesting as these samples that have been exhibited here. The wonderful thing about the show is the music by Harold Rome. Tony Martin has made a record of one of the songs, Eddie Fisher has made a record of another. These are two of the hit songs—so, drop into the Imperial Theatre and see *Wish You Were Here*.

What Sullivan accomplishes here is a subtle kind of synergy, decades before the term was coined. By mentioning the two hit songs (indeed, Eddie Fisher's recording of the title number was released the week of the Sullivan show and stayed on the charts for twenty-one weeks, even hitting the No. 1 spot in late August), it yokes the show's fortunes to its success in the music industry, as if to say, "See, record buyers like the show—you should, too." For millions of Americans contemplating a vacation to New York City some day, or for a suburban matron wondering what to request for a Mother's Day present, how could you find a better advisor for your consumer pocketbook than "nationally celebrated New York columnist, Ed Sullivan" (as he was described every week by the announcer)?

His personal seal of approval certainly seemed to do the trick with *Wish You Were Here*—even without the swimming pool. According to *Variety,* the show needed to make $30,000 a week to break even; for four weeks after the pans following its opening, the box office for *Wish You Were Here* hovered in the mid-$20,000 range; then, after the Sullivan appearance, it began picking up revenue, week by week. By the time Atkinson re-reviewed the show at the end of August (Logan had made some additional changes), he reported that the weekly box office grossed had "advanced from a low of $25,000 to a high of $47,000—give and take a few hundred dollars either way."[9] Never a show beloved among connoisseurs, *Wish You Were Here* would nonetheless go on to run 598 performances, a terrific amount for its time.

Sullivan had proven to Broadway skeptics that he—and his show—had the power, if not to make or break a show, certainly to give it a fair hearing among the television viewing audience. Considering that *The Ed Sullivan Show* routinely won its time slot for most of the 1950s and 1960s, this usually meant that, on Sunday nights, between 40 to 50 million Americans were given a "preview" of a Broadway show. Typically, Sullivan—still an inveterate first-nighter, because of his "Little Old New York" column—would pick and choose the numbers from the Broadway show himself. Sometimes, he didn't get to the show until well into its run (*Fiddler on the Roof* didn't appear on Sullivan with its then-current lead, Harry Goz, until five years after it opened); sometimes he was helpless to boost the fortunes of a terrible show (despite six minutes of airtime during its February 1970 previews, *Gantry*, with stars Rita Moreno and Robert Shaw, still closed on opening night). The numbers would always be performed live that night, in front of some simulacrum of the show's set, invariably capped off with some sort of ceremonial handshake or hug between Sullivan and the show's stars.[10]

If one simply uses the definition "Direct from Broadway"—the shows that Sullivan presented with the cast that was currently performing—the list of representative Broadway musicals where Sullivan showcased at least one number (and frequently two or three the same night) is astonishing by any reckoning. Here goes:

A Tree Grows in Brooklyn, Make a Wish, Wish You Were Here, Top Banana, Kismet, The Pajama Game, Fanny, Plain and Fancy, Ankles Aweigh, Carnival in Flanders, Happy Hunting, Pipe Dream, My Fair Lady (with cast replacements)*, West Side Story, The Body Beautiful, Say, Darling!, Goldilocks, Flower Drum Song, Destry Rides Again, The Sound of Music* (with Nancy Dussault or Martha Wright filling in for Mary Martin)*, Bye Bye Birdie, Do Re Mi, The Girls Against the Boys, Carnival!, The Unsinkable Molly Brown, Donnybrook, Wildcat, Camelot, The Gay Life, Let It Ride!, No Strings, Stop the World (I Want to Get Off)!, Oliver!, Little Me, Mr. President, Best Foot Forward, Tovarich, The*

Girl Who Came to Supper, Golden Boy, I Had A Ball, Do I Hear a Waltz?, Flora the Red
Menace, Roar of the Greasepaint, Half a Sixpence, Pickwick, Funny Girl (with Streisand's
replacement, Mimi Hines), *The Mad Show, Man of La Mancha, Annie Get Your Gun*
(1966 revival with Merman), *Sweet Charity, Walking Happy, Illya Darling, Hallelujah*
Baby!, Henry, Sweet Henry, I Do! I Do! (replacements Carol Lawrence and Gordon
MacRae), *Hello, Dolly!* (with Pearl Bailey), *George M!, How Now, Dow Jones, You're a*
Good Man, Charlie Brown, Mame, Fiddler on the Roof, Cabaret, Zorbá, Golden Rainbow,
Hair, Jimmy, Gantry, Promises, Promises, Look to the Lilies, Purlie, and *1776.*

The list concludes with *The Rothschilds* in December of 1970, three months before the
cancellation of *The Ed Sullivan Show.*[11]

As a contrast to this bounty, it's instructive to look at which shows Sullivan did *not*
invite onto his program. Of course, he was always bound by which producers wanted to
broadcast their shows at any given moment, but Sullivan also had his tastes—conservative and life-affirming—and was always protective of his carefully cultivated mainstream
Sunday night audiences. Mildly lubricious shows such as *New Girl in Town, A Funny*
Thing Happened on the Way to the Forum, Tenderloin, or *Irma La Douce* were excluded
because of their subject matter. Minor lyric changes in saucy songs—such as "Always
True to You (in My Fashion)" when it was performed as part of a Cole Porter tribute—
were typical in the 1950s, but Sullivan took his bowdlerization late into his career:
during a 1969 airing of two numbers from *Cabaret,* the Emcee refers to the Kit Kat Klub
girls not as "each and every one a virgin," but as "each and every one *innocent*"—which
totally kills the joke.

Performers could be dicey, too. Zero Mostel never appeared on the show, beyond an
early 1949 rendition of his nightclub routines; his left-wing affiliations might have run
afoul of Sullivan's politics—or perhaps, the highly principled Mostel didn't approve of
Sullivan.[12] Despite Sullivan's repeated plugs for *My Fair Lady,* the famously tetchy Rex
Harrison never performed a single moment from the musical on Sullivan's show; Harrison
was averse to giving "freebies." Beyond a brief bow from the audience in 1958, Mary
Martin never appeared on the Sullivan show; it might have been her affiliation with rival
network NBC (which broadcast *Peter Pan* repeatedly) or the whims of her husband/
manager, Richard Halliday. But these were the exceptions. The rule—at least, by the mid-
1950s—was that, by and large, if Broadway could deliver for Sullivan, Sullivan would
deliver for Broadway, as Alan Jay Lerner would discover to his enormous advantage in
the late winter of 1961.

Lerner and Loewe's *Camelot* had opened the first week of December 1960, to less-
than-stellar reviews. By February, according to Lerner in his autobiography, *The Street*

Where I Live, "There was hardly any window sale at all and people were walking out of the theater not by the dozens, but some nights by as much as two to three hundred."[13] Though hardly at death's door, *Camelot*, which had earned the largest advance sale in Broadway history before it opened, was losing money at the box office with each succeeding week throughout the early winter; it certainly wasn't selling out. To make comparisons worse for Lerner, *My Fair Lady* had just celebrated its fifth anniversary on Broadway and *Variety* had proclaimed it the most successful stage property of all time, earning an astonishing $48 million.

Ironically, it was *My Fair Lady*'s anniversary that opened the door to *Camelot*'s eventual success—what Lerner would refer to as "the miracle." Sullivan used the anniversary occasion to honor Lerner and Loewe on his March 19 broadcast; he proposed devoting the entire evening to the songwriters and their work. Lerner had a counter-proposal: "What I had in mind was to do very little from *My Fair Lady* and then spend the last twenty minutes doing all the best songs and scenes from *Camelot*, much more than had ever been presented before from any play running on Broadway...Ed, one of the most gracious gentlemen in television, gave us carte blanche."[14] In the week before the broadcast, *Camelot*'s director, Moss Hart, who had been sidelined in the weeks leading up to the opening night by a heart attack, went back into rehearsal at the Majestic Theatre and cut ten minutes and two songs from the show; *Camelot* would finally be in fighting trim for its showcase on *The Ed Sullivan Show*.

In his autobiography, Lerner conveniently claims that Sullivan bunched all of the *Camelot* material on the program into the last twenty minutes as a kind of socko finish. In fact, the *Camelot* songs are spread throughout, but even more marvelously, its stars—Richard Burton, Julie Andrews, and Robert Goulet—function as a mini-repertory company, singing Lerner and Loewe hits throughout the evening. Goulet and Andrews duet beautifully on "Almost Like Being in Love" from *Brigadoon*; Andrews gloriously reprises both "Wouldn't It Be Loverly?" and "I Could Have Danced All Night" from *My Fair Lady*. Goulet knocks three solos out of the ballpark: "They Call the Wind Maria," "Gigi," and "If Ever I Would Leave You." The two scenes from *Camelot* that feature Burton are spaced throughout the show; first, he sings the title number with Andrews, then launches thrillingly into a soliloquy about Arthur's ascension to his legendary kingdom. Later in the program, he and Andrews—in costume, in front of a condensed version of Oliver Smith's backdrop—perform "What Do the Simple Folk Do?"; Burton's vain attempt to vanquish unhappiness with a simple folk dance stops the show cold.

As if to confirm *Camelot*'s inherent worth, Sullivan tells Lerner and Loewe—sitting attentively in dapper tuxedos bestride a baby grand piano—that "Mrs. Sullivan and I were there for opening night. They brought all of us right out of our seats" and then cajoles them into performing a song from the show; Lerner obliges with "How to Handle a Woman," accompanied expressively by Loewe on the piano.

▶ Audio Example 9.1, "How to Handle a Woman" (Alan Jay Lerner / Frederick Loewe)

The Lerner and Loewe tribute was a high-water mark for the Sullivan show; expertly orchestrated with virtuoso performances, the program is enlightening, entertaining, and uplifting. "What do you do to follow a show like this?" asks Sullivan at the conclusion, not unreasonably. Lerner provides the punchline in his book: "The following morning, I was awakened by a phone call from an excited manager at the Majestic Theatre. . . . 'Just come and see what's going on at this box office.' . . . For the first time, there was a line halfway down the block. *Camelot* was finally a hit."[15] By the week of March 29, *Variety* reported that *Camelot* was selling out; it remained one of Broadway's few consistently sold-out shows—with the street's largest weekly gross of nearly $84,000—through to the end of 1961.

While it's fair to say that although Sullivan had no appreciable musical talent himself (or perhaps because of that fact), he was absolutely star-struck by songwriters, more so than by stage stars or even movie stars. He first brought Lerner and Loewe onto his program on March 3, 1957, to celebrate the one-year anniversary of *My Fair Lady* and its incredible success: "You've heard the music of *My Fair Lady* on Columbia Records, in hotels, in night clubs, on disk jockey programs, and on your car radios." The program's debt to CBS, the sole backer of *My Fair Lady,* was so extensive that Sullivan pointed out Goddard Lieberson himself from the audience, who bounded on stage with a presentation of his own for Lerner and Loewe: two framed discs of the *My Fair Lady* cast album. "Alan and Fritz," Lieberson told them, "I don't have to tell you what joy it is to present you with these plaques, celebrating the one millionth-selling record of [the cast album] to *My Fair Lady*. Because it's a long-playing record, it's actually seven million songs [per side]. And the fact that it sold a million records in only eleven months is a tremendous achievement and a recognition by the American people of your talent."

Beyond celebrating the commercial successes of songwriters, Sullivan loved poking and prodding them about their creative process: "I've Lerner and Loewe here at the piano; and here are some questions you'd like to address to them if they were in your living room: 'How did you decide to enlarge *Pygmalion* without doing damage to the play?' " It's quite possible that Sullivan actually believed that the millions of Americans watching the program from their own living rooms were bursting to ask Lerner and Loewe about their dramaturgical choices in adapting Shaw to the musical stage. Still, this was a question posed not on some esoteric Sunday morning omnibus presided over by Alistair Cooke, but for primetime television, on a program that was at the top of its time slot for decades.

From the very beginning of his tenure, Sullivan gave pride-of-place to songwriters. Walter Donaldson, Gus Kahn, Sigmund Romberg, Rudolf Friml—tunesmiths who hadn't had a hit since the Coolidge administration—were brought on stage to perform their works. Irving Berlin, who predated them all, was a frequent guest; as late as 1968 he performed "God Bless America," backed up by a massive choir of Boy Scouts and Girl Scouts. Jimmy Van Heusen, Sammy Cahn, Lerner and Loewe, Comden and Green, Jule Styne, Harold Arlen, and Anthony Newley all presented their songs, with some sort of background perspective about the creative process.

Sullivan devoted entire one-hour programs to certain songwriters, including, if one can imagine it, an evening celebrating the formation of ASCAP. The occasional two-part "life story" was given to titans of the field. Cole Porter received his special tribute in February 1952, which featured his greatest hits performed by the likes of William Gaxton, who had starred in the original 1934 *Anything Goes*, and Dolores Gray; Porter still had two Broadway hits and two film scores ahead of him. Sullivan would routinely be mocked by critics, impersonators, and the public for his often-garbled introductions and malapropisms (he once introduced Gray as "currently *starving* in the Broadway musical, *Sherry!*"), but he just as frequently framed the entertainment with important information and context. Sullivan's introduction to the first Porter evening invokes the gravity and scope of the program to follow and it bears repeating in its extensive fulsomeness:

> Cole Porter's Indiana has long claimed the ear of the nation. But Cole Porter from "PEE-rou, Indiana" has an added distinction; nothing ever quelled the song in his heart, no degree of discouragement ever silenced the music and the lyrics that ranged from the champagne frothiness of "My Heart Belongs to Daddy" to the intensity of such numbers as "Night and Day" and "Begin the Beguine." Even after his first big stage hit, you must remember that, for nine years, Cole Porter never had another show on Broadway, but he did have a song in his heart. For the past fifteen years, he has endured thirty-three operations, but they've never interrupted the stream of melody that poured out of him. To paraphrase one of his own hits, he's the top. He has another distinction, he is the only top Broadway composer that can boast that reviews of his first Broadway show were so alarming, that he went off and joined the French Foreign legion—that's true. That first show Cole Porter produced was oddly enough on this very stage, on this very theater, the Maxine Elliott, 37 years ago. I've assembled an all-star cast for a tribute to this musical genius.

His references to the injuries suffered from Porter's 1937 riding accident were both frank and relentless; Sullivan would mention it eight more times—as a symbol of Porter's courage—throughout the hour-long broadcast.[16]

Sullivan's longest and most satisfying relationship was with Richard Rodgers and Oscar Hammerstein, ever since their appearance on his first broadcast. Subsequently, Hammerstein appeared on Sullivan's program eight times, including a two-part tribute; the first to his work before Rodgers, the second to their collaboration. In addition, Sullivan scheduled an hour-long retrospective on Hammerstein two weeks after his death in late summer 1960. Including his joint appearances with Hammerstein, Rodgers was a guest on the program seventeen times, including four separate hour-long tributes devoted to his tunes—this was, of course, not counting the dozens of times one of his compositions was performed by some other entertainer on the show. Rodgers was easily Sullivan's most frequent non-performing guest during the show's twenty-three-year-long tenure.

For television audiences, Hammerstein and Rodgers made an odd couple; Hammerstein, pockmarked and towering over his partner, affected a bemused tolerance for the medium and for Sullivan, especially when the host continually referred to him as Oscar "Hammer-*steen*." Rodgers, jowly and cursed with ill-fitting suits, never seemed particularly comfortable on television (the result, perhaps, of several operations for cancer of the jaw), but always seemed enthusiastic about grabbing the baton to conduct the on-stage orchestra when it was proffered by Sullivan (although his conducting wasn't particularly elegant).

Still, the era's dominant songwriting team provided plenty of enlightened enjoyment for audiences. For a Christmas program in 1951, Hammerstein talked about his deep sorrow at learning about the fall of Paris to the Nazis, and, accompanied by full orchestra, recited his lyrics to Jerome Kern's melody of "The Last Time I Saw Paris"—one of the precious few recorded moments of Hammerstein "performing" his own work. It was one of Sullivan's favorite segments in the history of the show: "When Oscar was reading those lyrics aloud, and knowing the story behind them, you could have heard a mouse stumble in the theater," he told a reporter in 1969.[17]

This blend of cultural context and nostalgic sentimentality inspired something in Sullivan, and he frequently yoked the work of Rodgers and Hammerstein to his sense of patriotism and cultural values. He brought material from *Oklahoma!* out of the woodwork repeatedly. In 1955, he concocted a twelfth anniversary tribute to the show and brought the then-senator of Oklahoma, Robert S. Kerr, to New York to introduce the broadcast. Their exchange is fascinating:

SULLIVAN: Senator, what elements of *Oklahoma!* appeal to a universal audience?
SENATOR KERR: It portrays the basic urges and deepest emotions of ordinary people.
                 It captures the spirit of the pioneers; in beautiful songs, it tells of
                 their loves and even their hates. It speaks in a universal language.

SULLIVAN: The theme is not just American. It has played everywhere except behind the Iron Curtain. I think it would crack the Iron Curtain wide open, it would show them a picture of us they haven't got—as pioneers, as farmers, as loving husbands. It would be a tremendous thing.

SENATOR KERR: It might have succeeded even in—um, that state across the Red River—what's it called? *Texas!*

Given his relentless boosterism for the American musical, it was inevitable that Sullivan would eventually become a sort of brand name for the genre. In 1959, a record company based in Canada, the National Academy Record Club, set up a system where LP recordings were produced in London and then distributed for sale in various supermarkets up and down the Eastern seaboard. They were marketed as "Ed Sullivan Presents America's Great Musicals Series," with a color photo of Sullivan, leaning forward to "introduce" each title; the "great musicals" were essentially cover albums of popular scores—*My Fair Lady, Pal Joey, Annie Get Your Gun, Roberta, Kiss Me, Kate.* Sullivan—or a publicity flack—wrote an overview about each show on the back of the album. Part of the contractual agreement was that the singers on the albums—generically billed as "the Ed Sullivan All Star Cast"—could not be individually identified. Perhaps it was just as well—the singer of "Ol' Man River" on the *Show Boat* album is either a black man trying to sound white, or a white man trying to sound black. After the release of a dozen titles, the experiment folded in 1960.

That same year, Sullivan's symbiotic relationship with Broadway achieved its apotheosis: he became a character in a new Broadway musical. *Bye Bye Birdie* captured the cultural influence of the rock and roll phenomenon as a narrative for the Broadway stage. Given that Sullivan himself had been so seminal in bringing rock and roll to television audiences, with his three presentations of Elvis Presley on various broadcasts in 1956 (the second also featured fifteen astonishing minutes of *The Most Happy Fella*, "live from the Imperial Theatre!"), it seemed only natural to include him in Michael Stewart's original scenario of a rock and roll sex symbol's induction into the army (something that also, of course, happened to the real Elvis). In the course of the musical, the eponymous singer gets the press opportunity to kiss one lucky All-American girl farewell on *The Ed Sullivan Show*; it made perfect sense—where else would one stage such a miraculous moment?

At one point in the first act, the singer, Conrad Birdie, is bivouacked in the small Ohio home of the lucky girl, Kim MacAfee, and antagonizes her long-suffering father, Harry (played in a career-making performance by Paul Lynde). Birdie mitigates the situation by dropping the tidbit that the MacAfees—as part of their participation—will also get to appear (by remote camera) on *The Ed Sullivan Show*. MacAfee's jaw drops to the floor and he is transported: "Me? On *The Ed Sullivan Show*?? I've got a wonderful wife, two swell kids, a great job, and now *this!*" MacAfee, his family, and his neighbors join in unison to perform an extensive chorale: "Hymn for a Sunday Evening," which concludes:

I'll (We'll) be coast-to-coast
With my (our) favorite host
Ed Sull-i-van!!!

▶   Audio Example 9.2, "Hymn for a Sunday Evening" (*Bye Bye Birdie* original cast)

Of course, it was only a matter of time—two months after the Broadway opening—that "Hymn for a Sunday Evening" made it to Sullivan's own personal Sunday evening. At the conclusion of the number, Sullivan himself marches on stage and shakes Lynde's hand. Unfortunately, Lynde is either so dazed (or exhausted) that he never embraces the meta-quality of the moment. Nevertheless, the inclusion of Sullivan and his Sunday evening program into the plot of *Bye Bye Birdie* would ensure a kind of musical theater immortality for this most star-struck of Broadway enthusiasts.

By the end of the decade, it seemed as if the immortality of Broadway itself was in jeopardy. Tastes were changing rapidly and Sullivan was forced to present more and more rock acts—The Doors, Janis Joplin—that had little to do with his own personal sensibilities and more to do with the need to curry favor with younger audiences in order to boost sagging ratings. The rock scene was making its way into Sullivan's beloved Broadway musicals as well; on March 30, 1969, nearly a year after the show's premiere, Sullivan presented two numbers from *Hair*. Introducing the two numbers—"Aquarius" and "The Flesh Failures (Let the Sunshine In)"—Sullivan looks fatigued. He remarks that the audience is about to see songs from "Broadway's most discussed"—one expects him to say "disgusting"—"show from the Biltmore Theatre." The cast performs energetically and admirably; eventually bounding into the audience, jumping on top of seats, letting almost all of it hang out. At the conclusion, the cast festoons Sullivan with a garland of flowers and hands him some wilted daisies. He looks dazed and confused.

What's most interesting is not simply the numbers from *Hair,* but the surrounding acts that Sullivan intentionally programmed for the evening. As if to inoculate his more conservative audience from the hippie goings-on, he presented Steve Lawrence and Eydie Gormé singing Broadway standards and the Lennon Sisters, a middle-America quartet par excellence, performing "Strike Up the Band" as part of a patriotic Fourth of July parade. It's as if Sullivan is trying to cloak himself in a King Canute-kind of authority, vainly attempting to keep back the tides of change.

It would be fitting, in a way, if *Hair* were the actual end of Sullivan's Broadway presentations, but he had two more years to go before his program would be cancelled by CBS. The real eulogy for Sullivan's Broadway love affair would come during his Thanksgiving weekend show in 1970. He pulled out all the stops for his fourth—and final—full-hour tribute to Richard Rodgers, this time performed live from the cavernous Hollywood Bowl. The tribute was strangely cast, but oddly effective: Cass Elliott (from the Mamas and the Papas) gamely doing the Charleston to the tune of Rodgers and Hart's 1926 hit, "The Girl Friend;" Minnie Pearl effectively barking out "The Farmer and the Cowman" from *Oklahoma!*; Johnny Mathis, celebrating the inside joke by tackling "Johnny One-Note."

But, in the final moments, the broadcast shifts back to New York, to the stage of the Ed Sullivan Theatre, where, in a pre-recorded segment, Danny Kaye performs a number from Rodgers' latest musical, *Two By Two*, a whimsical look at Noah and the Ark. Sullivan joins him on stage, and he looks tired and old, with dyed hair and too-hip-to-be-true sideburns. Then, he brings out Rodgers himself, obviously frail and uncertain. Kaye, playing a

What do the simple folk watch on Sunday nights? On March 19, 1961, it was Richard Burton and Julie Andrews on *The Ed Sullivan Show*. By permission of SOFA Entertainment.

600-year-old man, looks downright sprightly compared with Sullivan and Rodgers, two venerated figures who were famous before Kaye had even made his stage debut in 1933. The trio is standing in front of a painted backdrop filled with marquees of all of Rodgers' hits, including *The Girl Friend, Jumbo,* and *No Strings*—shows utterly unrevivable and irrelevant in 1970. The whole segment seems to be straining to say, "Attention must be paid—this is history."

The Ed Sullivan Show would itself be history by the following March. Sullivan made his television debut a month before *Allegro* closed and concluded his tenure four months before *Jesus Christ Superstar* opened. The Golden Age of Broadway flourished between those two openings; its influence on American culture had much to do with Sullivan's curatorial enthusiasm. For the liner notes of a 1990 Columbia CD release of Broadway songs performed on *The Ed Sullivan Show,* former *New York Times* drama critic Clive Barnes wrote: "Sullivan made Broadway, particularly its musicals, a world of infinite dash, glamour, and sophistication, a cavern of wonders that had the very word Broadway resonating down every little Main Street in Middle America."[18]

All of which is true, but by the time Ed Sullivan brought his friend Richard Rodgers to the stage for one last farewell tribute in 1970, Broadway and Main Street were no longer singing from the same hymnal

The glorious K-series gatefold of the original cast album of *Camelot* celebrated the Broadway experience for home listeners. By permission of Sony Music.

CHAPTER 10

A Few of My Favorite Things

Movie Stars and the Soundtrack of Broadway

Billboard magazine doesn't provide discrete credit for the performers who front original cast albums or soundtracks—those are ranked under general categories, unlike pop or rock singers who get credit and gold records for their sales. That's a shame, because one superstar was among the very top-selling singers of the 1960s, and surely her name and her face adorned more LPs in more living rooms across America than anyone else's in that decade: Broadway's own fair lady, Julie Andrews.

As the decade began, the cast album to *My Fair Lady* was still a strong seller, in both mono and stereo. *Billboard*'s chart for album sales only went as deep as No. 50 until 1959, and *My Fair Lady* was continuing on the charts; in 1966, when the album charts had deepened to 150, the cast recording of the show was still charting. The television soundtrack to *Cinderella*, starring Andrews (but, of course, without *Billboard* acknowledgement) had charted into the new decade, but Columbia Records would seal its trifecta with Julie Andrews in its largest financial investment to date as the 1960s began: $425,000 to secure the rights to Lerner and Loewe's 1960 follow-up to *My Fair Lady*, *Camelot*. In addition to holding out for the largest investment amount ever from a record company, Lerner and Loewe (who produced the show with director Moss Hart) had their publisher and attorneys extract the highest mechanical rate ever paid for a commercial album. So, in addition to getting a full investment for their production of *Camelot*, Lerner and Loewe received the highest royalties per disk sold ever earned by a songwriting team.

Columbia managed to offset its investment by deploying as many possible artists in its stable to cover tunes from *Camelot*—eight separate albums of pop, jazz, and easy listening renditions, as well as six singles, recorded by the likes of Johnny Mathis and Jerry Vale—but the label's most meaningful expense was on the cast album itself. The visual splendor of the stage production was made for the "K" series gatefold treatment, this time with full-color photos on the inside and a gilded spine. As part of the chaotic last-minute opening of *Camelot*, the album hedged its bets by listing the song order on a little blue insert within the gatefold, rather than having the song list printed on the album itself (indeed, some of the songs would eventually be cut or shifted around after the show opened). The final product itself befitted the majesty of the story, and *Camelot* debuted in late January of 1961 at No. 4, which was remarkable for a commodity localized in New York. The album started climbing up the charts the same week as John F. Kennedy's inauguration, hit No. 1 by mid-March and stayed there for six weeks, ultimately keeping up on the charts for a total of 265 weeks.

That meant the LP was spinning on a lot of turntables in a lot of people's living rooms—apparently even at 1600 Pennsylvania Avenue. After the tragic events of November 22, 1963, journalist Theodore H. White was given an exclusive interview with Jacqueline Kennedy that would appear in a special issue of *Life* magazine that would be one of the most widely circulated and read publications of the decade when it reached Americans two weeks later. Toward the end of the essay, the First Lady made an association between her late husband's inspirations and the most elegant album in Columbia's catalog, better known to retailers as KOS 2031:

> When Jack quoted something, it was usually classical, but I'm so ashamed of myself— all I keep thinking of is this line from a musical comedy. At night, before going to bed, we had an old Victrola. He'd play a couple of records. I'd get out of bed at night and play it for him when it was so cold getting out of bed. It was a song he loved, he loved *Camelot*. It was the song he loved most at the end—The lines he loved to hear were: "Don't let it be forgot, that once there was a spot, for one brief shining moment, that was known as Camelot."[1]

When the *Life* magazine article appeared, Julie Andrews had long decamped from *Camelot*. Her run in the show had been an extended one, nearly a year and a half, but it was not without its other opportunities. In 1962, Andrews was performing a live television concert, *Julie and Carol at Carnegie Hall* (also recorded by Columbia and a big seller). Backstage, she asked her colleague, Carol Burnett, who had acquired more experience than she had outside of the theater, what to make of an offer from Walt Disney, who had come to see her as Guinevere—should she take him up on his offer to make her first film, as the practically perfect nanny, Mary Poppins? *Should* she?! Suffice it to say that the summer of 1963 found Andrews in Burbank, California, where she would be laying down tracks for her first starring role in a feature film at the Walt Disney Studios: *Mary Poppins*.[2] The movie would exponentially expand her reach to the American public, not just through the eventual release of the film, but of its movie soundtrack; that soundtrack, perhaps more than the film, helped to make a superstar out of Julie Andrews.

Once upon a time, when there were establishments called record stores, one could browse by category; you knew you were in a second-class establishment—perhaps even a department store—if the "Original Cast Albums" were filed under "Movie Soundtracks." Cast albums and soundtracks are emphatically not the same thing. The technology and the technique are different, but movie soundtracks based on Broadway musicals have spread the gospel of Broadway music near and far. A movie soundtrack allowed a Broadway score to make the rounds of homes along Main Street one more time, often in a more accessible and attractive package, allowing for a pleasant reacquaintance, perhaps a reappraisal, occasionally with far-reaching aesthetic and financial implications.

The differences between the two products begin with their creative inception: a cast album captures a live performance subsequent to its presentation, but the soundtrack of a musical is recorded often before principal photography on a film even begins. In the former case, the product follows the process; in the latter, the process follows the product. Also, a soundtrack recording is part of a larger financial package—the studio has already acquired, budgeted, prepared, recorded, sequenced, mastered, and paid for the music as part of the process of making the picture. On the face of it, it would seem as if a soundtrack release would be the easiest, and least expensive, recording product in the world.

In the beginning, however, preparing soundtracks for commercial consumption was extremely difficult. Before the arrival of magnetic tape, it was impossibly arduous to edit the musical numbers recorded directly on film for a 78 recording. RCA Victor released some limited "exclusive sound recordings from the actual film" of *Snow White and Seven Dwarfs* in 1938. Decca Records understood the commercial appeal of the songs from a musical film, but "the company's" solution—with *The Wizard of Oz* in 1939 and with Judy Garland and Mickey Rooney's *Girl Crazy* in 1943—was to take the stars into the recording studio and make analog versions of what they did/would do in the picture. For example, Garland's version of "Over the Rainbow" on the Decca recording is different from the version in the film, and she recorded "The Jitterbug," a song slated for the picture but cut from its release. Of course, recording stars such as Garland, Bing Crosby, Fred Astaire, and their peers would make commercial singles in the recording studio based on what they had been singing on camera.

MGM set up its own recording division in 1946 to promote its musical films; the label initiated decades of successful releases with eight selections from the company's Jerome Kern biopic, *Till the Clouds Roll By*, employing a laborious process of manually recording acetates off of other acetates. It wasn't until the 1950s that soundtracks became viable, because of the ability to transfer from tape and the increasing length of the LP. Hollywood musicals such as *An American in Paris* and *The Band Wagon* had reduced versions of their scores on 10" LPs released to the public on MGM.

The first real blockbuster soundtrack was, not surprisingly, *Oklahoma!*. When Fox released the film in Todd-AO in October 1955, its soundtrack LP, released by Capitol, had already been in stores for two months. The album shot through the roof, sitting at No. 1 for four weeks and staying on the charts for a total of 263 weeks. Its appeal to consumers was obvious: the entire score was conveniently on one LP, it had an attractive cover, it had one more song than the available Decca LP of the original show ("The Farmer and the Cowman"), and it sounded crisp, full, and robust. On top of which, the "souvenir" aspect of a movie soundtrack was considerably broader, as far more people would attend the film across the nation and around the world (*Oklahoma!* grossed more than $7 million in its initial outing).

Since the dawn of sound, film studios quickly realized that they could derive increased royalties that contributed to their own bottom line if they commissioned new songs for their adaptations of Broadway properties; dozens of Hollywood versions bore only a passing resemblance to their stage counterparts. But the narrative arcs and commercial triumphs (both as stage entities and as the wellspring for hit tunes) of the post-*Oklahoma!* era made it increasingly difficult (and ill-advised) for studios to employ such wholesale revisions to beloved classics. Although shorn of several of their original songs, the soundtracks of *Oklahoma!*, *Carousel*, and especially *The King and I* (which hit No. 1 for one week) were hugely popular and influential—and all of them were released on Capitol Records, which must have disappointed the folks at Decca, who bankrolled the original cast albums of all three of those shows.

Given the potential financial rewards, it was no surprise that Goddard Lieberson's concern extended beyond Columbia's acquisition of Broadway cast albums to the rights to the soundtrack releases from the scores already in the lable's catalog. In October 1956, well aware of the three consecutive Rodgers and Hammerstein soundtracks that were on the Capitol label, he wrote to Max Dreyfus: "I see that *South Pacific* is in the offing as a film. We would like to put in our bid for this, particularly to keep the tradition of *South Pacific* going at Columbia. Isn't it our turn to have a Rodgers and Hammerstein movie? I hope so. We're beginning to feel like Oliver Twist over here." After nine months of radio silence, he wrote to Dreyfus again: "I don't have to tell you that we are still interested in Columbia's having the film soundtrack for *South Pacific*. We seem to be able to get no information on this, and I hope this is not going to be another Rodgers and Hammerstein for Capitol." In the end, the soundtrack didn't go to Capitol; it went to RCA Victor. That must have hurt.[3] To his credit, Lieberson usually took these slights with grace; however, the *South Pacific* slight was not a slight slight; the soundtrack was the most popular album of 1958, and, buoyed by a stereo release in 1959, the soundtrack spent an astonishing thirty-one weeks at No. 1—the most for any album since the original cast album of *South Pacific*.

Lieberson would get his revenge when the original soundtrack to *West Side Story* was released by Columbia Masterworks in 1961. The cast album had done well enough for Columbia; it eventually went gold, but took several years to do so. In Hollywood, the Mirisch Company and United Artists saw huge potential for the bracing and tragic love story—especially when shot on location in New York City—and co-produced the film version. It was a success beyond anyone's wildest dreams, winning ten out of its eleven nominated Oscars. The soundtrack in particular was a handsome Columbia affair—with a gatefold and color photos, naturally—and it touched something in American consumers in fall 1961 that hadn't caught them back in 1957. In fact, it touched the record-buying public in unprecedented proportions. The soundtrack of *West Side Story* charted almost immediately after the film's release in October and wound up perched at No. 1 for fifty-four weeks—more than any album that has followed since, including cultural touchstones such as Michael Jackson's *Thriller*.

There are several possible reasons for the soundtrack's extraordinary success: the quality of the film; the quality of the album with its arresting Saul Bass cover graphic (as opposed to the awkwardly staged black-and-white photo on the cast album cover); the music, of course, which had collated all of the jazz, symphonic sway, Latin beats, Tin Pan Alley ballads, and teenage angst that spanned the pop charts into one unforgettable score (even if the movie's leads were dubbed by other singers); and the zeitgeist, which had caught up to the score's eclectic edginess. In 1964, Stephen Sondheim, the show's lyricist, told a reporter, "Everybody said they couldn't hum the score of *West Side Story* when it first came out. The only reason that it is 'melodic' now, or 'hummable' is that they have been exposed to it over and over again, so that it's come into their consciousness with some ease. There were no hit songs from the show until the movie came out three years later, and then the repeated hearings made people like the songs."[4]

West Side Story's smashing success led to a big bump not only in Columbia's original cast album sales, but in singles jobbed out to its stable of singers, notably Johnny Mathis's cover of "Something's Coming"—a song that practically nobody recorded back in 1957. The film release also sparked seminal and popular jazz recordings of Bernstein's score by the Stan Kenton Orchestra and the Oscar Peterson Trio. That marvelously tactile economic connection between cast album and soundtrack was out there, just waiting to be exploited again; it would require the right show and the right film. For Columbia, the next logical show from its catalog to exploit was *The Sound of Music,* released in December 1959. The cast album was a genuine blockbuster, spending sixteen weeks at No. 1 and continuing its incredible success by staying on the charts for 276 weeks; it would remain in the top five when Oscar Hammerstein II passed away in August 1960.

But for all the extraordinary success of its cast album, in the wake of the Broadway opening, none of the songs from *The Sound of Music* was a breakaway hit on the pop charts. Perhaps because of the specific nature of the setting and their organic relationship to the narrative, most of the songs in *The Sound of Music* didn't lend themselves to being taken out of context. Neither Frank Sinatra, Peggy Lee, Ella Fitzgerald nor Nat King Cole touched one note of its score. In the wake of the original production, Columbia put a lot of its resources into an "easy listening" orchestral version by Percy Faith, whose recordings could do very well, especially with members of the Record Club. Tony Bennett recorded a 45 single of "Climb Ev'ry Mountain" for Columbia and reprised it as part of his Carnegie Hall debut in 1962, but in the early 1960s, *The Sound of Music* offered comparatively little for major pop singers. Steve Lawrence's cha-cha version of the title number appeared on his 1960 *Lawrence Goes Latin* album, and Perry Como included "My Favorite Things" as a selection on a LP for RCA two years later, but the few singles covers appeared on smaller labels, including a young Anita Bryant's rendition of "Do Re Mi" for Carlton Records.

It's tempting to think that the behemoth of the original cast album simply obliterated all comers, but there were two vastly different approaches to its score that demonstrated the alpha and the omega of *The Sound of Music* and the idiosyncrasy of its appeal. The first was an LP released in 1960 by RCA Victor featuring "members of the Trapp Family Singers" performing songs from *The Sound of Music*. This *extremely* original cast album is a dolorous affair, where fidelity to the musical's source material obliterates all of its charm; it's like hearing the snappy score to *Guys and Dolls* played by a Salvation Army band. The second approach, however, was a monumental rethinking of "My Favorite Things" performed by the newly constituted John Coltrane Quartet. In the middle of 1960s, the famed saxophonist had left the Miles Davis band and formed his own group. Apparently, a song plugger—no one quite remembers who or from where—gave the sheet music from *The Sound of Music* to Coltrane. Thinking it was probably a good idea to render some popular standards, Coltrane included "My Favorite Things" on his third album for Atlantic, entitled *My Favorite Things*, released in March 1961. Coltrane brilliantly rethought the melody as a nearly fourteen-minute hypnotic roundelay, performed on soprano sax in 6/8 time; the song became Coltrane's most requested number. When asked in 2011 if the Quartet ever went to see the Broadway version of *The Sound of Music*, its pianist, McCoy Tyner, laughed and said, "That's unimaginable."[5]

▶   Audio Example 10.1, "My Favorite Things" (John Coltrane)

For all of these idiosyncratic experiments, it was the Columbia cast album that kept the sound of Rodgers and Hammerstein's music alive into the mid-1960s. The album was still on the charts by the end of 1963, when 20th Century Fox dusted off the property (which had been kept on the shelf for three years) and moved forward with its own feature-length film of *The Sound of Music*. Searching for a leading lady, director Robert Wise and screenwriter Ernest Lehman were less than enthusiastic with the choices buzzing about them—Leslie Caron, Audrey Hepburn, Doris Day—and asked the Disney studio if they could screen a rough cut of *Mary Poppins*. Disney obliged and within five minutes, they knew that the star of their film had to be Julie Andrews. And so, in March 1964, Julie Andrews reported for duty to the Fox lot in Century City to record the initial tracks for *The Sound of Music*. *Mary Poppins* wouldn't be released for another six months; neither Andrews, nor the world at large, knew how stupendously ubiquitous she would become.

Mary Poppins was eventually released the week before Labor Day in 1964; at roughly the same time, *The Sound of Music* was wrapping up filming in Hollywood, after an arduous summer shooting on location in Salzburg. The soundtrack album to *Mary Poppins*, released by Buena Vista Records in early October, plastered Andrews's invitingly smiling face on the cover (along with co-star Dick Van Dyke) under an distinctly un-Edwardian marquee assembled out of Broadwayesque lightbulbs; the cover looked like one of the ubiquitous "So-and-so Sings Broadway Hits" of the 1960s. The soundtrack made a slow climb up the *Billboard* charts, but by March 13, 1965 (the same week that *The Sound of Music* had its Los Angeles premiere), it was the No. 1 album in the country, beating back the backbeat of *Beatles '65*. After a brief tussle with the soundtrack to *Goldfinger*, the *Mary Poppins* album returned to No. 1 and stayed there for thirteen weeks, until July 3—when the *Beatles VI* was took the top position on the album charts.

With the incipient release of *The South of Music*, Columbia would have been perfectly confident to assume it was going to score big with the soundtrack version of one of its best-selling Broadway titles (in addition to the *West Side Story* soundtrack, Columbia had released the smash 1964 soundtrack to *My Fair Lady*—complete with gatefold, of course—but this was a property Columbia owned from the get-go). After all, this time the film would star the label's darling Julie, who had fronted three of Columbia's most successful albums of the previous nine years. The company was to be bitterly disappointed. RCA Victor put all of its chips on *The Sound of Music*, making a $100,000 offer to 20th Century Fox to promote the soundtrack to the film: "The campaign to sell a musical motion picture and the campaign to sell the soundtrack from that motion picture are inseparable," said an RCA executive, who won the competitive contest to release the album.[6] "We got a gold record for the original cast stage recording on *Sound of Music*," Lieberson told a reporter, who quoted him as "frowning." "But an attorney for the producers thought the film and stage records would sell better if each were promoted by a different company."[7] When *The Sound of Music* soundtrack was released in mid-March, the album racked up $1 million in sales within the month; no soundtrack had ever reached that goal faster.

In an era marked by the rise and triumph of Beatlemania, the ascension of the Motown Sound, and the beachhead of the British Invasion, the two most dominant LPs of the mid-1960s were, far and away, the soundtracks to *Mary Poppins* and *The Sound of Music*. In the middle of this showdown among an Edwardian nanny, a British secret agent, and four moptops from Liverpool, the soundtrack to *The Sound of Music* had skyrocketed far enough to be the No. 2 album in the country within eight weeks of its release; the No. 1 album that May was *Mary Poppins* and the two soundtracks toggled between those respective positions for the next four weeks. Pop culture has seen its share of singers whose singles are stacked one above the other on the charts—the Beatles, Michael Jackson, Mariah Carey—but to be the star performer on the No. 1 and No. 2 albums in the country—for a month!—was an unprecedented achievement for Julie Andrews.

National consumers besotted with the movie were able to bring home quite a handsome album with the RCA Victor soundtrack to *The Sound of Music*. While RCA Victor didn't go quite as far as a gatefold Columbia extravaganza, the label was clearly taking its cues from the kind of glamorous packaging that its competitors had deployed for original cast albums. The packaging of the RCA Victor release of the 1958 *South Pacific* soundtrack could hardly have been duller, but the *The Sound of Music* release contained a gloriously illustrated eight-page "storybook" insert with photos from the film and profiles of the stars and crew. The insert had a glowing "Tribute to a Partnership," a lengthy article of praise for Rodgers and Hammerstein, written (presumably months before the film's release) by Judith Crist, then the movie critic for the *New York Herald Tribune*. The joke was on her—or someone, maybe in the marketing department of 20th Century Fox—because when the film actually opened, Crist slammed it mercilessly in her column.

None of which stopped the juggernaut that was *The Sound of Music*, as both film and soundtrack. As the movie went on to become the highest-grossing movie of its time, the soundtrack hit No. 1 for two weeks in mid-November 1965. It would sit in the top five until May of 1966; in April, it would be joined on the charts by the hit soundtrack to *Thoroughly Modern Millie*, which also starred Julie Andrews. The soundtrack would stay in the Top 10 until the end of July 1966 and would remain on the charts for 233 weeks, nearly a year shy of *The Sound of Music* original cast album, but a considerable achievement nonetheless.

One important aspect that made *The Sound of Music* soundtrack different from *The Sound of Music* cast album was the inclusion of two new songs written by Richard Rodgers (who also supplied the lyrics, in the absence of Hammerstein): "I Have Confidence" and "Something Good." (Three songs were cut—none particularly missed—and "Something Good" was a far superior replacement for the show's duet between Maria and Captain von Trapp.) Hollywood films had routinely tampered with the scores to Broadway musicals, but good songs have also been added to the Hollywood soundtracks of Broadway adaptations. Several Hollywood additions (e.g., "Maybe This Time" from the film of

Cabaret) have eventually insinuated themselves in subsequent Broadway revivals. In the case of *The Sound of Music,* "Something Good" is a potent enough movie memory that theater audiences feel cheated if it's missing; certainly there are enough requests to interpolate the song into professional and amateur productions around the world.

⊳ Audio Example 10.2, "Something Good" (Julie Andrews and Christopher Plummer)

How did *The Sound of Music* album find its way onto so many living room hi-fi sets? How did it triumph over its more obstreperous rivals in the pop album world—the Beatles and the Beach Boys, the Monkees and the Supremes, Herb Alpert and the Tijuana Brass? Part of it can be chalked up to a sort of dime-store sociology, that in the uncertain times of the mid-1960s, a family-oriented musical about a family that stayed together rather than fracturing into a generation gap must have reassuring. Part of it must also be that, in the pre-VHS, pre-DVD days, any kind of precious souvenir of a beloved film would be treasured. Perhaps parents felt that the appearance of Julie Andrews on the cover, after *Mary Poppins,* represented a "safe pair of hands" for listening in the family den. "Even in the 1960s," observed Keith Caulfield, *Billboard's* co-director of charts, "no matter what it was up against, there's something to be said for something that's timeless, that's universal, that, importantly, can be enjoyed by both a younger and older generation."[8]

Of course, a huge part of the soundtrack's appeal is the sound of its music. The most astonishing statistic of all: the original cast album of *The Sound of Music,* which charted at the beginning of 1960, overlapped with the soundtrack of *The Sound of Music* on the charts from March to November of 1965; the soundtrack itself picked up the baton and charted until early 1969. Which means that, during the entire decade of the 1960s—those swinging, unsettling sixties—the most popular and enduring music in America was the score to Rodgers and Hammerstein's *The Sound of Music.*

Although Columbia was surely disappointed to run only the first half of the *Sound of Music* relay, there were some ancillary benefits. The interest in the movie moved nearly a half million more units of the original cast album (the *South Pacific* movie had bumped a million more units of the Columbia cast album),[9] and there were new cover versions of the songs by Columbia artists, such as the LP of *Eydie Gormé Sings the Great Songs From the Sound of Music and Other Broadway Hits.* Following Jack Jones's unforeseen inclusion of "My Favorite Things" on his eponymous Christmas album released by Kapp Records three months prior to the film's opening, that song would elbow its way into the ongoing Yuletide repertoire (perhaps those nose-grazing snowflakes made it seem justifiable). Subsequently, Barbra Streisand and Tony Bennett recorded the song on their own respective Christmas albums, both on Columbia. But, perhaps the best upside that Columbia could take away from *The Sound of Music* soundtrack was that it increased the value of its own assets—specifically, the music star whom it had nurtured from nearly the very beginning of her career, Julie Andrews.

Toward the end of 1966, *Camelot* began its long, tortuous slog as a Warner Bros. movie adaptation, shooting in various locations in Spain. None of the Broadway show's original stars were taking part in the film; a rueful irony because, in the six years since the Broadway debut of *Camelot*, each of them—Richard Burton, Robert Goulet, and Andrews—had seen their stars, as it were, in the ascendant: Burton and Andrews in blockbuster films, Goulet as a major recording artist. Warner Bros. cast three lesser-known non-singers in the roles for the film (to be fair, Richard Harris, Vanessa Redgrave, and Franco Nero were younger and better suited for the intimacy of the cinema). The soundtrack would go to the recently anointed Warner Bros. record label, and the studio planned a major publicity rollout for the movie and the soundtrack.

Columbia's marketing division sprang into action against its foes at Warner Bros., marshaling its sales reps with an appropriately lionhearted air:

> Both of these coups [the loss of the Rodgers and Hammerstein soundtracks to RCA Victor] were scored in spite of some of the fiercest competitive activity the enemy has ever initiated. We say enemy because: Gentlemen, *this is war!* They have the soundtrack and will fight like blazes. They have one advantage and they are sure to make the most of it by tying in the record closely with the film. But...! We have the Great One! We have *The Great Recording of "Camelot."*
> We were first in the field of combat.
> We have the STARS.[10]

Columbia fought back with a highly original stratagem: it reissued the cast album, but redesigned the cover—something fairly rare in the first few decades of the LP age. Normally, a cover graphic for a Broadway cast album, with the original poster, is the height of easily recognizable branding. But Columbia replaced the original cover—a kind of fey Gothic cartoon of knights, damsels, and trumpets—with three whopping color photos of Burton, Andrews, and Goulet, their names emblazoned above the title (Goulet had eighth billing on the original album cover). Columbia would take no prisoners with its rerelease in 1966, timed to compete with the European nobodies on the cover of the Warner Bros. soundtrack. Goddard Lieberson and his marketing staff at Columbia intuited that movies—and their soundtracks—might always be commercially available in some form, but the cast albums of Broadway's glory days, even though the shows had faded from view—or even, *because* the shows had faded from view—had transmuted, like some Arthurian alchemy, into legend. Even better, the stage stars who had given those

When the film version of *Camelot* hit movie theaters in 1967, Columbia Records showcased its stars by rereleasing the original cast album with a new cover. By permission of Sony Music.

legendary performances had the capacity to be catapulted from Broadway—often by virtue of these recordings—into another cultural stratosphere.

Nothing bore out the strategy more clearly than the Columbia-coordinated store displays and posters that read, simply and boldly:

BURTON
ANDREWS
GOULET

What better to go into battle than with a 12-inch vinyl shield adorned with those legends? Why ask for the moon, when you have the STARS?

Steve Lawrence and Eydie Gormé, both signed to contracts at Columbia Records, in 1963. By permission of Sony Music.

CHAPTER 11

Was There Too Much of a Crowd, All Too Lush and Loud?

Pop Singles and the Adult Contemporaneity of Broadway

Edith Gormézano and Brigid Lansbury were both children of the Depression, growing up halfway around the world from each other; the point at which they crossed paths was also the crossroads of popular music in America.

Edith was born in the Bronx in 1928, the daughter of a Sephardic Jew from Italy and his wife, who hailed from Turkey; she started her show biz career as a teenager, singing in big bands. She told her mother that she wanted to change her name to something more American, but her mother begged her not to: "It's bad enough you're going into show business, but if you become famous, no one will know we're related to you."[1] Brigid was born in London, three years earlier, to a British politician and an Irish actress; she also started her showbiz career as a teenager. Having moved to Hollywood as a refugee during World War II, she was cast in an MGM film at eighteen. The studio brass suggested she change her name to Angela Marlowe.[2]

Decades later, by the middle of the 1960s, they were both facing major

Angela Lansbury, in a recording session for *Anyone Can Whistle* (1964), with Goddard Lieberson in the wings. By permission of Sony Music.

career challenges. Eydie Gormé had become a successful recording artist; she married another successful recording artist, the dashing Steve Lawrence, in 1957—together they had gotten a contract at Columbia in 1963, and their albums and singles—separately and together—were frequent residents on the pop charts. Still, the popular tastes of America were swinging in another direction, away from the Broadway classics and the sassy bossa nova style that made Eydie Gormé's reputation. Angela Lansbury—she turned down MGM's suggestion to change her last name—had become one of Hollywood's most reliable character actresses by the late 1950s, but was constantly nettled by the fact that she often played mothers of other actresses only a year or two younger than she. Lansbury thought Broadway would be more hospitable and, indeed, it was—more or less. In the early 1960s, she starred in a hit play and a flop musical, but what she needed was a hit musical. Knowing a good thing when she saw it, Lansbury auditioned relentlessly and obsessively for Jerry's Herman's follow-up to *Hello, Dolly!*: *Mame*. The show's producers spent weeks hemming and hawing; Lansbury didn't have quite the marquee wattage for which they were hoping.[3]

As 1966 began, Jerry Herman was still writing the score for *Mame,* which had been signed up by Columbia Records, to the tune of a $100,000 investment. At the same time, Gormé had a hit single for Columbia of the eleven o'clock number from Alan Jay Lerner and Burton Lane's *On a Clear Day You Can See Forever*, "What Did I Have That I Don't Have." Before Herman had his leading lady—and quite a leading part Auntie Mame was, too—he had worked out *her* eleven o'clock number: "If He Walked into My Life," Mame's rumination over whether her unconventional child-rearing methods had served her nephew well. It begins, very specifically, with a reference to him:

> Where's that boy with the bugle?
> My little love was always my big romance;
> Where's that boy with the bugle?
> And why did I ever buy him those damn long pants?

And then it moves along, through a series of heart-rending regrets, concluding with:

> Were the years a little fast?
> Was his world a little free?
> Was there too much of a crowd,
> All too lush and loud and not enough of me?

Then, the rousing finish:

Would I make the same mistakes
If he walked into my life today?

While Herman was finishing up the number, esteemed music arranger Don Costa had stopped by the composer's apartment on Central Park West; Herman, naturally, played his latest song, fresh off the Steinway. As Steve Lawrence recounted: "Don grabbed the lead sheet and he said, 'I'm going up to Eydie and Steve!' Jerry lived just up the street, a block or two from us. 'I think I can get Eydie to record this. I think it would be sensational for her.' So, Don came very excitedly up to the apartment. He says, 'You gotta hear this song.' And he played it— *boom*. Eydie loved the song right then. She said, 'Oh God. This is such a killer song.' "[4]

Gormé would record "If He Walked into My Life" for release on a Columbia LP album called *Don't Go to Strangers*, released in mid-April 1966; by this point, *Mame*'s producers had come to their senses and hired Lansbury for their lead. Neither they nor Herman were prepared for the professional commitment and vibrant performance that Lansbury would bring to the demanding role in its out-of-town tryouts. "Not in years has an allegedly staid Boston audience given any musical opening such a tumultuous welcome," wrote the correspondent from *Billboard*. "Angela Lansbury comes to the forefront of musical comedy leading ladies."[5] While *Mame* was in its Philadelphia tryout a few weeks later, *Variety* wrote that Gormé's version of "If He Walked into My Life" "should put the songstress well up the Hot 100 chart." During the out-of-town tryout—before *Mame* even crossed the Delaware northward—Gormé was singing the number on the Jack Paar television show.[6]

On stage, Lansbury performed her version, simply yet effectively, seated by a small garden table. In the theater, she was indeed still singing about a "boy with a bugle"—in fact, "If that boy with a bugle / Walked into my life today" was repeated in the song's penultimate lyric. Lansbury built her version from an actor's point of view, asking herself questions about her behavior; each skeptical inquisition about herself leads to another, deeper question. (And, technically, she cuts off the note at the end of each question, where Herman has it sustained.) Lansbury delivers the big finish at the end, but it's arrived at by going deeper into her character with each step along the way.

▶   Audio Example 11.1, "If He Walked into My Life" (Angela Lansbury)

Gormé, not being tied down the character's context, had a different focus, cutting some of the lyrics; "She interpreted it like a lover," says Lawrence. "Not to the little boy with the bugle."[7] Supremely conscious of the tools at her disposal to create a musical architecture, Gormé employed longer phrasing across the bar, skipping over breaths, changing notes up to bounce herself further along to a climax. She has neither the time nor the predilection to be skeptically inquisitive; in the words of NYU/Juilliard voice professor Deborah

Lapidus, "She treats it like it's already a famous song and she's going to make it more famous."[8] Gormé builds to her patented effect of nearly growling the italicized words:

> Were the years a little fast?
> Was his world a little free?
> Was there too much of a crowd
> All too lush and loud and *not enough of me?*

Then, thoroughly confident of her dynamics, she goes in the opposite direction, pulling back, especially in the parenthetical lines:

> Though I'll ask myself my whole life long,
> What went wrong (along the way;
> Would I make the same mistakes
> If he walked into my—)

And, with the end in sight, here she goes, a step higher than the music, holding the last note twice as long as written:

> life . . .
> to . . .
> daaaaay!?

⏵   Audio Example 11.2, "If He Walked into My Life" (Eydie Gormé)

When the 1966 Tonys were awarded on June 16, 1966—less than a month after *Mame* opened, Lansbury easily walked away with Best Actress in a Musical. When the Grammy Awards were given out in March 1967, for music recorded the previous year, Eydie Gormé was nominated for Best Female Vocal Performance for her version of "If He Walked into My Life;" her competition included Barbra Streisand, Nancy Sinatra, and Ella Fitzgerald. By a twist of fate, Steve Lawrence had been scheduled to present the award to the winner that night at the Beverly Hilton Hotel. "I'd be thrilled to do it," Lawrence told them. "But, be prepared: If her name is not there, I'm going to say it anyway."

It was. In a year that featured such nominees as the Mamas and the Papas, the Beatles, Dusty Springfield, and Ray Charles, Eydie Gormé won with a song from *Mame* (and *Mame* itself won a Grammy for "Best Score from an Original Cast Show Album"). The parallel tracks of the British girl in Hollywood and the Sephardic girl from Brooklyn eventually crossed: "Angela once said to Eydie, 'I don't know how I will ever sing that song again. After your blankety-blank record I can't ever sing that song again,'" recounted Lawrence. "And Eydie said, 'Sure you can. Do you want your paycheck? Get up there and sing it.'"[9]

As much as Lansbury and Gormé were living in parallel universes—the Winter Garden Theatre and the Beverly Hilton—so, too, was popular music living in several parallel universes in the 1960s. On July 17, 1961, *Billboard*—the most prominent chronicle of the music entertainment industry—pulled twenty titles off its Hot 100 chart of pop singles and placed them in an ongoing category called Easy Listening. This category would evolve over the next few decades, being retitled Middle-Road Singles or Pop-Standard Singles, eventually landing on the title of Adult Contemporary. Joel Whitburn, the archivist who has collected the vast treasure trove of *Billboard* rankings, described the category: "Adult Contemporary has existed for generations as the serene side of the American popular music prism... It is the pop music that is contemplative, pleasing to the ears, and non-grating to the nerves."[10]

Billboard, ever cognizant of the shifts in both popular music and in the demographic groups that purchased it, had made changes in its charts before. In the late 1940s, it created separate charts for music from the South—eventually known as Country and Western music—and for records by black artists for black audiences, which transformed into Rhythm and Blues. Given the ever-evolving ways in which listeners across the country—which included more and more teenagers every year—were hearing singles in the 45 format, *Billboard* managed one more major conflation in 1958, bringing all of its "popular" sub-category charts—stores, disc jockeys, and jukeboxes—into one major category that now ranked the top one hundred singles, dubbed forever after as the Hot 100.[11]

The weeks leading up to the secession of the Adult Contemporary category in 1961 didn't feature the worst songs in pop music history. There were a couple of teenybopper hits, like "Runaway" by Del Shannon, with an overworked electric keyboard, but there was also "Stand By Me" sung by Ben E. King. However, in the spring of that year, two of the biggest hit singles were a syncopated version of "I've Told Ev'ry Little Star" rendered by a baby-voiced teen named Linda Scott and The Marcels's doo-wop stylings of "Blue Moon" (which was No. 1 for three weeks); the former song had been written by Kern and Hammerstein in 1932; the latter was written by Rodgers and Hart two years later. These weren't "easy listening" versions, but pop renditions of classics recreated for a youthful audience; the landscape of popular music in the early 1960s was complex, indeed.

Of course, if Hammerstein or Rodgers had looked in the opposite direction from their royalty statements, they might find much to dislike—or even despise—on the pop charts. The obvious culprit, of course, was rock and roll, the scourge of highbrow (and middlebrow) tastemakers from roughly 1954 on, when disc jockey and concert promoter Alan Freed applied the term "Rock 'n' Roll Party" to frame his rhythm and blues programming for teenagers. That year, Elvis Presley released his first single for Sun Records, "It's All Right" (the same week that Rosemary Clooney was hitting No. 1 with "Hey There"). As cultural historian Glenn Altschuler put it, "As Alan Freed provided a name, and Elvis an icon, Bill Haley gave rock and roll its anthem."[12] "(We're Gonna) Rock Around the Clock" also came out in 1954 and was picked up as the background music for the opening credits of *Blackboard Jungle,* a 1955 film about juvenile delinquency in a city school. Almost immediately, rock and roll was branded with a renegade stain, and as fast as it became a national pastime among the youth of America, denouncing the new form of music (and dancing) became a kind of hobby among many of America's elders. Frank Sinatra said that rock and roll is sung, played, and written for the most part by "cretinous goons, and by means of its almost imbecilic reiteration and sly, lewd, in fact plain dirty, lyrics, it manages to be the martial music of every sideburned delinquent on the face of the earth."[13] Rodgers himself said, in a television interview, "The worst I can say about [rock and roll] is that musically, it's repetitive; I don't know why it has to go on for 32 bars in the same way; even the chord structures are '1-5-4-5-1'; it seems to me, you could try something else every now and then."[14]

As this new kind of music received more radio airplay in the late 1950s through a growing cadre of national disc jockeys who could easily spin gold for their young fan base, it became increasingly threatening to the establishment of the traditional pop music world. *Billboard* called it correctly as early as 1955: "The horizons of the pop music business are broadening and development is not without its pain, turmoil and soul searching; [for example], the continued impact of rhythm and blues and the consternation and confusion it has caused among so many segments of the popular music business. Tin Pan Alley must integrate itself with a larger musical scene if it is to continue its traditional function of song purveyor to the nation."[15]

Alas, Tin Pan Alley spent most of its time and money in the 1950s segregating itself from the "larger musical scene." The convenient target was rock and roll, but that was really a stalking horse for bigger game: the wide range of musical offerings controlled by Broadcast Music, Inc. A decade and a half after its creation during the ASCAP boycott, the ranks of BMI's songwriters had grown exponentially; they had cultivated all the kinds of songwriters who excelled in genres that ASCAP had disparaged: country, rhythm and blues, rock, Latin, novelty numbers. These were also the genres that postwar Americans began to enjoy in greater numbers. Tapping into a wider market, and utilizing the AM broadcast radio stations that owned BMI, the company had the easiest and most appealing access to that market; by the end of the 1950s, roughly 70 percent of the most popular tunes on the radio were BMI tunes. ASCAP writers increasingly felt that they were being stifled by deejays favoring BMI tunes and that the interlocking interests of the broadcasters and BMI gave their writers an unfair competitive advantage, thus depriving the public of what ASCAP called "better quality" music.[16]

In 1953, led by composer Arthur Schwartz, thirty-three ASCAP songwriters (including Alan Jay Lerner and Ira Gershwin) filed a $150 million lawsuit against BMI for antitrust violation. The suit snowballed and eventually led to Senate hearings in 1958 in support of a bill that would pursue the antitrust case against BMI. Schwartz and Oscar Hammerstein were among the more than dozen musicians, composers, and scholars who testified on behalf of ASCAP and, more often than not, rock and roll—and its implied deleterious effects—was the cudgel with which they used to beat BMI. According to *Variety*, Hammerstein claimed that there was so much "unworthy" music cluttering the airwaves that it deprived the public of *South Pacific*-type tunes. "BMI songs have been rammed down the public's ears," he said.[17]

It was a rare moment of intolerance for someone so revered for his open-mindedness. It was inevitable that a creative personality or two would find the generational (and financial) struggle over rock and roll to be a prime subject for a musical comedy. Michael Stewart worked for years with the talented young songwriters Charles Strouse and Lee Adams on the musical that would put the contentious world of rock and roll on a Broadway stage for the first time; it would become *Bye Bye Birdie*. However, according to Strouse, it was difficult to get producers to share their enthusiasm, until his music publisher Edwin Morris called Goddard Lieberson for an appointment. The team played the score for him, it tickled Lieberson's sense of humor, and Columbia signed the show on the spot. With Columbia's investment in *Bye Bye Birdie*, the production was off and running.[18] It's easy to think of *Bye Bye Birdie* as a rock and roll musical, but it's not quite: it's a musical about America's *reaction* to rock and roll. The contemporary reactions are all there: the smitten youngsters, the slightly incredulous promoters, and, above all, the bewildered parents, the elder generation: "Why can't they dance like we did? / What's wrong with Sammy Kaye? / What's the matter with kids today?" It almost sounds like Strouse and Adams had musicalized Hammerstein's congressional testimony.

Most of the score to *Bye Bye Birdie* is straight up Tin Pan Alley—"Put on a Happy Face," "A Lot of Livin' to Do," "Talk to Me"—but there are only two attempts to create a real rock and roll sound (three, if you count a brief riff in "The Telephone Hour"): "Honestly Sincere" and "One Last Kiss." When *Bye Bye Birdie* debuted on Broadway in April 1960, it was literally bracketed by four No. 1 hits by the honestly actual Elvis Presley—one in 1959, three in 1960. One would think that the Elvis pastiches from *Birdie* would find a happy place on the charts, but there wasn't a significant cover of any of them, except for a single release of "One Last Kiss" by the 17-year-old teen idol Bobby Vee. On the other hand, "A Lot of Livin' to Do" and "Put on a Happy Face" were covered by dozens of pop artists—Sammy Davis, Jr., Louis Armstrong, Jack Jones, Peggy Lee with the former, and Matt Monro, Marilyn Maye, and most notably, Tony Bennett with the latter. Bennett released "Put on a Happy Face" one month after *Birdie* opened, on a Columbia 45. The original cast album, of course, came out on a beautiful K-series gatefold from Columbia as well.

As part of his Columbia contract, Bennett got first crack at Strouse and Adams's next show—also signed and produced on record by Lieberson—a somewhat convoluted tale about college football called *All American* (Mel Brooks contributed the book). Bennett recorded the show's big ballad, "Once Upon a Time," two months before it opened on Broadway, a tune with a madrigalesque delicacy that Strouse and Adams had been kicking around for a while. Strouse recalled a meeting with Bennett: "He loved 'Once Upon a Time.' He thought that was going to be the biggest hit, but he didn't know what to put on the B-side and he played me a demo of 'I Left My Heart In San Francisco.' I told him it was great and it went on the B-side. 'Once Upon a Time' never became 'I Left My Heart In San Francisco' but, because we were on the A-side, we made all the money that they made on 'I Left My Heart.'"[19]

Tony Bennett was chief among the reliable cohort of pop—or, rather, "Adult Contemporary"—singers who covered Broadway tunes on a regular basis throughout the turbulent 1960s. Most of the folks who felt at home with this material were signed with a major label (Columbia, RCA, as well as Mercury, MGM, and Atlantic—three vibrant postwar entrants to the recording field) and were equally comfortable recording an LP, a 45 single, or some combination of both. These singers had contracts that required them to record a certain amount of music every year, and in the 1950s and 1960s, a reliable source of good music came from Broadway. As writer David Dachs warned in his 1964 book, *Anything Goes: The World of Popular Music*: "Despite the lordly disclaimers that record albums provide much of the record company's revenues, the popular 'singles' business is of critical importance. The superior vocalists—Sinatra, Ella Fitzgerald, Peggy Lee—do original material on singles, but each have about six releases a year and of these there is a good amount from Broadway shows or title songs from movies."[20] Many of the more discriminating singers made sure they got to record the better songs to come from Broadway shows, and it was a win-win for the singer, the label, and the production. Steve Lawrence recalled: "The A&R folks went and saw how the song was used in a show. There were some songs that disc jockeys were happy to play and say, 'Not only is this a great song, but it's from the show *Such-and-such*.' So, the show's producers started appealing more to recording artists who felt that they could do a good job with that kind of well-written song."[21]

The Broadway cohort of pop singers tended to fall into several different categories. Some, such as Bennett and Sinatra, or Peggy Lee and Sarah Vaughan (or, for that matter, Bing Crosby, Nat "King" Cole, Ella Fitzgerald, or Judy Garland) never performed in Broadway shows at all. A smaller number actually gave up lucrative touring and Vegas singing gigs to perform in a Broadway musical. It's hard to overestimate the kind of sacrifice—both financial and physical—these performers made by committing to eight performances a week on Broadway, or how intricately they entwined themselves into the fabric of Broadway mythology and the demands of popular music.

Lena Horne had always been a big supporter of the prewar Broadway songbook—the Gershwins, Harold Arlen, Rodgers and Hart—and was not only a major recording artist for RCA, but a movie star as well. She returned to her stomping grounds in New York in 1957 to star in an original musical called *Jamaica*, written by Arlen and Yip Harburg, but despite some cleverly crafted specialty material for Horne, *Jamaica* wasn't a hit and the songs didn't transcend the show or translate into commercial recordings. Steve Lawrence had done an enormous amount of live television in the late 50s and early 60s before he signed with Columbia in 1962. When he landed the leading role of the unscrupulous Sammy Glick in *What Makes Sammy Run?* the following year, he quickly recorded a 45 single for the label of two songs from the show, "My Home Town" and "A Room Without Windows." Typically for the time, the single was released before the show was even in rehearsal; by the time the show opened in late February 1964, the theater audience was applauding those two tunes during the Overture. Columbia still had to invest $150,000 for the cast album, and although *What Makes Sammy Run?* ran for more than a year and a half (and Lawrence garnered a Tony nomination), the album didn't do as well as the singles releases.

▶ Audio Example 11.3, "A Room Without Windows" (Steve Lawrence)

Lawrence and Eydie Gormé—now with a hugely successful body of work, nightclub contracts, and Vegas venues behind them—made their Broadway debut as a team in a 1968 musical called *Golden Rainbow*. The show was set in Vegas, a reworking of a Frank Sinatra film, *A Hole in the Head*, which was originally set in Florida. Some critics felt the musical had been rather effortfully overhauled to accommodate the Lawrences, but their box-office appeal outmatched these reservations. They were the most successful romantic partnership on the "adult contemporary" charts and there they were, on Broadway, eight times a week. Songwriter Walter Marks gave Lawrence a terrific Act One closer, "I've Gotta Be Me"—an anthem of self-assertion, with a bolero underscoring—and he released it as a single on his new label, Calendar, a company that he and Gormé owned with promoter/producer Don Kirshner (RCA distributed their recordings). Lawrence's recording went as high as No. 6 on the Easy Listening charts, and the song became a standard in his act.

But, as times were a-changin', there was something about the defiant definition of self in "I've Gotta Be Me" that struck Lawrence as transcendent: "I heard it one day and I thought this song would be great for Sammy Davis on so many levels. The lyric was now interpreted by a black man in society at that time, this man who is different than anybody else. It was a bigger statement coming from him than it was from me."[22] In Sammy Davis, Jr.'s impassioned rendition, "I've Gotta Be Me" was certainly a bigger commercial statement. Late in 1968, his version of the song zoomed up the Easy Listening charts and stayed at No. 1 for seven weeks; perhaps more impressively, in early 1969, it reached No. 11 in the "Hot 100." It was Sammy Davis's chance, as the song itself goes, to have it all.

▶ Audio Example 11.4, "I've Gotta Be Me" (Sammy Davis, Jr.)

If any pop singer of the postwar era gave his all to the cultural significance of Broadway, it was Sammy Davis. Raised as part of a song-and-dance trio, Davis grew up with the Broadway catalog from the 1920s forward as the soundtrack of his performing life. After a brief and ultimately disappointing recording contract with Capitol beginning in 1949, Davis switched to Decca in 1954; his first single with them happened to be a recording of "Hey There," a month following the Broadway opening of *The Pajama Game*. Although it didn't chart quite as high as Rosemary Clooney's version, Davis's single hit No. 16—a remarkable achievement in a remarkable time, when multiple renditions of the same song could be popular with national listeners simultaneously.

But Davis did Clooney one better by debuting on Broadway two years later in *Mr. Wonderful,* a vehicle created expressly for him. *Mr. Wonderful* was the kind of show that *My Fair Lady,* which opened the same season, was rendering obsolete—a thin story about the rise of a nightclub entertainer (Davis), which culminated in Act Two with the actual nightclub act that Davis had been touring across the country for a decade. *Mr. Wonderful* yielded two standards: the title number (covered by Sarah Vaughan, Peggy Lee, and Teddi King) and "Too Close for Comfort" (a hit for Davis, but also for Mel Tormé and Ella Fitzgerald). Because of Davis's contract with Decca, the label recorded the cast album (although rights issues precluded the recording of his full "nightclub routine" in Act Two); luckily, Decca was also a fertile proving ground for Davis's enthusiasm for recording first-rate material. From 1956 to 1960, Davis ransacked the Broadway catalog, covering the most demanding solos from contemporary shows—such as "Gesticulate" from *Kismet* and "Trouble" from *The Music Man*—as well as two stunning albums of duets with Carmen McRae, one of which exploited Davis's performance as Sportin' Life in the 1959 film version of *Porgy and Bess.*

When Davis's contract with Decca was under renewal, Goddard Lieberson inquired of his A&R staff whether or not he was worth signing to Columbia, as his "star status would be useful to the Record Club," but the general feeling was that Davis would be better off with Sinatra, Dean Martin, "and others of that coterie," as a staff producer replied.[23] Indeed, Davis moved over to Sinatra's start-up label, Reprise (backed by Warner Bros.) in late 1960. Sammy Davis's early tenure at Reprise was full of the same quality standards—Rodgers and Hart, old Jolson songs—and new, ongoing relationships with the British tunesmiths Leslie Bricusse and Anthony Newley with a 1961 recording of "What Kind of Fool Am I?" from their *Stop the World* (*I Want to Get Off*) that would land on the *Billboard* charts for fifteen weeks. By fall 1963, however, Davis was offered the opportunity to return to Broadway as a serious leading man in a groundbreaking musical update of the Clifford Odets play *Golden Boy.*

The new *Golden Boy* was unique for its era as a serious inquisition into race, passion, and betrayal on the Broadway musical stage. Strouse and Adams were hired to tailor the score expressly for Davis's talents, and the show's producer, Hillard Elkins, obtained a re-lease from Davis's Reprise contract to allow him to record the cast album for Capitol. Elkins also got Capitol to kick in more than $250,000 toward capitalizing the production of *Golden Boy*, including $20,000 for marketing and promotion. Davis's role as a prize-fighter was one of musical theater's most demanding: nine songs, plus an intense boxing match for the finale. This nightly ordeal did not put a dent in Davis's active nightlife, how-ever, nor his two-pack-a-day smoking habit; when he recorded the cast album a week after the October 20 opening, his vocal chords were severely frazzled. Although Davis gave a dynamic performance on the original Capitol recording, it was not his finest moment vo-cally. Davis went back into the recording studio seven months later, re-recorded five of the show's major songs, and had them dubbed onto the cast recording for subsequent press-ings. It was a smart idea—the show ran for another year and Davis toured it in Chicago and in London until the end of 1968—and Capitol was no doubt grateful to have a more pol-ished product to sell. From the singles perspective, he recorded three songs from the score for Reprise in advance of the Broadway opening—"Yes, I Can," "There's a Party Going On," and "Night Song," his character's soulful, striving opening number. Ironically, the first two songs would be eliminated before the show opened—a rare case of cutting a potential hit song off at the knees—and, although "Night Song" would be beautifully covered by a wide range of singers, including Sarah Vaughan and Nina Simone, it never became a hit for Davis.

In "Night Song," the lyrics refer specifically to the race of Davis's character: "Where do you go / When you want to break out / But your skin is your cage?" So, it would seem odd for the chiseled Canadian baritone Robert Goulet to cover that number. But, through the early to mid-1960s, it seemed as if there was nothing from Broadway that Goulet *didn't* cover. Making his Broadway debut as *Camelot*'s narcissistic heartthrob Sir Lancelot in 1960, Goulet seemed a natural to carry the Broadway songbook on his reasonably broad shoulders. After a particularly impressive solo turn on *The Ed Sullivan Show* in 1962, Columbia signed him to a contract, where he routinely churned out more than two LPs *per year* for the rest of the decade—a total of nineteen.

With his good looks (always front and center on the record jacket) and masculine charm, Goulet was, quite literally, Columbia's poster boy for Broadway material. His initial LPs had only a dollop of Broadway songs, but by the mid-1960s he released *On Broadway*, which contained a dozen current Broadway tunes (including a more generalized version of "Night Song"); two years later, he released *On Broadway, Volume 2*, with another dozen tunes currently being sung (or easily recalled) on the Great White Way. Taken together, these albums are an anthology of nearly every Broadway tune worth recording between 1964 and 1968; Goulet renders "Ciao Compare," an upbeat ballad from the score to Bob Merrill's *Breakfast at Tiffany's*—a show that didn't even make it to Broadway. At the same time, he starred in three very credible primetime television versions of *Brigadoon*,

Carousel, and *Kiss Me, Kate,* as well as assaying a terrifically egotistical Frank Butler opposite Doris Day on the studio album of *Annie Get Your Gun* in 1962. Goulet combined the best qualities of John Raitt and Alfred Drake, only this time packaged into a personality known—and beloved—by housewives across the nation.

Goulet was nearly unique among the Broadway cohort for beginning his recording career in the 1960s; all of the other members—Sammy Davis, Steve and Eydie, Tony Bennett, even Johnny Mathis—had been singing songs from Broadway since the 1950s. It would take an intrepid soul to stake a claim with Broadway material in the mid-1960s and, at the time, no one in the popular recording world was more intrepid in this regard than Barbra Streisand.

As early as 1961, when she was still a teenager, Streisand and her manager, Marty Erlichman, arranged for an audition with Goddard Lieberson at CBS's offices, believing that a recorded demo wouldn't do justice to her unique style and material. But although Lieberson met with her twice at Columbia—the second time in a studio, where he recorded her to see how she sounded on playback—the admitted eccentricity of Streisand's manner made her an odd fit for a label that had such mainstream singers as Doris Day, Eydie Gormé, and Johnny Mathis. Too odd, in fact: Lieberson turned her down, concurring with his A&R staff that, while Streisand's voice was thrillingly expansive, the whole package seemed limited to her fans from tiny, smoky, tatty Greenwich Village clubs.[24]

Then, in 1962, Streisand was cast in a brief but attention-getting role as a romantically frustrated secretary named Miss Marmelstein in Harold Rome's Broadway musical adaptation of *I Can Get It for You Wholesale.* As luck would have it, the show's cast album would be recorded by Columbia. During the tightly scheduled recording session itself, she told Lieberson she wanted to make some changes in the musical arrangements of her big solo, "Miss Marmelstein;" he took her quietly aside, shared some private exchange with her, and Streisand went back and sang the number as written in the show. Lieberson may well have been the last record producer to tell Barbra Streisand what to do. Still without a recording contract per se with Columbia, she went back into the studio to record its archival version of Rome's 1938 hit, *Pins and Needles.*

Streisand continued her *Wholesale* chores eight times a week and then off she went, performing in nightclubs uptown and downtown, as soon as she could beat it out of the Shubert Theatre stage door. Lieberson came to see her at the Blue Angel and it was enough to convince him; Streisand was signed by Columbia in October 1962. In 1973, Lieberson told the *Boston Sunday Globe,* "Now there is an original!...Barbra says that at first I didn't want to sign her, and she also says that I thought that she was colored, both of which are untrue, but we had very strong connections, that girl and I." Although Lieberson, of course, *didn't* want to sign her, Columbia and the singer began a relationship that would last for five decades and counting.[25]

The executives at Columbia wisely realized that the breadth of her emotional, but thoughtful, repertoire would work better on an LP than on singles. As 1963 began, she went into the studio and wound up repackaging much of her nightclub material on an LP, entitled *The Barbra Streisand Album*. The selections on the album—artfully arranged by Peter Matz—were atypical for the time, but would signal the kind of material Streisand would put on her first few albums. There were two songs from the Off-Broadway show *The Fantasticks*; an obscure Rodgers and Hart number; an obscure Harold Arlen; and a Cole Porter song so obscure—"Come to the Supermarket in Old Peking"—that it wasn't even on Broadway (it came from a television special from 1958, *Aladdin*). By the summer, her debut album had cracked the Top 10, peaking at No. 8, and stayed on the charts for another eighteen months.

A second album—aptly titled *The Second Barbra Streisand Album*—continued very much in the same vein of repertory: four slightly less obscure Harold Arlen songs (one from *Bloomer Girl*, one from *St. Louis Woman*); two songs from the new team of John Kander and Fred Ebb: a pop hit ("My Coloring Book"), as well as an impassive ballad called "I Don't Care Much," which would eventually make a brief appearance in a musical they would write two years later, *Cabaret*. Most female singers might have covered the big torchy ballad, "As Long as He Needs Me" from *Oliver!*, which had just opened, but Streisand recorded another, more offbeat number from the show, "Who Will Buy?" Her follow-up album performed even better than the first, spending three weeks at No. 2.

By the time Streisand released her third album—inexorably called *The Third Album*—in February 1964, she was already deep into rehearsal as the lead in *Funny Girl*, the Broadway musical biography of Fanny Brice. When the show opened on March 26, Streisand joined the pantheon of Broadway's greatest stars; within two years, she had recorded five albums—three of which went gold for Columbia. But, the cast album of *Funny Girl* went to Capitol (*Variety* claimed that Columbia didn't "exercise their option"—ostensibly on Streisand's contract—to pick up the show). Capitol also put a substantial investment into the show, and, for Streisand's services, Columbia negotiated four singles from the score to be sung by her on its label. The cast album of *Funny Girl*—filled with Jule Styne and Bob Merrill's effectively showbizzy score (and its simulacrums of Brice's biggest hits)—was released two months after *The Third Album* and moved to No. 2 on the charts for three weeks; it was the fastest-selling cast album in Capitol's history. Capitol used its, well, capital to get a singles recording of "People" out to the public in advance of *Funny Girl*'s opening, but not by Streisand; Nat "King" Cole's rendition is up-tempo and not very effective. Streisand's reclaimed the song as her own as a single a few weeks later; her single of "People" sat at No. 1 on the Easy Listening charts for three weeks (and went to No. 5 on the Hot 100—no mean feat), making a tidy sum for Columbia.

▶ Audio Example 11.5, "People" (Nat King Cole)

Columbia still received the residual benefit of Streisand's association with Brice and *Funny Girl*; her fourth album for the label, released while she was performing the arduous title role at the Winter Garden every night, was called *People*—it would be the biggest hit of all Streisand's releases in the 1960s, sitting at No. 1 for five weeks and earning Streisand her second Grammy for Female Pop vocal. Containing her first crack at Rodgers and Hammerstein ("My Lord and Master" from *The King and I*—a surprisingly submissive choice for a performer who tortured nearly every technician and arranger with whom she ever worked), she took on some other extremely unconventional choices from the Broadway canon. "How Does the Wine Taste?" was from a flop called *We Take the Town* that never made it to New York; "Autumn," by Richard Maltby, Jr. and David Shire, didn't even make it past an attempt to stage a Broadway musical version of *Cyrano de Bergerac*.

Streisand held certain show tunes solicitously in her hands as if they were birds with broken wings; she would continue to take up songs—excellent though they were—that had escaped from some of Broadway's greatest calamities only through her good graces. She would record four songs from *The Yearling*, a casualty that ran only for three performances. When her husband at the time, Elliott Gould, garnered the lead in a cops-and-robbers musical spoof called *Drat! The Cat!* in 1965, Columbia agreed to record the cast album and invest a fairly nominal $50,000 in the show. (It was rumored that Streisand herself invested $100,000.)[26] To help the chances for the musical, Streisand recorded a singles release of two songs from the show: the A-side was "He Touched Me" (in the show itself, "She Touched Me"), released about a month before the show opened, and it stayed on the Hot 100 for ten weeks. Such reflected glory didn't do much for *Drat! The Cat!*, however, which ran only eleven performances.

In many ways, Streisand was building on Frank Sinatra's visionary idea of a decade earlier: using the LP as a landscape to work out inventive renditions of Broadway material. But as Streisand was building her own career in the early 1960s, Sinatra was taking the possibilities of the LP to another level. He had formed Reprise Records, an independent label devoted to the mission of recording artists he admired (including himself, of course) without undue commercial pressure and with some degree of artistic freedom; by 1962, he had acquired a stable of singers that included Sammy Davis, Jr., Dean Martin, Keely Smith, and Jo Stafford. Sinatra would release some definitive albums of his own at the beginning of the Reprise venture—*Ring-a-Ding-Ding, Sinatra with Strings*—but he needed a signature project for the label itself. He hit upon the idea of four full classic Broadway scores, each one recorded by his ever-deepening bench of pop singers. Sinatra put his chips on the Reprise Musical Repertory Theater series, being "personally involved in the production" of the series, according to *Billboard*.[27]

The series would include four critically acclaimed scores, each of which had opened on Broadway between 1947 and 1950: *Finian's Rainbow*; *Kiss Me, Kate*; *South Pacific*; and *Guys and Dolls*—the sine qua nons of Broadway's golden age. The criterion used in selecting the shows was "what the competition was and which shows had the largest number of hit songs to spread around to the many performers involved."[28] The "repertory" cast would be spread over all four LPs, and it featured the most accomplished pop singers of the day: Sinatra, Martin, Davis, Stafford, Smith, with "guest" appearances by the likes of Bing Crosby and Dinah Shore (who were gravitating toward Reprise). There had, of course, been "cover scores" back in the 78 rpm era, but Sinatra's enterprise stretched farther and deeper than anything before: each LP would contain a full 40-plus minutes of songs, including an overture, in the order they appeared in the show (more or less) so that the narrative would be preserved. In addition, there was song material that no commercial singer had recorded before.

The logistics alone were mind-boggling: Morris Stoloff, the music director on the project, had to coordinate multiple sessions with multiple singers at multiple times, given the geographical dislocation of so many popular singers with professional engagements. If that weren't enough, it was Reprise's intention to release all four records—for a combined cost of $19.50 in stereo—in a set for distribution through a mail-order subscription in plenty of time for Christmas 1963. The entire project cost more than $150,000 to record and promote, roughly 50 percent more than the attendant costs of recording four cast albums at the time.[29] Sinatra expert Charles L. Granata explains what the project meant to Sinatra: "Telling the world that Reprise has some of the greatest artists in America on its roster was really clever marketing, but Sinatra also appreciated the whole score in context and wanted to expose more people to the whole score of a Broadway show sung by a roster of stars."[30]

Taken as an entire anthology, the Reprise Musical Repertory Theater tells a lot of different stories. The first, to get it out of the way, is the use of Reprise's benchwarmers—folks like Lou Monte, The Hi-Lo's, even parody comedian Allan Sherman—who may have needed the exposure, but who don't contribute much to a consumer's appreciation of the scores. Yet, there are many pleasures, large and small. Sammy Davis, Jr. is cast throughout the series, stereotypically or not, as the "outsider"—Nicely-Nicely in *Guys and Dolls*; singing "Too Darn Hot" in *Kiss Me, Kate* (written for a black performer); "Necessity" in *Finian's Rainbow* (also written for black singers). On the *South Pacific* album, Davis is given "You've Got to Be Carefully Taught" from *South Pacific* (interpolated from another Reprise album that he performed with a subtle guitar accompaniment by Laurindo Almeida); it's a moving rendition, not the least because the song had never been recorded before outside of cast or film recordings of the show, and its message of tolerance fitted Davis extremely well.

And then there's Sinatra himself. Commentators have mentioned how selflessly he appears to promote himself on the recording; indeed, he only appears on two or three songs per album, giving such confident renditions of "Old Devil Moon" and "When I'm Not Near the Girl I Love." On the *Guys and Dolls* album, however, he takes on the role of Sky Masterson for the first time, having been elbowed out of the part in the movie by

Marlon Brando eight years earlier. "I've Never Been in Love Before" is a duet in the show, but Sinatra sings it as a solo; far more essential is his version of "Luck Be a Lady," which he had never recorded before the Reprise album. His rollicking, optimistically delusional version would become a cornerstone of his concert performances ever after.

But "Luck Be a Lady" was a no-brainer. His true courage as a producer and as a performer comes on the *South Pacific* album, the best of the quartet. Sinatra, taking on the role of Emile de Becque, joins with Keely Smith to sing "Twin Soliloquies"—the exquisite monologue/duet that leads into "Some Enchanted Evening"—and then takes off on that solo. Sinatra had recorded "Some Enchanted Evening" back in 1949, but no other popular singer had taken on "Twin Soliloquies," which is an essential part of the more well-known ballad. Sinatra honors the intentions of Rodgers and Hammerstein by putting the score in its proper context; later on the album, he tackles "This Nearly Was Mine"—a song that musical theater expert Ted Chapin calls the show's "stealth ballad"—the eleven o'clock number written for Ezio Pinza that no one before Sinatra had the temerity to record on a popular album.[31]

▶ Audio Example 11.6, "Twin Soliloquies" (Frank Sinatra & Keely Smith)

It would nice to reveal that there was a happy ending for the Reprise Musical Repertory Theater, but, alas, it did not reach the American public with the broad embrace that it intended to have, or that it deserved. Sinatra's most recent biographer, James Kaplan, suggests the reason may be "[that by] 1963, the golden age of the Broadway musical, which these four uplifting shows of the 1940s and 50s richly represented, had passed," but surely that's as ill-formed as it is unkind.[32] The Reprise Musical Repertory Theater may have suffered because of its unconventional mail-order distribution (a year later, the albums were released to store owners for direct sale); or its rather fey and unattractive graphics; or even the fact that they were released the same week as John F. Kennedy's assassination—and no one had much enthusiasm for anything celebratory through the end of 1963.

Whatever the reasons, as Sinatra settled into Reprise, and then worked past his Repertory recording project, he gave increasingly little time to contemporary songs from the Great White Way, certainly with none of the enthusiasm that he embraced the then-current hits of Broadway in the 1940s and early 50s, when he was recording for Columbia. Indeed, although Jule Styne had written some early hits for Sinatra, the singer recorded practically nothing of the composer's music from the mid-1950s to the mid-1970s; Sinatra was quoted by Will Friedwald as saying, "I'm the only person who never sang 'People.' "[33] Occasionally, in the 1960s, he would help out a pal (or pals); when his go-to songwriting team in Los Angeles, Sammy Cahn and Jimmy Van Heusen, wrote their first Broadway musical together, *Skyscraper*, in 1965, Sinatra recorded a 45 with two of the songs from the show that was released in advance of the opening. And in June 1964, from his podium at the United Recording studio, accompanied by the Count Basie Orchestra, he kidded an old pal from way back when:

Hello, Satch!

This is Francis, Louis—

It's so nice to see you back where you belong!

Louis was, of course, Louis Armstrong, who had made one of pop culture's great come-backs six months earlier with a recording of Jerry Herman's "Hello, Dolly!" Jack Lee of E.H. Morris Music publishing gave the song to Armstrong in December 1963 as a possi-ble single; Satchmo changed the tempo for his recording on the Kapp label and gave it a Dixieland background. Herman recalled that when "the publishing company called me and said, 'Louis Armstrong wants to record that,' I laughed. I thought it was the silliest idea that I had ever heard. But I said, 'Let him have a good time. I'm delighted,' you know."[34] Released at the end of January, two weeks after the show opened on Broadway, Armstrong's single of "Hello, Dolly!" received only a middling review in *Variety*: "an okay, if strictly conventional number that Satchmo can work over with his usual vocal savvy."

Armstrong promptly forgot about the recording and went on tour with his All-Stars across the Midwest in the beginning of 1964. To his bewilderment, crowds kept shouting "Hello, Dolly!" and Armstrong had to ask his sidemen what they were yelling about. He quickly relearned the tune from some sheet music ordered on the road and added it to his concerts: the crowds went berserk. This was at the height of the American edition of Beatlemania, with the British group commandeering the charts for thirteen weeks beginning on February 1, 1964; one Beatles song or another was consistently at No. 1 (for the week of April 4 the top five singles were all Beatles recordings). However, for one brief shining moment, the week ending May 9, Armstrong knocked them off their exalted pop chart perch (the song would continue to be No. 1 for nine weeks on the Easy Listening charts). At the age of sixty-three, Louis Armstrong had become the oldest person ever to have a No. 1 hit record; one week later, he too was knocked out of the No. 1 spot—the new champ was Mary Wells's version of "My Guy." Still, Armstrong's achievement was a fluke created by the zeitgeist; his take on the number—so retro as to be timeless—was a banner planted by the mainstream, telling America's infatuated Beatlemaniacs that their musical tastes belonged on the landscape, too.

In addition, this spotlight made Armstrong extremely attractive to the A&R men at various labels who figured they could get a financial reprise of "Hello, Dolly!" Satchmo recorded a bevy of show tunes in the mid-1960s (mostly for Kapp): some were natu rals—such as "Mame" (already a Dixieland number)—others simply bizarre, and beyond Armstrong's ability to make charming: "You Are Woman, I Am Man" originally a duet from *Funny Girl*. It was almost inevitable that, prior to the Kander and Ebb musical, *Cabaret*, going into rehearsal, Satchmo would get a crack at the title number. He recorded

Original Cast Album Available Soon!

An intoxicating musical based on "The Man Who Came to Dinner"

The Original Broadway Cast Recording

SHERRY!

An intoxicating musical

RCA VICTOR
The most trusted name in sound

A sign of the times. During its Boston tryout, *Sherry!* looked like an intoxicating addition to the 1966–67 Broadway season; alas, its lead George Sanders (pictured here as the acidulous Sheridan Whiteside) didn't make it to New York. Although the show eventually ran 72 performances, the anticipated cast recording never happened either. Credit: Photofest.

"Cabaret" as a single for Columbia in August 1966 and sang it on September 11 on *The Ed Sullivan Show*—where audiences received a special preview of a song that hadn't even been staged yet.

Eventually, of course, *Cabaret* would come together on the stage, directed by Harold Prince, and it began its tryouts in Boston at the end of October. Composer John Kander remembers how the title number helped to sell the show: "When I was unpacking my suitcase at the old Bradford Hotel in Boston in the fall of 1966, before there'd been a performance of *Cabaret*, I turn on the radio and there were I think about five songs from it on the radio—before there'd even been a performance. That was kind of standard, at least with a lot of the big shows. And [in the performances] when they played the entr'acte or the exit music and they played the song 'Cabaret,' people stayed—they stayed down and listened and applauded because they knew the song already. And that wasn't unusual. That had been going on for quite a while."[35]

Cabaret would move into New York in November and become a whopping hit, winning eight Tony Awards; the cast album, released by Columbia, would also do extremely well. But, as Kander and Ebb moved toward their next project, a musical version of the play *The Happy Time*, produced by David Merrick, starring Robert Goulet, and scheduled for a Broadway opening in January 1968, there was a subtle shift in the landscape of popular music. Kander recalls:

> The next show of ours that came out was *The Happy Time*. There would certainly have been songs from it, which would have been recorded ahead of time, but none were. The only song they could get recorded was Goulet singing "The Happy Time" because he was a star. And I think that was true of just about everything that came afterward. I can't really explain it. Up to that time if there was a Broadway song, lots of people sang it, lots of people recorded it. And that ended, pretty much. I actually date the beginning of the withdrawal of theater music from the popular market as sometime in the middle of 1967—between *Cabaret* and *The Happy Time*. It's almost as if you could put your finger on the date that the separation began to happen.

In spring 1967, Eydie Gormé was honored at the Grammy Awards for her rendition of "If He Walked into My Life"; the album of the year was Sinatra's *A Man and His Music*. A year later, when *The Happy Time* was early in its Broadway run, the Grammys awarded the Beatles *Sgt. Pepper's Lonely Hearts Club Band* with the album of the year. The awards were on February 29—it was a leap year. You could put your finger on it.

Goddard Lieberson (l.) and Stephen Sondheim have each other to lean on, during the session for *Anyone Can Whistle* (1964). By permission of Sony Music.

CHAPTER 12

Losing My Timing This Late in My Career

The Rock Scene and the Middle of the Road for Broadway

On Saturday, April 4, 1964, *Billboard* announced the jaw-dropping news that the Beatles had captured all top five slots on the Hot 100, an unprecedented and unmatched achievement in popular music history. Fans of the Broadway musical, however, might have been more intrigued by the new show opening that night at the Majestic Theatre.

Anyone Can Whistle was a contemporary satire with direction and a book by Arthur Laurents and a score by one of the bright lights of the next generation of Broadway songwriters, Stephen Sondheim. By the time *Billboard* would announce the next week's Hot 100—"Hello, Dolly!" had inched into the No. 5 spot—the scenery for *Anyone Can Whistle* was being carted away into the alley behind the Majestic Theatre; it had run only nine performances.

The show's brief run had done little to dampen Goddard Lieberson's enthusiasm for Sondheim, his work, and his promise. Lieberson had known Stephen Sondheim since the *West Side Story* cast recording, where Sondheim took over from a hors de combat Leonard Bernstein in the studio to make last-minute adjustments; they also worked together on the *Gypsy* album in 1959. Although producer Harold Prince brought Sondheim's debut show as composer and lyricist, *A Funny Thing Happened on the Way to the Forum*, to Capitol, Columbia committed to the album for Sondheim's next show in this capacity without any more than a token financial investment. *Anyone Can Whistle* was not received well by out-of-town critics, and there were rumors that it would close before it came to New York. Lieberson publicly stuck by the show.

Columbia's contract allowed for a minimum of twenty-one performances before it was obligated to record the album, but Lieberson not only committed to the recording,

Columbia put it in a very attractive K-series gatefold cover (they were probably all sitting in the Bridgeport factory anyway). Columbia took out a full-page advertisement in *Variety* and proudly announced it was taking a loss:

> It is an unhappy fact of life on Broadway that the theatre's complex economics sometimes force a show to close when too few people have had the opportunity of judging it for themselves. Columbia's Original Cast Recording of ANYONE CAN WHISTLE cannot give you everything you would have experienced if you had seen the show at the Majestic Theatre. But at the very least it allows you to hear Stephen Sondheim's lyrics and music for the Arthur Laurents book and to form your own opinion of them....
>
> We believe that the Sondheim-Laurents kind of originality and invention needs the hearing and rehearing made possible by recording.[1]

In the early 1960s, no other company in its right mind would have knowingly issued a cast album to a show that had closed before the recorded product could reach consumers; in fact, it would be decades before a major company would release an album from a show with such a comparably disastrous track record.[2] But, in addition to his loyalty, Lieberson had the vision to see that the ever-expanding boundaries of popular music would require an investment in the future, and the future of the Broadway musical was in the hands of its next generation of songwriters.

For one thing, the old guard was becoming less reliable. In 1961, Broadway wags were left speechless when, following the death of Oscar Hammerstein and the temporary dissolution of the Lerner and Loewe partnership, Alan Jay Lerner announced he was teaming up with Richard Rodgers as his next collaborator. Eventually, they would land on a new, original idea for a musical about ESP called *I Picked a Daisy*, and Lerner began his painfully slow writing process in 1962. To lose a new project by the creative geniuses behind Columbia's crown jewels—*South Pacific, My Fair Lady, The Sound of Music*, and *Camelot*—was something that Lieberson could not countenance. At what was surely considerable expense, he had Columbia's marketing department create a bound 12″ x 12″ brochure as a promotional pitch to Rodgers and Lerner (and to their respective lawyers, as well as their music publishers). The proposal—liberally illustrated with photos and sales reports of the songwriters' past successes with Columbia—offered some unprecedented enticements. They included printed sleeves advertising *I Picked a Daisy* inside every Columbia album; an exclusive nationwide radio premiere of the album; and a promise that read "We will insure that no other Original Cast album will be released for a specified time following your Broadway opening."[3]

Never in the field of cast album competition was so much spent for so few—and for so little return. On June 18, 1963, Lieberson wrote to Rodgers: "I don't have to tell you that I was terribly disappointed to learn that Irving Cohen [Lerner's lawyer] had informed us that your new show is going to Victor. We're beginning to get an inferiority complex over here. We don't think it's our recording or sales abilities. Could it be some dread unspoken social disease?"[4] As it turned out, Lieberson probably wrote more for the promotional booklet than Lerner ever wrote for Richard Rodgers. Rodgers, annoyed by Lerner's indolence, walked off the project and, within three weeks of Lieberson's letter to Rodgers, the musical was temporarily cancelled. When *I Picked a Daisy* came back to life two years later as *On a Clear Day You Can See Forever*, now with Burton Lane as composer, RCA put out the cast album, and an advertisement in *Variety* trumpeted not only the album, but *twenty-five* separate covers from the score, sung by performers ranging from Eydie Gormé to Ann-Margret and from Peter Duchin to Lawrence Welk.

In the meantime, Rodgers had taken his new score of *No Strings*—for which he contributed lyrics as well as music—to Capitol. "Mr. Rodgers never has allowed record companies to invest in his shows and he says he intends to abide by this rule; 'I wouldn't want a record company or a network telling me how a show should be produced or how I should write a song,'" he told the *New York Times*. "My selection will depend on which company will give me the best service. My company will put up the money needed for the recording. What I want is the company that will do the best musical production on the album and also the best job in promoting it in stores and with disk jockeys."[5] Rodgers apparently hoped readers would forget that the production of *Allegro*—fourteen years earlier—had been paid for, in part, by RCA.

In spring 1965, Lieberson made amends with Rodgers. Columbia underwrote a partnership between the songwriting generations, this time for the composer's only collaboration with Sondheim, *Do I Hear a Waltz?*, which, although it had a "K" designation, was the company's first non-gatefold cast album since *Camelot*; its illustrated record sleeve looked like a design for a gatefold, hastily reconceived. There was a flurry of subsequent Columbia acquisitions in the mid-1960s: *"It's a Bird…It's a Plane…It's Superman!"* (which would have made for a great gatefold, but it did have a witty back cover purporting to be an edition of the *Daily Planet*); *The Apple Tree*; *Cabaret*; *Sweet Charity*; *Mame*; and *Hallelujah, Baby!*. *Mame* went gold (which meant that it eventually made more than a million dollars, at the wholesale price, the Gold Album designation back then), and both *Mame* and *Cabaret* won Grammy Awards. RCA had two tremendous successes in mid-1960s, *Hello, Dolly!* and *Fiddler on the Roof*. The cast recording of *Fiddler* never charted very high, but its long run enabled it to go gold. Still the cast album game was a "mad scramble" as RCA's general manager, Norman Racusin, told *Billboard*—not surprising, as almost all of the companies took a bath on the anemic offerings for the 1967–68 season.[6] Still, the fight for original cast album rights was the oldest established permanent floating crap game in New York, even if the history of the recent past was not entirely encouraging. There had been some spectacular speculations that ended in total disaster: RCA Victor lost $300,000 investing in the Arlen/Mercer flop *Saratoga*; Capitol threw away $200,000 on the short-lived Schwartz/Dietz *The Gay Life*; a new entrant to the field, Warner Bros. Records, poured $200,000 down the drain on the Judy Holliday train wreck, *Hot Spot*. But one didn't have to be a neophyte to lose one's bearings; Columbia invested the full $400,000 in a Pancho Villa musical starring Robert Preston called *We Take the Town*. It never came *into* town and lost every penny. Joseph Linhart, who was appointed music director in charge of musicals for RCA, told the *New York Times* in 1961, "If you add up all the Broadway musicals, you will find many more losses than successes. The position of my company is that we don't want to invest per se. We want to sell albums. But the competitive bidding for albums has forced us to invest."[7]

Such common sense didn't seem to penetrate the boardrooms of the major recording companies—it's as if some of them just couldn't *wait* to lose money. In June 1963, ABC-Paramount formed a $1 million partnership with Jule Styne to invest in three shows; only one of the initial offerings even made it into rehearsal—*A Girl to Remember,* which became *Fade Out-Fade In*, starring Carol Burnett—and that went down in flames. Three years later, RCA threw its lot in with producer David Merrick, investing an undisclosed amount—rumored at $1.5 million—for exclusive first rights to a half dozen upcoming Merrick shows; the only one of the announced shows actually to open was *I Do! I Do!* (the rest of the investment was eventually put into some other shows—*The Happy Time*, for example—that did open on Broadway). MGM Records started to get into the Broadway scene in earnest. It made a lot of money on Merrick's *Carnival!*, which was based on one of its films, *Lili* (it was actually the No. 1 album in the country for one week). MGM committed to a two-disk recording of Bock and Harnick's valentine *She Loves Me*—no company had recorded a multi-disk package since *The Most Happy Fella* seven years earlier. It was a handsomely produced set, but not a huge seller. MGM followed that up with what was reported as a "substantial" contribution to the 1965 Sherlock Holmes musical, *Baker Street,* which lost buckets of money. Again, it was a handsome package—a gatefold with a lot of color photographs on the back cover—but the recording itself was ineptly produced. It had no tension, no mystery, no narrative arc—it just ended with a second-rate, irrelevant, chorus number. Had Goddard Lieberson been in the control booth, listeners could have heard Sherlock Holmes turning upstage and walking "off into the London fog as the curtain falls" at the end of the record, just the way that Harold Prince staged the production.

But by then, Lieberson himself had moved out of the "mad scramble;" he was giving some of the cast album producing duties to associates in the Columbia ranks, including a young classically trained musician named Thomas Z. Shepard, who had joined Columbia in 1960 as an associate producer. Shepard assisted on several of the in-house recordings of popular scores in the 1960s and, in 1964, he produced the album for *Bajour*, a terrible show, remarkable only for being the last K-series gatefold from the label for years (although the "K" designation would continue for other, flatter, less elaborate and glamorous cast albums). In June 1966, Lieberson was promoted, as part of an alignment in the CBS corporate structure, to president of the CBS-Columbia Group, a new unit of the Columbia Broadcasting System, dedicated to diversifying into other music formats. He chose Clive Davis, former general counsel and general manager of Columbia, to take over his post at Columbia Records. Davis had his eye more on the contemporary music of the time and, in his own somewhat aggressive manner, acquired rock acts for Columbia—Janis Joplin, Laura Nyro, Santana, Blood, Sweat & Tears—with the kind of enthusiasm that Lieberson exhibited for a more, shall we say, serene musical idiom. Within a few years, Davis made rock music the most dominant and profitable unit at the company, turning Columbia into a contemporary music juggernaut.[8]

Davis wasn't the only executive straying from safe mainstream territory; there was an increasing contingent of record companies going Off-Broadway for their product. In the 1950s, MGM had done extremely well with an Off-Broadway revival of *The Threepenny Opera* (translated by Marc Blitzstein), which ran for six years and brought the score back to the public (inspiring, among other renditions, the Bobby Darin cut of "Mack the Knife" that held the No. 1 spot on the Top 10 for nine weeks); the label's recording of *You're a Good Man, Charlie Brown* in 1967 would become a perennial. In October that year, RCA traveled south of 14th Street to sign up the first production done at Joseph Papp's New York Shakespeare Festival's Public Theatre at Astor Place: a non-linear, self-stylized "American Tribal Love-Rock Musical" called *Hair*.

Hair was a rare out-of-the box project for RCA, which—despite its ground-breaking promotion of Elvis Presley—wasn't particularly hip with the rock scene in the late 1960s. *Hair*'s score, with music by Galt MacDermot and lyrics by Gerome Ragni and James Rado, wasn't rock per se, but rather an inventive—and a dramatically appropriate—mixture of funk, folk, rhythm and blues, ragas, girl groups, and rock and roll. The Off-Broadway album, although it had one of the most unattractive covers ever for a musical (a collage of Native Americans and the authors, on a pale fuchsia background), caught the attention of folks who wanted to expand their horizons. *Variety* said the album was "promoted by the nation's 'underground' press which is read by the hippies and the intellectuals."[9]

It was by no means an inevitability that *Hair* would transfer to a larger venue, but, after a brief stop at a discotheque, a revised production opened on Broadway at the Biltmore Theatre at the end of April 1968. RCA was contractually obligated to record the score again if the production moved uptown; that proved provident, as the score was in better shape (with the addition of some teeth-rattling numbers, such as "Hashish," "Sodomy" and "Colored Spade") and was performed by singers who had a better grasp of the rock idiom. Before the Broadway album was released in late May 1968, it caused some concern for RCA because of the rough nature of some of the lyrics, but the company swallowed hard and decided not to tamper with or bowdlerize the score. It was a good decision. As *Variety* wrote, "The distance between 'Bye Bye Birdie' and this Off-Broadway musical tells how far to the end of the limb the pop musical has traveled in the in the last few years. The lyrics would have been unthinkable a few years ago, but nobody today even raises an eyebrow." One of the unintended consequences of those cutting-edge lyrics was that certain songs from the album weren't getting much play on AM radio, to the songwriters' dismay.[10]

The reticence from broadcasters was silly; the resistance was futile. It took most of the summer for *Hair*'s cast album to hit the charts (it debuted on August 3 at No. 159; the cast album to *Camelot* was at No. 143, seven and a half years after *its* debut), but it began a relentless, inexorable climb. The scabrous and racially charged lyrics didn't damage the album's appeal at all, of course, and its largely upbeat conglomeration of pop chart styles sat well with the changing demographics of the listening population. In a 2007 piece in the *New York Times*, tagged to a Broadway revival, Charles Isherwood wrote: "A decade before, every household with pretensions to any sophistication had to have the original-cast album of 'My Fair Lady.' The cast album of 'Hair' was similarly a must-have for the middle classes. I grew up in a non-show-tune-loving household, but even we had the album of 'Hair.' "[11]

The score to *Hair* would eventually spawn all the singles business that any songwriter could possibly want, from the sublime—Nina Simone singing "I Ain't Got No"—to the ridiculous—The Four Lads covering "Where Do I Go?." Major hits came from Three Dog Night's rendition of "Easy to Be Hard" (peaking at No. 5); Oliver's "Good Morning Starshine" (peaking at No. 3); and "Hair," covered by the bubble-gum group The Cowsills (peaking at No. 2). The week the Cowsills reached second place, the No. 1 song on the Hot 100 was the Fifth Dimension's tight-harmony medley of "Aquarius/Let the Sunshine In (The Flesh Failures)"—it stayed at No. 1 for six weeks during the summer of 1969. The cast album itself, on RCA, stayed at No. 1 on the Top LPs charts for thirteen weeks in the middle of 1969 (and for several weeks, the Fifth Dimension's album *The Age of Aquarius* was the second most popular album in the country). By fall 1969, the score to *Hair* had achieved a ubiquity, in terms of the mixture of singles hits and original cast album appeal, not seen in mainstream popular music since the score to *Annie Get Your Gun* in 1946—and in many ways surpassed it.

▶ Audio Example 12.1, "Ain't Got No—I Got Life" (Nina Simone)

It would be a mistake, however, to assert that the transition from mainstream pop music to rock-oriented music happened overnight in the summer of 1969. What occurred, throughout the late 1960s was a kind of porosity that allowed all sorts of music to flow up and down the LP charts. Certainly, the Beatles' albums always rose to the top when they were released, as did albums from The Monkees, The Rolling Stones, The Doors, Led Zeppelin, Simon and Garfunkel, Big Brother and the Holding Company, Creedence Clearwater Revival, Jimi Hendrix, Joe Cocker, and other (increasingly) hardcore rockers. But, they coexisted with the soundtracks to *The Sound of Music, Dr. Zhivago,* and *Romeo and Juliet,* and with the Supremes, Glen Campbell, Herb Alpert, Andy Williams, Johnny Cash, and Tom Jones. Members of the former and latter camp might pass each other on the way up and down the charts all the time. In the absence of prognosticators of the rock scene (who read the entrails with a more nuanced knowledge), one might date the transition to the week of April 4, 1970, when *Tom Jones Live in Las Vegas* dropped out of the Top 10 Album chart, leaving the remaining ten albums exclusively composed of rock group performers for the first time. The debut of the *Woodstock* soundtrack album in June of that year solidified the transition to rock on the Top 10 charts—although occasionally the Carpenters or the Partridge Family would peep through.

But one thing was certainly true: when the original Broadway cast album of *Hair* slipped off the charts at the end of the week of October 25, 1969, it would mean the last time any cast album would ever appear in the Top 10 for the next five decades.

The new mad scramble would be for Broadway to access some of that popular sound. Clive Barnes would frequently use his bully pulpit as chief drama critic of the *New York Times* to beseech Broadway producers to induce major pop and rock composers such as Lennon and McCartney, or Simon and Garfunkel, or Bob Dylan, to write a new Broadway musical. "Pick up a transistor radio and twirl it at random. The sounds you are likely to hear will not be like 'Henry, Sweet Henry' or 'How Now, Dow Jones.'... It is obvious, I think, that we are slowly, and gingerly, approaching a crisis on the musical."[12] The board of directors at RCA supposedly told the A&R folks to "get with it."

One of the first people to "get with it" in a serious fashion was, unpredictably, David Merrick, who was traditionally more comfortable being a hidebound curmudgeon. But it was Merrick who reached out to the most successful non-performing songwriters in pop music in the 1960s, Burt Bacharach and Hal David. The songwriters of *Hair* were complete unknowns, but Bacharach and David had a string of international hits in their arsenal when Merrick signed them to adapt Billy Wilder's film *The Apartment* to the Broadway stage as *Promises, Promises*. The material was perfect for their contemporary sensibilities—urban, witty, rueful, alienated but passionate—and, when the show opened in December 1968, they turned in a score that sounded like nothing before it. Bacharach, who used all the elements of the recording studio as part of his compositional palette, brought in record producer Phil Ramone to redesign the sound system of the theater. The players in the orchestra pit were grouped by section into four separate clusters, each surrounding a microphone that would relay the sound to a console in the back of the theater where it would be mixed live (a shocking idea, at the time). There was also a quartet of female singers in the pit to add non-verbal ambient sound. The technical innovations apparently unnerved Merrick: he admonished Ramone and Bacharach by saying, "I don't want the audience walking out of the theater saying, 'It's a recording.'"[13]

The resulting cast album, alas, was not the kind of recording that had listeners walking out and saying, "It's the theater," either. Although the tunes themselves were terrific and suited the material perfectly, the cast album itself—from United Artists, who owned the rights to the original film and backed the show to the tune of $600,000—doesn't quite convey the show's excitement or its huge commercial success (it was an ugly album, too, with no photos of the show). The cast album itself performed miserably—never getting higher that No. 95—on the Top LPs charts, bested by a country mile by *Hair*.

Far better for Bacharach and David was the singles activity for two of the songs from the show; their blockbuster vocal muse, Dionne Warwick, had a hit song with the title number, which came out before the show opened, charting as high as No. 7 on the Adult Contemporary chart. During the Boston tryouts of *Promises, Promises*, there arose a need for a duet between the two leads—something charming and low-key. Bacharach and David came up with "I'll Never Fall in Love Again," which, because of the late date, was orchestrated simply, mostly with guitar. It became the hit of the production, but because of its late addition, it couldn't really be covered until the show opened; another kind of unintended consequence that drives music publishers crazy. Singers of all stripes made up for lost time; "I'll Never Fall in Love Again" was covered by Ella Fitzgerald and by the country singer Bobbie Gentry, who had a No. 1 hit in the UK. Both Johnny Mathis and Bacharach (with an instrumental) had versions that made it to the Adult Contemporary chart, but Warwick had a huge smash with it on the same chart, hitting No. 1 for three weeks in the beginning of 1970; in fact, of all the astonishing songs she recorded in the 1960s, "I'll Never Fall in Love Again" was the only No. 1 hit she ever had. It would also be the very last song to originate on Broadway to reach No. 1 on any of the *Billboard* singles charts.

▶   Audio Example 12.2, "I'll Never Fall in Love Again" (Dionne Warwick)

The "new sound" quest wasn't over by a long shot. In a front-page interview for *Billboard* on February 22, 1971, Alan Jay Lerner drew some battle lines: "The original Broadway cast album will come back into its own as a highly marketable property within the next two years because music of the theater is better than anything else.... In the 1920s, the theater dictated, in a sense, the style of music of the country and the world, but nowadays it's no longer true.... The gap [between music theater and rock] is going to be closed because a man today, a contemporary composer who has his own voice, writes for the musical theater."[14]

If this were just abstract thinking, Lerner's interview might be dismissible fulmination, but he had an actual contemporary composer in mind. John Barry had come by "his own voice" honestly. Born in York, England, in 1933, Barry was equally influenced by classical piano, film scores of the 1940s, and the sounds of the American big bands. In the early 1950s, he formed his own jazz combo, the John Barry Seven, and began scoring films. This led to a phone call from the producers of a spy picture entitled *Dr. No*—they needed someone to arrange and complete parts of the soundtrack. John Barry's ongoing assignment with the James Bond series became one of the most exciting and enduring relationships in film music of the 1960s. He expanded his reach in the mid-1960s to write the soundtrack (and title song) to *Born Free*, as well as a short-lived West End musical entitled *Passion Flower Hotel*. When Lerner reached out to Barry to compose his latest project, he was bringing on board a three-time Academy Award winner, experienced in film, theater, and pop music.

What Lerner brought Barry *into* was another story entirely. Never one to shy away from adaptations of challenging material, Lerner acquired the musical rights to Vladimir Nabokov's provocative 1955 novel, *Lolita*. The notion of a European pedophile—no matter how cultivated—preying on a prepubescent American girl as the subject for a musical was certainly open to question, but hadn't Lerner worked miracles on Bernard Shaw? In this case, the ace up his sleeve was Barry, who could bring a contemporary sensibility to the show (the story would be updated to the 1970s). Barry employed various technological advances in the pit: a Moog synthesizer, a Duovox amplifier, and an electric accordion. Lieberson had a lot of faith in Barry's talent; he, too, thought Barry was the Next Great Thing and Columbia had made heaps of money with Andy Williams's rendition of the *Born Free* title theme. Columbia made an investment of $400,000 for the cast recording of the new show, now called *Lolita, My Love*, which was headed for a Broadway opening at the end of March 1971. Barry completed his task artfully; it was he who did most of the heavy lifting to make the show feel contemporary, as some of Lerner's lyrics strained to sound "with it." As a sign of optimism for the project, Robert Goulet cut a single of Humbert Humbert's rueful ballad of lost youth, "In the Broken Promise Land of Fifteen," and Shirley Bassey—who burnished Barry's "Goldfinger" into a pop legend—recorded a song from the show, a lament about the way of the world called "Going, Going, Gone."

Going, going, gone, indeed. *Lolita, My Love* had a horrendous tryout in Philadelphia in the early spring; the director and its eponymous nymphet were fired; and it went back into rehearsal for its Boston tryout. Thomas Z. Shepard, who had, more or less, inherited Lieberson's mantle of resident cast album producer for most of Columbia's cast albums of the late 1960s and early 1970s (*1776, The Rothschilds*), took the train to Boston with some of his Columbia colleagues in late March: "Goddard caught the show in Philadelphia. He said, 'This thing looks like a Krafft-Ebing spectacular.' Still, it was a nice score. But, when we [*sans* Lieberson] saw the show in Boston, we knew right away it just didn't play—and not just because it was a Boston audience. So, whatever our out clause was, we exercised it. It's terrible thing to have to do—unless you hate the guts of the person who wrote the show."[15]

►   Audio Example 12.3, "How Far Is It to the Next Town?" (*Lolita, My Love* demo)

Lolita, My Love closed out of town, following its Boston engagement, never to be seen again. The Columbia cast album joined that increasingly busy graveyard in the 1960s and 70s of cast albums ebulliently announced in *Playbill* or *Variety* that never got recorded, including *Nowhere to Go But Up* (Columbia); *Sherry!* (RCA); and *Gantry* (also RCA). At least *Anyone Can Whistle* had opened on Broadway; the idea of recording a show that had already *closed* would have been seen a sign of madness in the high-stakes world of studio costs and album sales.

It's amusing to see such arduous pursuits within the recording industry attempting to discover a new sound for Broadway when it had been staring it in the face all along. Stephen Sondheim's *Company* had all the attributes that the record companies were looking for: it was vibrant, contemporary, urban, and engagingly discordant (it shared an orchestrator with *Promises, Promises*, the gifted Jonathan Tunick, who also placed a female chorus in the orchestra for *Company*). Perhaps it was too mature for the adolescent and college market, but its rock-inflected score, with its infusions of soaring ballads and Latin rhythms, perfectly mirrored the pop music charts pivoting between the end of the 1960s and the beginning of the 1970s.

The cast album of *Company*, recorded at Columbia's 30th Street studios on May 3, 1970, achieved its own kind of immortality, as the first cast album recording session to be committed to documentary form, courtesy of filmmaker director D. A. Pennebaker. The documentary was supposed to be the first of a series—incredible as it seems from today's perspective—on primetime television, devoted to the recording of Broadway cast albums. Although it was the only "episode" that remains, the *Original Cast Album: Company* documentary is one of the most cherished artifacts of life backstage in the real world of the theater.[16] For most viewers whose hearts are not made of stone, the most affecting section is Elaine Stritch's climactic and excruciating peripeteia while attempting to perform "The Ladies Who Lunch" correctly. The sheer pressure of the recording situation—almost always done at that point from 10 a.m. to 1 a.m. on the Sunday after the show's opening, with appropriate and carefully monitored union breaks for the orchestra—comes through when Susan Browning, a supporting actress featured in two important numbers from the show, turns to the camera with the terrifying realization that "this is the one shot we get. This one is *forever.*"

The producer for this recording session was Thomas Shepard, who had a chance not only to put his own stamp on the label's cast album repertoire, but to employ his own brand of recording techniques: "Some people just record the songs, but I've always liked the connective tissue. An album should convey the dramatic thrust of the show in addition to being just a listening experience. Are you making the recording as a souvenir for somebody who's seen the show, or are you making it as a standalone? I'm the standalone guy."[17] Shepard's predilections revealed a kind of signature, certainly one that violated some of Lieberson's long-held tenets. Shepard would add more dialogue than Lieberson would ever have dreamed possible—before, during, and after songs (the insertion of dialogue into the middle of a song was often truer to the original intent of the songwriters). He could masterfully manipulate the left-to-right and back-to-front dynamics of the stereo recording, as in the overture to the *1776* album, when Shepard had the fife-and-drum band sound as if it appeared from the distance and marched away at the end—something the house orchestra at the 46th Street Theatre couldn't quite accomplish. The cast album to *Company* allowed him to add his cherished sound effects: karate kicks and body thumps in "The Little Things You Do Together," and tap-dancing in "Side by Side by Side."

▶ Audio Example 12.4, "The Little Things You Do Together" (*Company* original cast)

The *Company* album won the 1971 Grammy Award for Best Score from an Original Cast Show Album; there were some concomitant issues when the original lead, Dean Jones, left the show early in its run; he was replaced by Larry Kert, who was brought into the studio to rerecord some of the tracks for subsequent release on the CBS pressing of the score for the UK. Sondheim and *Company*'s director Harold Prince followed up *Company* with *Follies,* which opened almost a year later (it was trying out in Boston at the same time as *Lolita, My Love*). *Follies* was an opulent, acid-tinged, memento mori, with a massively complex score, filled with artful pastiches of songs of the 1920s, 30s, and 40s, while contrasting them with the more emotionally scabrous musical numbers set in the present. It was one of the most ambitious scores ever attempted in a musical, but the eventual cast recording has long been considered one of Broadway's great heartbreaking disappointments.

The shadow that stretched over the cast album of *Follies* was a film directed by Harold Prince called *Something for Everyone*. Released three months after *Company* opened, *Something for Everyone*—set in Austria, and starring Angela Lansbury—attempted to be an elegant sex farce, but was met with overwhelming indifference by audiences and flopped. The film was produced by Cinema Center Films, a subsidiary of CBS, and one of the many new media units overseen by Goddard Lieberson, subsequent to his promotion. "Hal was sore at CBS," Lieberson was quoted as saying in the 1988 book, *Sondheim & Co.*, "[He] didn't like the way we handled [promotion] for the movie, so he wouldn't allow us to record *Follies*."[18]

The cast album to *Follies* went instead to Capitol Records. It was a pointed reminder of how little power the creative talent of a musical has when a score is recorded by a commercial company subject to deals between producers and music publishers. Composer John Kander said, "The issue of what company recorded an album was primarily a matter taken care of between the publisher and the producer. I don't ever remember anybody coming to me or Fred [Ebb] and saying, 'Well, it's up to you guys.'" Lyricist Sheldon Harnick left the decisions about the recording of his songs to his publisher, Tommy Valando. Valando, head of Tommy Valando Music Publishing, arrived on the scene as a promoter and one-time partner of Perry Como in the 1950s, and grew his stable by embracing the new generation of Broadway songwriters—Bock and Harnick, Kander and Ebb, Sondheim—and bringing them into the BMI fold. "I hoped that Tommy would be able to get albums, I was absolutely tickled any time we did get an album," said Harnick. "It was always kind of a miracle to me. I was delighted when he did, but not surprised when he didn't."[19] Harnick's second and third scores with Jerry Bock—*Fiorello!* and *Tenderloin*, both produced by Harold Prince as the 1960s began—had been recorded by Capitol.

Capitol had a long history—dating back to *St. Louis Woman*—of getting involved with Broadway cast albums in sharp bursts, and then losing interest. *The Music Man* had been a tremendous hit for the label—staying at No. 1 for twelve weeks—and had floated the company financially for some years. Capitol could often be relied upon to create a well-conceived album with a nice, full-grained, theatrical sound such as *The Unsinkable Molly Brown* or *Golden Boy*. After two flops in the mid-1960s, both written by Sammy Cahn and Jimmy Van Heusen (*Skyscraper* and *Walking Happy*), Capitol pretty much took a series of beatings on shows that never returned on its investment—including Hal Prince's thrilling production of *Zorbà*—and it must have made the executives at Capitol wary.

The ambivalence at Capitol was thrust upon the shoulders of the album's producer, Richard Jones. According to *Everything Was Possible*, Ted Chapin's detailed account of the making of *Follies*, "[Dick Jones] felt the show deserved and needed two discs, but the company was adamantly opposed to it.....all the departments at Capitol felt that a two-disc set would cut into the sales potential enormously, although they were more than happy to squeeze as much *Follies* onto one LP as possible. In the end, Dick Jones lost the fight."[20] According to Chapin, producer Jones fought with Capitol until six days before the recording date of the album, which was scheduled for a one-day session in a rented ballroom at the Manhattan Center, near Penn Station. The final decision to produce only one LP intensified the already stressful situation of recording *Follies*—or any cast album. As Kander states, "It was always the first thing you talked about when recording the cast album: How many minutes can we have and where would the cuts come? It was always very frustrating."[21]

Particularly frustrating in this case was that practically every song required some sort of internal cut or alteration, which meant the changes had to be decided, typed up, and learned within days, if not hours. Important songs were recorded then cut from the final album—the faded operetta pastiche "One More Kiss," for example—and the session had a great deal of inexplicable technical problems as well. The complexity of *Follies* would have taxed the imagination and skill of a producer with *two* LPs at his disposal, but with only 50 minutes to work with, the final result was an insufficient record—in every sense of the word. "If you didn't see the show, you would have no idea what it was about," said Shepard.[22] Prince responded, "Of course, I realize how egregious a decision it was because the cast album for *Follies* only presents a portion of the score and, obviously, I regret that."[3] Stephen Sondheim was apparently never pleased with the decision; he responded to a congratulatory opening night telegram from Lieberson by thanking him, then tersely lamenting that Columbia should have been recording *Follies*.[24]

As Chapin put it, "To add insult to injury, the show that beat out *Follies* for the Tony in the Best Musical category, *Two Gentlemen of Verona*, had a two-LP cast album, albeit on a smaller label [ABC Records]."[25] But, in spring 1971, if one were looking for a powerful two-LP set of highly charged theatrical music in a narrative context—*plus* a score that would appeal to young people—one only had to look across the record racks at Sam Goody's to find something extraordinary that had arrived from across the pond via Decca Records: the two-LP rock opera "concept" recording of Andrew Lloyd Webber and Tim Rice's *Jesus Christ Superstar*.

Originally planned as a stage production, *Jesus Christ Superstar* was based on the final days of Jesus Christ, as seen from the perspective of Judas. The rock opera's creators, Lloyd Webber and Rice, turned to the recording studio to create one of the most ambitious demos in music history—more than sixty musicians and singers—produced by two British unknowns in their early twenties (Lloyd Webber played the piano and the Moog on the original concept album). Decca Records in the United States realized it had a potential bonanza—if it could get around the perception of sacrilege from offended consumers; before the albums were completed, the company released a trial balloon in the form of a 45 single at the end of 1969, entitled merely "Superstar" (taking no chances) with Murray Head delivering the vocals.

Having seen the single make a brief but significant impression on the U.S. Hot 100 without having its headquarters burned to the ground, Decca moved to have the two-album set released in the United States in late 1970. Demonstrating that packaging is, if not everything, certainly *something*, Decca wisely jettisoned the British cover to the concept album produced by its U.K. affiliate MCA—it looked like scrambled eggs dropped onto a lava lamp—and substituted it with a rich, walnut-toned, boxed set (with printed libretto), embossed by a Gemini of sleek, gilded angels, designed by graphic artist Ernie Cefalu. It was the magic touch: the two-LP set of *Jesus Christ Superstar* was released right before Thanksgiving 1970 and eventually went to the No. 1 spot on the charts one week after *Follies* opened. The concept album stayed at the top for three weeks and remained on the charts for 101 weeks. As one writer put it succinctly: *"Jesus Christ Superstar* seemed to pick up where the Who's *Tommy* (also a Decca release) and *Hair* had left off.... Teenagers who didn't know from Jesus, opera, or oratorios liked the beat, the hard rock sounds, and the singing and bought the album, as did parents who felt that the record offered a chance to understand some aspects of this youth culture around them, and especially its music."[26]

The commercial success of *Jesus Christ Superstar* led inevitably to a stage production, which debuted on Broadway eleven months after the U.S. release of the album. The production did well enough—running 711 performances—but its original cast album (also on Decca), with the score condensed to one LP, did far less business, only reaching as high as No. 31. In the meantime, the Adult Contemporary charts had two hit records from the score, both of "I Don't Know How to Love Him." Yvonne Elliman (from the concept album) had a version that reached No. 15, while Helen Reddy's rendition went as high as No. 7. On the Hot 100 charts, it reached the rank of No. 13—a lucky 13, as it turns out; it would be the highest rank a song derived from a musical theater piece would ever achieve on the Hot 100 charts to date.

It was quite a paradox, especially when *Follies* earned seven Tony Awards at the 1972 Tony Awards and *Jesus Christ Superstar* won none; *Jesus Christ Superstar* was a smash as a two-album set, while the ostensibly less expensive one-LP versions of *Follies* and the Broadway *Superstar* did poor to middling business in record stores.

The commercial failure of *Follies* on Broadway had made it difficult for Prince to get investors for his next venture with Sondheim—the anxious operetta *A Little Night Music*—so an infusion of cash from a record company would be invaluable. When it came time toward the end of 1972 for Sondheim and Prince to audition the score at Columbia, their first stop, the changes in the music industry were palpable. By this point, Sondheim's biggest fan, Goddard Lieberson, was high up in the corporate structure of CBS and the task of adjudicating cast albums had fallen to Clive Davis. According to Prince: "Steve and I auditioned *A Little Night Music* for Davis and a room full of executives. He would play the songs and I would briefly describe the plot. And there was almost no interest. And, by about the third number, Clive Davis's secretary came in and whispered something to Clive and he stepped out of the room. Over the next several songs, this happened with all the other executives and, by the end of the presentation, Steve and I were presenting the show to a room full of mailroom workers."[27] A few days later, Tom Shepard was dispatched to inform Prince that Columbia was going to "pass on this one," though he himself had admired the music greatly.

A Little Night Music ventured on to its Boston tryout at the end of January 1973; it still hadn't procured a record contract. A staff producer, Charles Burr, was sent to Boston to report back to Columbia. His report admires the genius of the score, but concludes that "as an original cast album, it offers relatively little beyond prestige. No hit tunes and so no great sale.... I don't see it as a good risk either as an investment or a show from which we could break even one single."[28] A few weeks later, *A Little Night Music* opened in New York—*still* without a commitment from any company to record an album. The critics were rapturous: "heady, civilized, sophisticated and enchanting," wrote Clive Barnes in the *New York Times*. It sounded like just the kind of show that Goddard Lieberson would love.

Apparently, he did; "I previewed the show and fell madly in love with it," he told the press, "it seems like a traditional show, but it isn't."[29] "Goddard pressured Columbia into doing it," in Prince's words. The month of March 1973 was a period of high vulnerability for Clive Davis; he and some members of his staff were being investigated internally for possible misuse of funds and padding expense accounts. Lieberson used that moment to grab back the reins of a property he highly valued (Lieberson would take over, temporarily, as head of CBS Records when Davis was fired in May). In fact, Lieberson announced not only that Columbia was going to acquire *A Little Night Music*, but that he would produce the album himself—the first time he would do so since 1966. A Columbia executive told a reporter, "He's the highest placed executive in the entertainment world to take on the chore of producing a show disc."[30] On Sunday, March 18, the company of *A Little Night Music* assembled at Studio C on East 30th Street to record the score under the supervision of Lieberson. "The recording of the musical would have been an event anyway, but with Goddard as producer," said Shepard at the time, "there was more electricity in the air."[31]

The cast album for *A Little Night Music* was released to the market by the end of March. A "K" designation with a gatefold—with charming black and white photos—it also contained a 12″ x 12″ insert, with all of the delectable lyrics—the first time complete lyrics had been in a Broadway cast album in decades (perhaps it had been inspired by the *Jesus Christ Superstar* insert). Prince wrote to Lieberson, thanking him for the work on the album, referring, in passing, to the disappointing initial audition for Davis, "But I figure 'Goddard's Album' will make it different for us."[32] What remained was to see how this classy package would be received by consumers in spring 1973, when "Love Train" and "Tie a Yellow Ribbon 'Round the Old Oak Tree" were dominating the pop charts.

The days in which a music publisher such as Max Dreyfus had the power to weigh in on million-dollar decisions had vanished with the 1960s, but, still, Tommy Valando's brief, of course, was to wrangle as many commercial recordings of his client Sondheim's work as possible. Soon after the release of the *A Little Night Music* cast album, he besieged the A&R departments at Columbia for increased singles opportunity for the score. The responses from Columbia's staff reflect, rather illuminatingly, the situation in American popular music, more than the (considerable) quality of Sondheim's music. Lieberson wrote to Shepard, "What do you think the possibilities are of getting an instrumental version on NIGHT MUSIC? If this were only the old days, LITTLE NIGHT MUSIC would be a perfect show for that purpose." Shepard suggested, somewhat wearily, that they might try to interest André Previn and the London Philharmonic, or even pops arranger and pianist Peter Nero, who had a big instrumental hit for Columbia with the theme to *Summer of '42*.[33] Kip Cohen, an A&R man with a background in progressive rock who had been hired by Davis, regretfully concurred in an internal memo to Lieberson (the "MOR" he refers to stands for "Middle of the Road," a contemporary classification for Easy Listening): "I feel that a well-made MOR recording of any of the songs will do nothing whatsoever to generate album sales, publishing income, or show attendance (e.g., the Sarah Vaughan version). Unlike the 'old days,' we cannot force any artist to cover a Broadway tune."[34]

This was a brilliant assessment of the state of popular music—or, rather, of a signal moment when Broadway and Main Street veered in opposite directions. One of the casualties at the crossroads would be what David Dachs called a "quiet hit," referring to Broadway show tunes such as "I Believe in You" or "Once Upon a Time" that had a dogged longevity rather than massive exposure: "Besides large individual song successes, there have been countless 'quiet hits.' These are musical theater compositions which often do not reach the teen-oriented hallowed best-selling charts in flamboyant rocket-like fashion. Yet, they are recorded, rerecorded, and heard on AM and FM, and in the better night-clubs. They make money on performances on radio and TV. There are dozens of these unspectacular money-making hits."[35]

Cohen's memo concluded on one vaguely optimistic note: "[It] seems that only 'Send in the Clowns' even leans toward a commercial Top 40 single market. Here it should be noted that I personally forwarded acetates of the song to Liza Minnelli, Barbra Streisand

and Carol Burnett long before the cast album was released. Needless to say, there is no way to compel them to cut the record, and I am not certain that it would even be in their best interests to do so."

About the same time as this internal discussion at Columbia, a delivery person arrived with a thick envelope at the poolside of Frank Sinatra's desert home in Palm Springs; it contained the music for "Send in the Clowns." Sinatra expert Charles Granata revealed that "Frank was extremely enthusiastic about it. He went on to a poolside guest for a few minutes about how he loved this song, and the message, and Sinatra told his guest, 'You really have to read into what is being said here. I'm going into the studio and I'm going to record it.'"[36]

Sinatra was in the middle of a brief, self-imposed retirement, but he went into the recording studio in late spring 1973 to record a new LP, *Ol' Blue Eyes Is Back*. With an overly soupy arrangement by Gordon Jenkins, Sinatra recorded "Send in the Clowns" in June, only three months after the debut of the song of Broadway; he put his rendition on the album and also released it as a Reprise single. He performed it at his comeback concert, "The Main Event," at Madison Square Garden, the following October and kept it in his repertoire. Cabaret singer Bobby Short also included "Send in the Clowns" in his act around the same time. Without the usual machinery of 1960s song promotion, it took a while for the song to reach a wider public. In 1975, the plaintive folk/pop singer Judy Collins recorded the song

Traditions were crumbling by the end of the 1960s; here is the full cast and orchestra for *Fiddler on the Roof* (1964), assembled at RCA's go-to recording space, Webster Hall. By permission from Sony Music.

for her album *Judith* and released a single on Elektra; this version made it as high as No. 8 on the Adult Contemporary chart. It also hit the Hot 100, but only went as high as No. 36. However, "the charts turned over very quickly, beginning in the early 1970s," said Keith Caulfield, *Billboard*'s current co-director of charts, "'Send in the Clowns' didn't chart very high, but it stuck around for almost thirty weeks—half a year. That was significant then, that

Frank Sinatra showcased "Send in the Clowns" in his live New York concerts throughout 1974, while *A Little Night Music* was still running on Broadway. Credit: Photofest.

was a big deal."[37] By 1976, the song had become ubiquitous enough to be named "Song of the Year" at the Grammys—three years after its Broadway debut.

Sinatra continued to sing "Send in the Clowns" in concert, evolving it into something else, something deeper, as he tended to do with songs he reprised in the November of his years, depending on his mood and perspective. Sinatra eventually got rid of the over-determinate Jenkins arrangements; he would frequently pull forward either Tony Mottola or Al Viola on guitar, or just pianist Bill Miller, and perform it as an intimate duet. It had become the perfect song for him to connect with audiences in the 1970s and 80s, who had followed him this late in his career.

Indeed, Sinatra's respect for the songwriter—in this case, Hammerstein's protégé, Sondheim—gave him liberty to share some of his thoughts about the song and the writer with his audience. Typically, as he performed the song into the 1990s, he would preface it with some version or other of the following:

> There's been a show running—it opened about a year ago, *A Little Night Music*, and it's a winner. This is a very beautiful song, and it's poignant and it's sad. It tells the story of two adult people who've been together and one of them gets restless and moves on. Whether it's the man or woman who left is unimportant. It's a break-up. And it's a lovely marriage of words and music by Stephen Sondheim.

It's unlikely Sinatra ever made it to the Shubert Theatre in New York to see *A Little Night Music* and, even if he had, he would have had no interest in recounting the plot about a wistful actress and a buttoned-up lawyer rekindling their love affair in turn-of-the-century Scandinavia. His intro told audiences not to worry about "farce" and "clowns"—that was "unimportant." What counted was the sentiment, which was universal. And he'd frequently conclude with a coda, when the rueful ballad had run its course:

> Isn't it rich?
> Isn't it queer?
> Losing my timing this late in my career.
> And where are the clowns?
> There ought to be clowns
> Well, maybe next year....

▶ Audio Example 12.5, "Send in the Clowns" (Frank Sinatra)

"Isn't that a glorious song—a marvelous song?" Sinatra added. "And it's such a breeze of delight that has come through the music business to get a song like that every once in a while, as opposed to the acid rock 24-hours-a-day."

Stephen Sondheim (l.), producer Thomas Z. Shepard, and Bernadette Peters connecting the dots on RCA's recording of *Sunday in the Park with George* (1983). By permission of Sony Music.

CHAPTER 13

"You Never Seen a Show Like This Before!"

Compact Discs and the Digitization of Broadway

On Wednesday, May 25, 1977, a science fiction film opened for Memorial Day weekend—something called *Star Wars*—but the curiosity of show tune fans might have been piqued by a short article that appeared in that morning's *Variety*. Whereas movie fans might be looking to the future that day—in a galaxy far, far, away—the recording industry was investigating the commercial potential of the past.

Variety's article concerned the back catalog of out-of-print cast albums: "Many out-of-print Broadway show albums, some selling at $75 or more in stores dealing in such rarities, are being reissued, a bonanza for show buffs and a possible source of coin for such diskeries as RCA, Capitol, and Columbia." Among the titles that had been recently restored to the sales catalog from which they vanished long ago were *Anyone Can Whistle*, *Golden Boy*, and *Call Me Madam*, occasionally in revised packaging with revamped liner notes. Thomas Shepard, then working as a producer at RCA, was quoted as saying, "it was too early to determine which...shows had the most appeal, whether familiar oldies or more esoteric material." The headline read: "Diskeries Mine Legiter Lode; As Cutouts Return to Catalog, Labels Could Make Lotsa Coin."[1]

The idea that an old cast album of a show no longer running could actually mint gold from a mother lode would have been met with incredulity by record executives a decade earlier; however, beginning in the mid-1970s, a new evolution in technology would once again upend the record industry and reframe the narrative experience of a recorded musical—living or dead—for a home audience. The advent of compact discs would have its greatest impact on the duration of a given recording, completely altering how Broadway scores—and what kind of score—could now be recorded. The duration of a cast recording had, of course, bedeviled producers since the very beginning, certainly since Jack Kapp had to add a second volume to cover *Oklahoma!*'s score, but the new technology raised an unanticipated question for home listeners of Broadway material: what was the ideal length for a cast album?

An initial technological advance was the introduction of lightweight cassettes in the mid-1970s. Cassettes were compact and portable, and their appeal was boosted by the introduction of Sony's Walkman cassette player in 1980, which allowed for listening as an entirely personal experience beyond the confines of one's living room.[2] The introduction of cassettes didn't do much for Broadway cast albums one way or the other. Of course, major titles—*My Fair Lady*, the soundtrack to *West Side Story*, and so on—were quickly reissued on cassette, but although one had the relative pleasure of skipping down the street to the tune of "Do Re Mi," the narrative experience was similar to that of LPs; you still had to flip the cassette over for Act Two. Furthermore, the diminution of size in the packaging was a distinct drawback. Even the worst cast album had a full-color 12" x 12" cover and some liner notes, but on a cassette, the material was folded up and crammed into a little plastic box. Occasionally, one might get a slight bonus; the CBS Masterworks two-cassette release of the score to Maury Yeston's *Nine* in 1982 promoted that "This special value cassette package contains over 80 minutes of music"—a good chunk of music originally recorded in the studio, but unreleased on LP.

A more pertinent issue for the recording and promotion of cast albums was the increasingly apparent epiphany throughout the 1970s that they were no longer the chartbusters they were back in the 1960s. The highest charting cast album of the 1970s was Stephen Schwartz's *Godspell*, following on the heels of the contemporary sound of *Hair* and *Jesus Christ Superstar*, which peaked at No. 34 in mid-1971. The 1977 musical *Annie* appeared to have everything going for it, not the least of which was the first family-friendly score in years; *Newsweek* had called it "the season's prayed-for big musical."[3] Columbia had put $100,000 toward the show's $800,000 production budget and naturally for its investment Columbia owned the recording rights. The company would have to sell out its initial shipment of 100,000 albums at $7.98 per LP—$1 more than most pop LPs at the time—in order to make a reasonable profit on its investment and its studio costs. In the 1970s, that was a dicey proposition for a cast album. *Annie* would eventually sell through its copies tenfold, but it would take years to do so; its peak chart ranking at No. 81 in 1977 would do little to inspire a corporation board used to the skyrocketing quick release/ quick return world of rock and pop music.[4] The musical's most ubiquitous song, "Tomorrow," received barely any airplay as a cover single; Grace Jones released a disco version in 1978, which seemed more like a put-on, and although Barbra Streisand recorded the song in a samba-inflected version as the first track on her *Songbird* album the same year, she never released it as a single.

Expenses only exacerbated the situation; according to a *New York Times* profile on Thomas Shepard in 1983, it cost a major label between $125,000 and $175,000 to make a cast album—nearly on a par with recording a major rock act for an LP—while recording a classical symphony cost the company about a third of that.[5] Union rules for musicians and actors (who were paid a full week's salary for their one-day studio contribution to the recording) hadn't changed—anything that went beyond the strict boundaries of the nine-hour Sunday recording session was prohibitively expensive; woe to the producer who exceeded that time constraint. In addition, the recession of the 1970s made companies less adventuresome than usual, and the promotional perks were slowly vanishing; AM radio stations that played cuts from Broadway scores were giving way to rock-oriented stations. An entire generation of popular singers emerged who wouldn't be caught dead singing a show tune. Barbra Streisand, still at Columbia, had been steered to a contemporary sound by Clive Davis as the seventies were beginning; her 1971 album *Stoney End* was a major pivot in her career, with nary a show tune in sight. She successfully diversified her vocal portfolio, with only the occasional foray to Broadway for the next fifteen years.

Other Adult Contemporary singers from the 1960s were not so lucky; many of them—Tony Bennett, Sammy Davis, Jr., Steve and Eydie—saw their contracts terminated by the major labels. They then turned to Vegas, nightclubs, or touring, grabbing onto a possible crossover Broadway ballad such as "What I Did For Love" from *A Chorus Line* as if it were a bobbing life preserver in a roiling sea of rock music. Following *A Little Night Music*'s unfortunate precedent, several major shows of the 1970s and early 1980s opened on Broadway without any recording contract or commitment: *42nd Street*, *Sophisticated Ladies*, and *Nine*, for example. Eventually they were lucky enough to be signed by RCA and Columbia respectively (at bargain basement investments and budgets) after they opened, while a very popular retro-valentine to burlesque, *Sugar Babies*, starring Mickey Rooney and Ann Miller, ran 1,208 performances without a commitment from a major label during its entire run.

The general trepidation of the major labels toward Broadway cast recordings had another unintended, if not uninteresting, consequence; it brought some other more independent, or affiliated, recording companies into the mix. Clive Davis bounced back after he was fired from Columbia and, with support from Columbia Pictures (a sister organization), started his own label, Arista, which inclined toward soft-rock artists such as Barry Manilow, Tony Orlando, and Melissa Manchester. Arista had incorporated Bell Records, a former children's label that recorded the Partridge Family; Arista's first foray into cast albums was Stephen Schwartz's commercially resonant *Godspell* in 1971. In the mid-1970s,

Arista then picked up Schwartz's *The Magic Show* and Kander and Ebb's original production of *Chicago*. Herb Alpert's A&M label, home of Cat Stevens and Captain and Tennille, recorded the Christopher Plummer musical version of *Cyrano* as a rare two-LP set with extensive dialogue tracks, constituting practically the entire show.[6] Casablanca Records, the home of KISS and Donna Summer, turned the disco floor over to the Marvin Hamlisch/Carole Bayer Sager romantic musical comedy *They're Playing Our Song*. Even Motown got into the act; the cast album recording rights to Schwartz's *Pippin* were shopped around and the guarantee of three singles from the score by Motown artists was part of the deal—including a cover of "Corner of the Sky" released in 1972 by the Jackson 5. For Schwartz, the aberration of a cast album on Motown was the thrill of a lifetime: "I don't know that I would have been a 'pop' writer without the influence of the Motown sound, at least certainly not to the same extent. So actually to have a cast album on Motown was not only thrilling for me, it felt like a kind of validation."[7]

▶ Audio Example 13.1, "Corner of the Sky" (Jackson 5)

The major studios, mostly RCA, Columbia, and MCA Records (which had taken over both Decca and Kapp Records in 1971) were still capable of interesting work. Columbia went through the most transition; in 1974, Shepard moved on, accepting an offer to run RCA's prestigious Red Seal label. This brought Goddard Lieberson back to the fold, returning to CBS Masterworks as a subcontractor to produce the LP of *A Chorus Line*. It was an extremely complex and high-profile project, given the amount of visual and physical integration that Michael Bennett's choreography had with the score by Hamlisch and Ed Kleban. There were cuts, elisions, compressions, but it was still an artful recording, despite the challenges. It had, of course, a gatefold (though not a "K" designation), a shiny metallic design, and Lieberson even wrote an elegant set of liner notes. The *Chorus Line* cast album was, in many ways, everything he stood for: innovation, mastery of a complex form, and a mixture of panache and restraint. It would be the perfect way to end a charmed career; Lieberson retired from Columbia for good, after the *Chorus Line* recording. Although it barely cracked the top 100 albums in 1975, the *Chorus Line* recording eventually sold more than two million copies over the decades in various formats.

Goddard Lieberson died of cancer on May 29, 1977, at the age of 66. Alan Jay Lerner was writing his own memoirs when he heard the news and two weeks later wrote the following: "With his passing went another drain on the world's fast-diminishing supply of charm…the pleasure of Goddard's company was the joy he brought to others."[8] Columbia managed some wonderful albums in the shadow of Lieberson's legacy, often bringing in a show's composer to co-produce the album: Charles Strouse on *Annie*; Cy Coleman on *On the Twentieth Century* and *Barnum*—all gorgeous albums, both inside and out, especially *On the Twentieth Century*, which was inventively coproduced with Mike Berniker, and featured a wonderfully bedazzled cover based on the poster art with a faux chrome finish that continued onto the gatefold.

Thomas Shepard was certainly the one producer who was consistently following in the footsteps of Lieberson's aspirations. Part of his brief was RCA's cast album division, which hadn't done much since *Hair*; his first assignment was to record the West End cast album of *A Little Night Music* in 1975, and, with that, he began an extended, productive, and eventually contentious collaboration with Stephen Sondheim. There was something nearly Oedipal about Shepard's decision to record the London version of *A Little Night Music*; Columbia had turned down the offer to record it, citing less than enthusiastic sales of the Broadway version, and RCA leapt into the breach. Shepard added his own signature by making some changes to Lieberson's "design" for the original album: inserting a "frog-in-the-throat" cough for the singer at the top of the opening number; adding more dialogue in certain spots; boosting musical accents in others.

The military theorist von Clausewitz once said, "War is the continuation of politics by other means;" for Shepard, a recording was the continuation of theatricality by other means: "Whatever I feel is legitimately in the minds and hearts of the creators of the show, which they were able to express with sets, lights, and costumes—if I can reinterpret that or reshape it so that what was in their hearts and minds has an aural equivalent on the recording, I think that's not only my right, I think that's my job."[9] Working with his associate producer, Jay David Saks, Shepard began in earnest on his first collaboration of an original Broadway show with Sondheim in 1976, the extraordinary *Pacific Overtures*.[10] The next Sondheim show, *Sweeney Todd, the Demon Barber of Fleet Street*, was one of, if not the most, ambitious and challenging musicals of the 1970s; Sondheim, Shepard, and Saks were up to the task of composing, producing, and mixing the album, a two-LP set that relentlessly drove its narrative home. The RCA recording of *Sweeney Todd* was as ambitious as its source and, arguably, the finest cast album of its time. Shepard and his staff has reimagined the twisted musical tale of cannibalism and revenge as a kind of 1940s radio horror anthology, such as *Inner Sanctum* or *Lights Out*, with grisly sound effects and melodramatic accents; they were entirely appropriate to the source material and made for a high level of home listening (an insert of Sondheim's complex lyrics didn't hurt, either).

Shepard saw himself, in his capacity at RCA Red Seal, as the steward of Sondheim's recorded works, often releasing concerts and boutique shows of Sondheim's material that had little chance of mass consumer appeal, but affirmed the label's dedication to the composer's work. That stewardship was sorely tested with the 1981 musical, *Merrily We Roll Along*, which ran only sixteen performances. As was the case in 1964 with Columbia and *Anyone Can Whistle*, RCA was not contractually bound to record the score after such a short run, but Shepard went out on a limb and procured the recording budget, saving a magnificent score from oblivion. Frank Rich wrote in the *New York Times*, "Listening to this masterful score, in its lush recording by RCA, you wonder how it possibly could have failed?" After *Sunday in the Park with George* in 1983—another exquisitely rendered and textured album of a challenging Sondheim score—Shepard moved on to MCA, to take over its division of classical and Broadway songs, while Sondheim stayed with RCA and the producer Jay David Saks to record several other complex and highly regarded albums of his work, including the scores to *Into the Woods* and *Assassins.*

Still, at the end of the day, no matter what kind of bold, commercially challenging decisions Shepard was making at RCA and MCA, he had to appeal to corporate executives for his budget and expenses. What was missing, since the heyday of Lieberson, was someone who had enough enthusiasm and clout to push through a cast album project in the timorous days of recording in the 1970s and 80s. In 1982, exactly that person came along—a youthful, energetic Hollywood mogul who grew up in Brooklyn and had saved his pennies in the late 1950s to take the subway to the Mark Hellinger Theatre, where he bought an orchestra ticket to *My Fair Lady* for $2.85.[11]

David Geffen had the right combination of ambition and outsized personality at the right time. When he made his first Broadway investment in 1982, he was not yet forty years old; still, his rise to fame and fortune was the stuff of showbiz legend. He had worked his way up through the mailroom at William Morris to become manager of several successful rock acts, such as Laura Nyro, the Eagles, and Crosby, Stills, Nash and Young. He formed his own record company, Asylum, and merged his company with Elektra Records, producing albums with John Lennon, Elton John, and Peter Gabriel. As the 1980s began, he was a vice president for Warner Bros. pictures, a real-estate magnate, and the head of the newly coined Geffen Records.

Geffen's interest in the theater came through an admiring friendship with director/choreographer Michael Bennett. Bennett—who was always impressed by wealthy, self-made people—invited Geffen to a workshop of a new musical he was sculpting at his 890 Studios on Broadway, a dynamic show about the bruised egos and merciless ways of the music business, as told through the rise and fall of a black girl group in the 1960s. Geffen was impressed with the show and was more than happy to put in his stake for one-third of the budget—nearly a million dollars of his own money. For his investment, he got the rights to the cast album. Next to Burt Bacharach and Phil Ramone, perhaps, Geffen was the first person to view the original Broadway cast album from a rock producer's point of view. He felt that cast albums weren't intrinsically soporific and old-fashioned; they simply had to be produced with the same canny professionalism that went into producing a rock album. It helped, of course, that Bennett's new show had a terrific, driving pop/rock score, courtesy of Tom Eyen and composer Henry Krieger. Geffen himself offered very little in the way of critical opinion or interference on the show for his 33⅓ percent investment, but he knew his way around the recording business and offered a few creative suggestions to Bennett during the workshop process. For starters, throw out *Big Dreams* as a title: Geffen preferred *Dreamgirls*.[12]

The album for *Dreamgirls* was recorded in New York, but mixed in Los Angeles for release on Geffen Records. Geffen had no interest in the old-school scrum of rushing master tapes to Bridgeport, Connecticut, so that the LPs could hit Korvette's or Sam Goody's within the week. "Most cast albums are cut the Sunday afternoon following the opening," he said, "We worked on the *Dreamgirls* album for four months and put $400,000 into the production."[13] The *Dreamgirls* album was happy to embrace the apprehension that David Merrick had with the *Promises, Promises* recording; it was pointedly an album first, a theatrical souvenir second. Content mattered more to Geffen than context; *Dreamgirls* was produced and edited like a pop album, so that all of the tracks could, theoretically, be played as single cuts on a radio station; the longest track—Jennifer Holliday's "And I Am Telling You I'm Not Going"—was barely more than four minutes long, and most of the other tracks hovered around the three-minute mark. *Dreamgirls* didn't spawn the breakout pop singles that Geffen had envisioned, but the cast album peaked at No. 11 on the album chart (and No. 4 on the Rhythm and Blues chart); it also sold more copies than any cast album since *Hair*, fourteen years previously. "Theater is as shaky as every business," said Geffen, who had mastered every element of the entertainment business, "but if you succeed on Broadway, it's extremely lucrative."[14]

When he gave that interview to *Billboard* in the summer of 1982, Geffen was anticipating the American opening of the West End musical *Cats,* written by Andrew Lloyd Webber. The show had opened in London in spring 1981 and would transfer to the Winter Garden Theatre in fall 1982. Barbra Streisand had released a single recording of "Memory" on Columbia nine months before the show opened on Broadway—the first time in a long while that a single was on the charts in advance of an opening. (It charted at No. 52, but was backed with Streisand's monumental "Love Theme from *Evergreen.*") Geffen once again provided one-third of the money to bring the show over, in concert with the Shubert Organization—his personal exposure was close to $2 million. Also, as part of his deal, Geffen again snatched up the recording rights. A British two-LP (and two-cassette) recording of *Cats* had already been released in England on Polydor; it had been selling extremely well as an import to the United States and/or bought enthusiastically by American tourists who had seen the show in the West End. Geffen acquired the rights to the Polydor recording and released it in the United States under the Geffen Records label. Then, a few weeks after the Broadway opening, he recorded the Broadway company (at the cost of between $250,000 and $400,000) and released *that* on a two-LP set to the American market (as well as an album of highlights from *Cats*—what would have been called "Gems from *Cats*" back in 1922), also on the Geffen Records label. If it was going to be *Cats*, it was going to be Geffen, too.

The two-LP versions of *Cats* were part of an Andrew Lloyd Webber continuum: the original concept album for *Jesus Christ Superstar,* the concept album for 1976's *Evita,* the Broadway cast album of *Evita*: these were all two-LP sets released by MCA (although the West End cast album of *Evita* with Elaine Paige was effectively rendered and released on only one LP). They presaged not simply a surfeit of music, expanded expensively on disk through the clout of their composer, but a sea change in what kind of experience the listener wished to recapture and/or enjoy. In a 1982 article in the *New York Times*, Michael Kerker, a record collector who also worked as an executive for ASCAP, was quoted as saying, "Up until the '60s, you had to have a hit song or hit songs to sell a musical. Now it's the *concept* musical, everything together—the set, the costumes, the choreography, the staging. Those are the important things."[15]

Back in the late 1940s, it was historically coincident that the LP arrived when there were also dozens of musical theater pieces with extended, organic narratives. Before *Cats* opened, the closest recorded analog one could get to a through-composed concept musical would be a well-produced recording that contained as much music as could be crammed onto a two-LP set. Within a year of the Broadway debut of *Cats*, the "pop-operas" that began to dominate the West End and, concomitantly, Broadway, found a recording medium that suited its needs: the compact disc.

By the early 1980s, when LP albums were declining in sales and cassettes were over-saturating the market, the Japanese engineering labs at Sony were working to perfect a new digital platform for recorded music. Music had been sampled by computer in studios since the late 1970s—taking sound waves and "bundling" them into millions of pieces of numerical information that could be reproduced with unprecedented exactitude by a laser beam that interpreted the data back as a sound wave. Those bundles would arrive to the consumer as an 11.9-centimeter polycarbonate disc, so compact that its very accessibility gave the platform its inevitable name. Compact discs—and the entirely brand-new decks required to play them though one's stereo system—were introduced to the American market by 1983; the initial repertory offerings were a mixture of standards from the classical catalog and reissues of swing band anthologies from the 1940s.[16]

Unlike the introduction of cassettes, the potential effect of CDs on the recording of cast albums had enormous implications. For a contextual narrative piece such as a Broadway musical, these changes were profound—now, there could be up to 50 percent more music from a score. Perhaps of more tactile consequence, for the first time, one no longer had to turn over the music to hear Act Two, which would influence how the score could be sequenced and programmed by the listener as one extended musical arc. Programming itself was now in the hands of the consumer, since with the tracking system on the CD (as opposed to the grooves on an LP), listeners could decide for themselves what they wanted to hear, when they wanted to hear it, and how often.

Progress has, of course, its trade-offs. The portability of the compact disc reduced its actual size from an LP by about two-thirds. The full panache of an LP cover showcasing a glamorous Broadway poster—let alone the occasional marvels of a gatefold—would vanish, as would the tactile glories of liner notes, inserts, lyric sheets, or even quality photographs. The booklets for CD cast album recordings (when they existed; for a while, Columbia's reissues only provided a folded-over piece of paper) were the bane of every show tune fan's existence, with their diminished capacity, microscopic printing, and the inevitable shredding that happened when one attempted (vainly) to jam them back through the plastic tabs that guided the booklet into what was called, without irony, the "jewel case." In reality, the jewel case transformed the real jewels of the LP age—elegant and evocative packaging for a multitude of cast albums—into a utilitarian storage unit.

Initially, compact discs took longer to produce than LPs; coordinating simultaneous releases of LP, cassette, and CD would be a challenge; for years, recording companies released their products in all three formats, despite the differences among them. RCA won the Broadway CD sweepstakes, being the first company to release a new original cast album on the format with *La Cage aux Folles,* which hit the market in November 1983, three months after the LP was released (on the day the show opened—a clever marketing move). By the end of the year, Geffen Records had put out both *Dreamgirls* and *Cats* on CD, and the gates flew open. And if the majority of successful musical shows in the 1980s—*Evita, Cats, Les Misérables, The Phantom of the Opera,* etc.—had scores that were bursting at the seams, it only made sense to have a recording format that could accommodate them.

The commercial success of these shows, often produced by Cameron Mackintosh, provided another unprecedented lifeline to the perpetuation of the cast album. The CD format was perfect for being branded and sold in the ever-increasing souvenir kiosks found in the theater lobbies of Mackintosh productions. In addition to, say, *Cats* T-shirts, coffee mugs, and umbrellas in the lobby of the Winter Garden, one could buy the cast album of *Cats* on a convenient-sized CD. Despite the fact that these CDs could be found much more cheaply in almost any nearby record store, audience members embraced the easy access of the product and dozens, if not hundreds, of copies were routinely sold at each performance.

"You can't market an album if you have no show," remarked former Broadway Decca executive Brian Drutman, who supervised the U.S. marketing of all of Andrew Lloyd

Webber's and Mackintosh's cast albums.[17] In the case of the most successful of their shows of the 1980s and 1990s, the productions were running ten, twenty years—longer than any shows in Broadway history. (*The Phantom of the Opera* has been running for three decades with no end in sight.) When the *Phantom* 2-CD set on Polygram hit the U.S. market in February 1988, it cracked the *Billboard* 100, reaching No. 98, due to an unusual amount of radio airplay, aided by the "synthesizer-catchy" title number, and the publicity buzz from the production itself. An advertising executive for a music store chain told *USA Today,* "The two things that seem to be important are the publicity that has been generated and the name of Andrew Lloyd Webber. People who are familiar with his other work want to see what he has to say today."[18]

Although a similarly promoted title back in the 1960s—say, *Camelot*—would have sent its album up to the top of the charts, *Phantom* simply hung in there for the long haul—and a long haul it would prove to be. One unprecedented creative solution contributed mightily to its longevity. Lloyd Webber and Mackintosh decided to promote the brand of the show by only releasing the West End two-CD set in America rather than rerecord the Broadway version (the two leads from London—Michael Crawford and Sarah Brightman—appeared in the New York production as well). Although there was also a successful "Highlights" CD, this had the effect of putting all of *Phantom*'s chips onto this one recording. Typically, if a hit show such as *Hello, Dolly!* had replacement casts of impressive enough individuals in New York and London—Carol Channing, Pearl Bailey, Mary Martin—separate recordings might be made, more for posterity than anything else. However, if you were one of the millions of fans of the score to *Phantom* over the decades, you were given the choice of only one basic English-language recording, despite the innumerable shifting cast members in productions across the globe: the West End version. The wisdom of this decision is borne out by the numbers: the combination of the two-disc CD and highlights of the London *Phantom of the Opera* make that score the best-selling cast recording of all time: more than twenty million units sold, and counting. If, as Drutman posits, the best way to promote an album is to have a popular show running, the recording of *Phantom* will continue to be commercially successful in perpetuity.

Perpetuity also seemed to go hand-in-hand with the accessibility and durability of the CD format. Beginning in the mid-1980s, the major companies went directly to their back catalog to rerelease successful titles on digital format, as they discovered many consumers who were willing to repurchase their entire collections on compact disc. The classic Broadway musical scores were still sought after by the consumer, and the record companies did their best to make new purchases more attractive. Columbia set up an entire in-house division called Columbia Special Products to deal with CD rereleases of Broadway material; by mid-1987, it had released 24 back titles on CD, from the original 1956 *Candide* to the London *My Fair Lady*, which sold units within a year of its rerelease. MCA and Capitol followed suit with major cast album titles, such as *The King and I* and *Funny Girl*, respectively. RCA did them all one better, rereleasing its 1964 *Fiddler on the Roof* original cast album with two tracks recorded back in the day, but never released on LP—miraculous "bonus tracks."

▶ Audio Example 13.2, "Wedding Dance" (*Fiddler on the Roof* original cast)

Bonus tracks became the Holy Grail for CD rereleases, correcting errors and omissions from days gone by, when technological limitations (and occasional limits of the imagination) kept compelling material off the original LP release. This was the musical theater equivalent of a mulligan—another shot at remodeling recordings from the past with slightly longer narratives, more in keeping with the authors' original intentions. Other bonus treats included tracks from demo recordings, jazz covers, and radio interviews— usually tucked into the final tracks of the CD—for the devoted fan. Additionally, albums could be re-sequenced to conform to the original theatrical playing order, as CDs no longer required certain tracks to fall in certain places on the LP for the sake of sonic fidelity. (The score to *Camelot*, for example, reordered the tracks to conform to the song order of the original production.) The luxury of CD rereleases had some unintended consequences: the two-LP set of *Sweeney Todd* was actually too *long* to fit on one CD, and the score was initially released as a reduced "Highlights" CD; likewise, the "80 minutes" of music from *Nine*'s cassette set was reduced to 68 minutes for its first CD release in 1984 (eventually, a 2-CD "Expanded Edition" was released in 2004).

The back catalog of out-of-print cast albums—now available in droves on CD—far outpaced the expectations that *Variety* held for LP rereleases in the 1977. In fact, in much the same way that Sinatra brought back obscure songs from the 1920s and 30s on his LP releases from the 1950s, the CD Broadway catalog reissues in the 1980s brought back obscure scores from the 1950s. William Rosenfield, former vice president of A&R for RCA/ BMG, recalled, "I was sitting behind my desk at RCA and someone from accounting came in and asked if I had the address for a Richard Rodgers and Oscar Hammerstein. I asked why and she said she had a royalty check for them because their recording of *Me and Juliet* has finally recouped, thanks to the CD reissue. It only took forty years, but they got their money back, just the same."[19]

The complex and copious wave of cast album rereleases on CD was so monumental for the collector that it occasioned its own Sunday column in the *New York Times* by the resident drama critic Frank Rich. Entitled "Broadway Flops Go to CD Heaven," Rich was at once bemused, enchanted, and exasperated: "With considerable energy, technical expertise, and expense, these labels have revived the original-cast recordings of often unrevivable musicals from the mid-1940s to the mid-1970s.... Great artistic claims can be made for few, if any, of these second-rung recordings, although in almost all cases they are far superior to the shows themselves.... the last dying gasp of the Broadway musical as an abundant mainstream American entertainment industry."[20]

The resurrection of the Broadway catalog through the CD format was the natural extension of a trend in the late 1970s and early 80s to record shows for posterity on independent labels, under tight budgets, pioneered by Ben Bagley's "Revisited" series on Painted Smiles, which initially recorded recondite material by great composers of the 1930s and 40s (and eventually a score or two) on LP. Flops were now able to cultivate devoted followings. Despite having the highest-charting cast album of the 1970s, Stephen Schwartz was not inured to Broadway disaster. In 1976, David Merrick produced Schwartz's period adaptation of the French film *The Baker's Wife*. It had a legendary trial by fire on the road, losing songs, book scenes, directors, actors, and stars on its journey from Los Angeles to Washington, where it closed. Two Broadway show tune fans, a married couple from Connecticut named Bruce and Doris Yeko, heard the score out of town and loved it. They wanted to commit it to a recording for posterity and got in touch with Schwartz. The Yekos only had the money and resources to record the non-ensemble numbers and gathered the four leads (including a young Patti LuPone) in a Greenwich Village apartment and, with Schwartz at the piano, saved *The Baker's Wife* from oblivion. It was hard to find the "Take Home Tunes" LP, but it made a distinct difference in the show's fate. Recalls Schwartz: "I don't think there had ever been a commercially available recording of a show that had closed out of town before. It was what kept the show alive. It was that experience that taught me that it is the cast album that is the lifeblood of any show; once the original production is gone, the cast album *becomes* the show."[21]

In the wake of the digital revolution a few years later, several small, independent labels sprang up to commit flop shows, Off-Broadway productions, lost scores, and other marginalized material to the CD format; CDs being easier to master, produce, and warehouse than LPs. Companies such as Varèse Sarabande, DRG, That's Entertainment, Original Cast, and others widely expanded the range of show material to consumers, even though most of those consumers were only hardened collectors. The magic number seems to have been 5,000 fans—no doubt an anecdotal figure routinely quoted; if a studio CD of a rare or obscure show sold 5,000 units, it could make its money back.

The barrage of recording firms tackling Broadway scores on CD weren't all devoting themselves to the Aisles of Misfit Toys; there was also a serious uptick in firms and individual producers who wanted to go back—much the way that Goddard Lieberson and Lehman Engel did in the 1950s—and reclaim great scores that had either gone unrecorded or that had been recorded in an inauthentic or compromised fashion. In 1985, *Of Thee I Sing* and *Let 'Em Eat Cake* finally got sterling recordings of their full scores by Columbia, subsequent to a live concert of both shows at the Brooklyn Academy of Music. Those recordings were an embryonic initiative of Roxbury Records, funded by the Ira and Leonore Gershwin Charitable Trust. Under the guidance of producer Tommy Krasker, Roxbury partnered with the Library of Congress to record five Gershwin scores on Nonesuch, including *Lady, Be Good!,* in impeccable studio recordings, painstakingly researched with authoritative arrangements and liner notes. The Trust also supported the recording of six additional rare Gershwin scores on various other labels.

But the mightiest archival project of all came from EMI, based in England, under the sterling (and often stern) baton of John McGlinn. McGlinn was a classically trained arranger and conductor with a fondness for the American stage classics of the pre-Depression era—written by Herbert, Kern, Gershwin, Porter—that bordered on an obsession. He claimed his interest was enflamed when he read some original orchestral scores from the period in the research room: "The original versions often had more bite, energy, and exuberance, and conveyed more the emotional power of the composer's work, and hearing modern recordings began to seem like listening to Mozart with saxophones."[22]

McGlinn's ambition to enshrine many of these unheralded or adulterated scores on archival recordings was greatly enhanced by the remarkable discovery in 1987, in a Warner Bros. warehouse in Secaucus, New Jersey, of the original scores to dozens of musicals by composers such as Jerome Kern, George Gershwin, Cole Porter, and Vincent Youmans. Combining these discoveries with the advent of the CD and his eye for detail, McGlinn was able to preserve this music in studio recordings. "These songs are presented in a form as close to the original as possible. In all cases, the earliest published sources have been used, and the composer's original manuscript—when it still existed—was consulted. The music is not 'stylized' in the current fashion, but sung absolutely straight, with the pitches and rhythms that the composer intended," he warned in one liner note.

Jerome Kern was McGlinn's favorite composer, and, in 1988, he went into the EMI Abbey Road studio in London to realize his greatest ambition: recording a definitive *Show Boat* in a seminal archival recording produced as a three-CD set for EMI. (He was aided greatly by some of the newly discovered Secaucus material.) McGlinn, working in collaboration with scholar Miles Kreuger, was acutely aware that, for decades, stage and film productions of *Show Boat* had applied a thick sugarcoated patina of sentimentality to the show. For the EMI recording, McGlinn's objective was to restore the original score, in its original order, and with the original orchestrations by Robert Russell Bennett; he also included cut numbers, numbers introduced in revivals, numbers added to the motion picture versions of *Show Boat*: in short, every single note Kern ever wrote for any

Jerry Orbach and Tammy Grimes, stars of *42nd Street*, one of several shows that opened in the 1980s and ran weeks before getting a recording contract. Credit: Photofest.

iteration of the show. It was a profound, if overweight, musicological achievement that ran for a combined 221 minutes—nearly four hours.

McGlinn could be an exacting fellow; he often demanded his orchestras in concert play every single note of a score, no matter how trivial or inconsequential. He loudly and frequently belittled several generations of popular singers—everyone from Sinatra and Sarah Vaughan to Tony Bennett and Ella Fitzgerald; in his eyes, they had ruined and traduced the original intentions of the composers from a bygone era.[23] But at the end of the day, with the 3-CD *Show Boat* and the half-dozen scores he subsequently recorded, McGlinn accomplished something that only his vision, tenacity, and the technological innovations of the CD would have made possible "When John produced [the EMI recording], he put all the pieces of the puzzle out there," says Ted Chapin, "and he implicitly invited a new generation of artists to put it together whatever way they wanted."[24] In fact, Harold Prince's successful 1992 Broadway revival of *Show Boat* was inspired by the riches revealed by McGlinn, and many of McGlinn's discoveries were interpolated back into the show.

▶   Audio Example 13.3, "Cap'n Andy's Ballyhoo" (Robert Nichols)

"You never seen a show like this before!" exclaims Cap'n Andy, one of the characters in *Show Boat*, extolling the virtues of the *Cotton Blossom*'s riverboat entertainment. But music archivist Bruce Pomahac sees a huge paradox in McGlinn's copious compendium:

> I always think the greatest four-and-a-half-hour musical in the world must have been *Show Boat* when it opened in Washington in 1927, but the show was diminished once [Kern and Hammerstein] had to come down to a timing that the audience could deal with. If John McGlinn gave one thing to musical theater, he gave us all that *Show Boat*—but it's a complete lie. There was never a performance of *Show Boat* anywhere, anytime with all the stuff in there he had recorded on those CDs.[25]

Was it finally possible, finally conceivable, after all the years and struggles with cutting, condensing, eliding, traducing, compressing, and compromising Broadway music to get it to fit on a 78, or an LP, that, because of the CD innovation, there was finally a Broadway cast album that was simply *too long*?

A musical that captured the zeitgeist is itself captured by the chronicle of popular music: the Broadway musical meets *Rolling Stone*. By permission of *Rolling Stone*.

CHAPTER 14

History Has Its Eyes on You

The Internet and the Mixtape of Broadway

Late in the second act of *Camelot*, a chorus of knights and courtiers intones the fate of their tragic queen, underscored by an appropriately galloping martial strain in Frederick Loewe's music: "Oh, they found Guinevere / With her brave cavalier…" Most listeners would never think to characterize that number as having "the dopest beat you'll ever hear in your life." But then, most listeners aren't Lin-Manuel Miranda.

On a segment on CBS's *60 Minutes*, following the breathtaking success of Miranda's brainchild, *Hamilton*, Miranda takes the host, Charlie Rose, on a tour of the record shelves of his childhood. After extolling the virtues of Richard Kiley on the *Man of La Mancha* cast album, Miranda plunks an LP of *Camelot* down on the phonograph and starts grooving away to "Guinevere." "The number one album [in our house] was *Camelot*," he tells Rose. "Remember I grew up not seeing Broadway shows, but loving cast albums." Branded with the imprimatur of Lin Manuel Miranda, the hippest purveyor of stage music of his generation, that would appear to be a ringing endorsement to the younger generation for the relevance of the Broadway musical score.[1]

However, in the early twenty-first century, among the younger generation, the Broadway musical had already become, if not totally dope, certainly pretty cool for the first time in four decades. In its own paradoxical way, the age of Internet streaming and digital downloads—which would hardly seem conducive to the world of live theater—unlocked new opportunities for the music of Broadway to reach Main Street again. The charge was led largely by the younger generation—"millennials" in popular discourse—who coolly controlled and manipulated the Internet and its ability to send compressed, digitally coded music to anyone and everyone, sometimes without permission, often without context, always without liner notes.

The notion of downloading a Broadway score in bits (or bytes) and pieces would have been anathema—or at least, hardly conceivable—to record producers of Goddard Lieberson's generation. Many of the values to which they aspired, Lieberson in particular—narrative coherence, attractive packaging, recognizable branding—would be granulized and atomized by search engines and online music distribution powerhouses such as iTunes, Spotify, and Amazon Music.[2] But what the MP3 file represented in demolishing the old order, it gained in terms of fluidity and access; entire libraries of Broadway material, standards, and esoterica, could be acquired with a few keystrokes. Listeners could assemble playlists of their favorite tunes and juxtapose them against each other. Mixtapes, which began as homemade cassette tapes, morphed into playlists available to anyone with an iPhone; what was once, in the 1910s and 1920s, called "the medley" became the mash-up. The deconstruction of a structured Broadway score might have been a catastrophe for theatrical composers and songwriters, but for home listeners, it was a boon to exploration and experimentation; it would even lead to some of the most vibrant creative moments of Broadway music of the last few decades.

This notion of putting the final editing stages of a discrete piece of musical material into the hands of the consumer is something that Glenn Gould toyed with back in the 1960s and 70s; he had a sense that technology inspired a kind of freedom that might horrify the "suits" in a media corporation, but would inflame the imagination of the listener. In a live conversation with Yehudi Menuhin for the television series *The Music of Man* in 1979, Gould wielded an explicitly theatrical analogy: "If an actor wants to deliver a proper rendition of 'To be or not to be,' he may do that in the context of the play *Hamlet*, as we know it, from first word to last. Or he can take that speech and perform it as part of a traveling routine, the way John Gielgud used to do [in *The Ages of Man*] and read selected excerpts —why then is it not possible [in the recording studio] to cut in on one particular note and say *that* is the tenor, that is the emotion of that note?" While Gould was referring to a piece of piano music, the effect is the same for the digitally minded consumer: he/she is now capable of detaching content from context and recontextualizing it. In a way, the mixtape age has undone all the careful work of Jack Kapp and Goddard Lieberson.

But these were technological innovations; without a shift in the narrative focus of American musicals, the younger generation might have shrugged off Broadway with indifference. From many different quarters—network television, animated films, rock-oriented composers—there appeared the canny creation of new musical role models and characters that would capture the interest of Gen-Xers and millennials. The middle-aged music men, milkmen, and matchmakers of their parents' (and grandparents') generation gave way to more accessible characters who confronted similar problems as their enthusiasts. "At the end of [the previous century] is when everything started to change," said Keith Caulfield. "It was really the early 2000s when people started to transition away from albums. This was back when the only way to get that music from *Rent* was to actually buy the album or to go see the show."[3] When a former girlfriend took Lin-Manuel Miranda to see *Rent* on his seventeenth birthday, it was, for him, "a revelation—that you could write about now, and you could have musicals that really felt contemporary."[4]

When *Hair* debuted at the end of the 1960s, critics declaimed that there was finally a Broadway score that could reach and move a new, younger generation of theatergoers. When Jonathan Larson's *Rent* debuted nearly three decades later in 1996, critics declaimed much the same thing all over again. With his admitted enthusiasm for both Stephen Sondheim and Peter Frampton, Larson was able to create a Broadway narrative with a popular sound, bound up in a story that would actually speak to the "now" of young people. The score to *Rent*—and the buzz that it elicited across the generations—was tailor-made for producer David Geffen's sensibilities. He saw the immense commercial potential of a score with such crossover appeal: "I think *Rent* is incredibly entertaining. It's an important work."[5] Geffen supposedly outbid Sony Music Entertainment (which acquired Columbia Records in 1991) and RCA—which were rumored to have put up anywhere between $500,000 to $750,000 for the recording rights—by offering $1 million, an all-time record. But, given Geffen's experience and the eclectic nature of the score, the deal was a no-brainer. The show's co-producer, Kevin McCollum, told *Billboard*, "David Geffen lives at the crossroads of popular culture—from Nirvana and Guns N' Roses to *Cats* and *Little Shop of Horrors*."[6]

Geffen spotlighted *Rent*'s contemporary relevance by hiring one of the most respected record producers of the industry, Arif Mardin, to helm the *Rent* cast album. Mardin had cut his teeth in the 1960s working at Atlantic Records with a range of important singers such as Aretha Franklin and Dusty Springfield, and was responsible for transforming the Bee Gees into the most commercially successful musicians of the 1970s. Mardin was the perfect producer to corral the eclectic score of *Rent* into something coherent; he produced a two-CD set for DreamWorks Records at a reported cost of $400,000. When *Rent* hit the stores—back in 1996, when there were record stores—it sold an extraordinary 43,000 units in its first week.

One of the reasons that Geffen was initially so excited about the score was what he anticipated in terms of "covered" singles: "I hear a lot of people doing these songs," he said.[7] In the end, however, Geffen only heard those people in his imagination. With the exception of Stevie Wonder, who recorded a track of "Seasons of Love" with the cast that was appended to the two-CD release, no commercial singles from *Rent* ever really landed or ever really charted. "By the late 1990s, popular musical tastes had evolved to the point where it was nearly impossible to crack through the *Billboard* Hot 100 with any-thing even remotely sounding like 'Broadway,'" remarked Caulfield.[8] Back in 1965, even a zeitgeist also-ran such as *On a Clear Day You Can See Forever* had better luck with single releases. There would be an inevitable *Selections from Rent* single-CD release, but the dawn of the age of digital download would obviate the need for such a studio-directed conflation; within a year or two of *Rent*'s release, listeners could make their own selections from the full cast album on their own personal computers.

"Sweetheart, it's just not commercial—it's not what's selling nowadays—it's like your old stuff," goes the cacophony of bureaucratic chatter. It's not from a publicity conference at Atlantic Records or DreamWorks or Sony Music; it's the beginning of "Putting it Together," the first track on Barbra Streisand's *The Broadway Album*, her 1985 release of fifteen songs, all from Broadway, spanning more than fifty years of show tunes. Streisand had been toying with an all-Broadway album for years, provoking, no doubt, the same wearied responses from Columbia executives that she satirized at the beginning of her first track. But a year earlier, her previous album, *Emotion*, a mixed bag of contemporary songs, charted only as high as No. 19—below the expectations of an artist of Streisand's stature. "One reason I made *The Broadway Album* is that I felt I had to stop recording songs that any number of other people could sing as well if not better than I could," Streisand candidly told the *New York Times*. "It was time for me to do something I truly believed in. This is the music I love, it is where I came from, it is my roots."[9]

Although Broadway had obviously been the main stem of Streisand's roots for two de-cades, she changed up her songbook to reflect the times—or at least the prestige—of Broadway's leading practitioner in the 1980s: Stephen Sondheim. Incredibly, Streisand had not recorded one word or note of Sondheim's prior to *The Broadway Album*, other than an unreleased song from *Anyone Can Whistle*. For this disk, she went nearly all in: eight songs with lyrics by Sondheim, six of which he composed as well. Streisand also managed to con-vince Sondheim to alter the lyrics to three songs, including "Send in the Clowns." Nearly every popular chanteuse of a certain age had recorded that number in the dozen years since its debut; the song had been waiting for Streisand to make her own entrance with her usual flair. She intuited that the pop version of the song had elided several important dramatic moments from the actual stage version of *A Little Night Music* and that, as a one-off on an album, "Send in the Clowns" needed to be restructured and slightly revised, particularly in the bridge. Sondheim obliged and although he was very vocal in his appreciation of Streisand's sensitivity and prowess, he demurred about sending the revised version out into the world beyond Streisand's album: "It's a self-sufficient song," he told the *Times*.[10]

The success of *The Broadway Album*, released the week of Thanksgiving week in 1985, surprised everyone, except probably Streisand. It lasted on the charts for fifty weeks and hit No. 1 for three of those weeks. It wound up selling four million copies and even spun off a single release, a rather ethereal version of *West Side Story*'s "Somewhere," that charted as high as 43—not bad for a song from the late 1950s. A follow-up album in 1993, *Back to Broadway*, which was heavy on Andrew Lloyd Webber compositions, also hit No. 1 (for one week) and lasted nearly as long on the charts. Streisand's affection for Broadway extended into the twenty-first century: a 2016 release with the ungainly title of *Encore: Movie Partners Sing Broadway* encompassed the full range of her Broadway interests, including a Rodgers and Hart song and yet another bird with a broken wing: a tune intended for the 1986 flop, *Smile*, that never even made it into rehearsal. This album, too, hit No. 1 on the *Billboard* 200. With this trio of Broadway albums—bestsellers over the course of three decades—Streisand easily inherited the baton from Frank Sinatra as the pop world's most gregarious and successful ambassador of the Broadway songbook, making its most accepted standards and its newer discoveries vital and relevant to listeners into the twenty-first century.

She might well have made Broadway music more relevant that she would have liked. In 2011, Nancy O'Dell, a host for *Entertainment Tonight*, asked Streisand what she thought of the popular television show *Glee*, which, beginning in 2009, successfully integrated tunes from the Broadway and pop songbooks (including "Don't Rain on My Parade") and placed them within the internecine rivalries of a Midwestern high school glee club: "Barbra, the TV show *Glee* uses interpretations of your songs; would you ever consider appearing on the show?" "Not if I can help it," responded Streisand. "I have seen some of the episodes. My niece, my young niece saw *Funny Girl* on DVD and said, 'How come you're singing so many songs from *Glee*?' "

During its five-season run, *Glee* sang a lot of songs from a lot of sources: not just *Sweet Charity*, *Funny Girl*, and *Dreamgirls*, but Celine Dion, the Dixie Chicks, and Jay-Z. The program was nothing if not eclectic. But the ensemble cast of *Glee* lent their youthful imprimatur to their varied repertoire in a healthy, egalitarian way: show tunes were not the exclusive domain of nerds, dweebs, and outcasts on the show. *Glee* also gave credibility to Broadway by not only tapping legit alums for its cast—Matthew Morrison (*Hairspray*, *South Pacific*) and Lea Michele (*Spring Awakening*)—but also enticing guest performers with 42nd Street chops such as Victor Garber and Kristin Chenoweth, who conferred her Broadway benediction on the show by performing "Maybe This Time" from *Cabaret*. The *Glee* cast expanded into the world of digital music by releasing sixteen soundtrack albums, six compilation albums, eleven extended play specials, and 450 singles on iTunes and other sites—the downloaded sales would total an astonishing 36 million units.[11] Among those digital tracks were 119 songs with a provenance from the musical stage—everything from *My Fair Lady* to *Fiddler on the Roof* and *Wicked*.

The cast album to 2003's *Wicked* was also pitched to a younger generation, both in its style and its subject matter, and it, too, became successful, selling an average of 12,000 copies a week of its CD on Decca Broadway in the months following its opening. It has gone to sell more than six million copies. Its composer, Stephen Schwartz, put all his chips on the original Broadway album, despite numerous requests to record the West End or touring versions out of concern that subsequent editions would dilute the brand. "It's a lesson learned from Andrew Lloyd Webber, who is one of the most business-savvy composers of all time," admitted Schwartz.[12] Schwartz sees the increasing power of musical theater being communicated by properties such as *Wicked* and *Glee,* which promote strong characters in a musical idiom that straddles pop and Broadway: "I actually think there is *more* openness now on the part of pop artists to covering songs from shows than there was when I started out, when being associated with musical theater could be death to a pop singer's credibility."[13]

Cultural touchstones from Broadway in the twenty-first century in mainstream entertainment included Gwen Stefani sampling tunes from *Fiddler on the Roof* and *The Sound of Music*; Beyoncé employing Bob Fosse moves; or Susan Boyle storming the ramparts of popular culture by singing "I Dreamed a Dream" from *Les Misérables* on the English program *Britain's Got Talent,* which became a YouTube sensation in 2009. Perhaps the most pervasive mash-up of a show tune into the popular consciousness began when rap artist Jay-Z overheard a DJ sampling instrumental beats from *Annie*'s "It's a Hard-Knock Life" during a Puff Daddy tour. Supposedly, white members of the audience went bonkers for it, but for Jay-Z, "It immediately brought me back to my childhood." The rapper had grown up in Brooklyn watching the film version on television and immediately bonded with "the struggle of this poor kid in this environment and how her life changed…I knew right then and there that I had to make that record, and people would relate to the struggle and the aspiration in it, as well."[14] Jay-Z's "Hard Knock Life (Ghetto Anthem)" proposed to sample sections from the Columbia original cast recording through Jay-Z's counter-rap, and he knew that permission to use the Broadway track would be expensive—and dicey—to acquire. He wrote to Charles Strouse and Martin Charnin, *Annie*'s songwriters, with a heartwarming tale of how the young Jay-Z—Shawn Carter at the time—won an essay contest at his rundown Brooklyn junior high school and was rewarded with a once-in-a-lifetime chance to see *Annie* on Broadway. The trip paralleled little Annie's own optimistic dreams of tomorrow; it was also a total fabrication. Nevertheless, it did its job; released in October 1998, "Hard Knock Life (Ghetto Anthem)" was Jay-Z's biggest hit to date and reached No. 5 on the *Billboard* Hot 100. It was the highest ranking that any original Broadway tune—well, a sampling of part of a Broadway tune—would achieve in decades.

▷ Audio Example 14.1, "Hard Knock Life (Ghetto Anthem)" (Jay-Z)

Television invited the Broadway tune book into primetime once again; the *American Idol* competition devoted entire evenings to the songs from the Great White Way, and

Broadway returned the favor by inviting former *American Idol* contestants to play the leads in such diverse shows as *Spamalot, The Color Purple,* and *Rock of Ages.* Even the popular dance contest television program, *So You Think You Can Dance?* introduced a new audience to the moves of Bob Fosse, Jerome Robbins, and Michael Kidd (and identifying them as such), while playing the show tunes that provided the foundation of their greatest work.

However, with the demise of *The Ed Sullivan Show* in 1971, there was a real vacuum for a more extensive network exposure of show tunes. There were a few television specials into the 1970s, celebrating Irving Berlin or George Gershwin in primetime, with artists as varied as Steve Lawrence and Eydie Gormé on one side, and the Supremes on the other—these were just the last gasps of the variety show format. But narrative musicals eventually made a surprising comeback. Beginning with a 1993 television version of *Gypsy* starring Bette Midler, the producers Craig Zadan and Neil Meron, who also produced the Oscar-winning film of *Chicago,* brought Broadway back to primetime with acclaimed television versions of such classics as *The Music Man, Cinderella,* and *Annie.* These versions were occasionally rethought for twenty-first century audiences, but the tinkering was mild in comparison with their respective film versions and they were backed up with Broadway professionals, on camera and behind the scenes.

In 2012, Zadan and Meron upped the ante by proposing a live broadcast of *The Sound of Music*; its potential success hinged on the fact that the broadcast wasn't going to be a second-rate remake of the movie but, rather, a first-rate production of the stage musical. Zadan and Meron combined Broadway stalwarts such as Audra McDonald, playing the Mother Abbess, with pop stars with mass appeal such as Carrie Underwood, who undertook the role of Maria von Trapp. The live broadcast was more or less an exact replica of the original Broadway text, and audiences only familiar with the film version got to see "Do Re Mi" and "The Lonely Goatherd" in their original contexts, although the television correspondent from *Time* magazine apparently didn't get the memo, complaining that the producers repurposed "My Favorite Things" for the Mother Abbess, just so that "Audra got to sing it."[15] The immense ratings success of *The Sound of Music Live!* inspired two more live television events—versions of *Peter Pan* and *The Wiz,* which performed less well than *The Sound of Music Live!,* but well enough. In February 2016, Fox's *Grease Live!* was a ratings success with 12.2 million viewers, most of them in the most sought-after 18–40 demographic. It was followed that year by *The Rocky Horror Show* and *Hairspray,* both of which, it must said, had perfectly fine and respectful film versions; *Bye Bye Birdie,* with Jennifer Lopez, was announced for live network broadcast in 2018. The television cast recordings were released within days or hours of the live event—often teased out as special previews—via digital download, with eventual hard copies of CDs following swiftly in the wake of the MP3 versions.

If television accessed Broadway's mainstream appeal, the Internet broadened its ability to market product and promote its brand. Every musical that opens on Broadway today has its own website, providing backstage chats, rehearsal footage, and new songs and material. It's all streamed on the Internet with much attention paid to the bragging rights of consumers who have access to a sneak preview or a first glimpse of a new production number. The Internet has also helped producers, publicists, and marketing gurus carve up a potential audience more efficiently by using social networking and the rapid response rate of cyberspace to create niche marketing.

This has proven to be a successful pathway for one of the newest of recording entrepreneurs, Sh-K-Boom Records, whose chief executive, Kurt Deutsch, began the company in 2000 as an option for both performers and producers who prefer a more personal business model; in fact, Deutsch said he formed the company for talented performers, equally at home with show tunes and rock, who were getting more Broadway exposure because of the change in music on Broadway. "These are folks who wanted to record an album, but wouldn't be caught dead singing a show tune on it." Setting the adage of "without a show, there's no market for an album" on its head, Deutsch has a different mantra for the twenty-first century: "Without an album, there's no show [to market]."[16]

Deutsch's philosophy affirms that a show album can give a stage production the kind of credibility that, in the absence of a recording, it might otherwise lack. Sheldon Harnick remembered the ignominy of his first full Broadway production, *The Body Beautiful*, which crashed in early 1958 after only 60 performances: "And then the big heartbreak for me: we were supposed to have an album and then whoever the recording company was [Columbia] read the reviews, they said, 'We're not going to do this.' The producers accepted a $5,000 check for advertising [as a buy-out], but there was no album. And for the next year or so, as I passed Sam Goody's and I saw other people's albums, I was just sick at heart."[17] Deutsch realized that, in an age where ancillary income could be derived by small-scale revivals, or university productions, it was the theater producers who now needed the recordings: "The way that our business model works is that we will executive produce the album, and put the investment for the recording together. So, if I put in 25 percent, the show's producers may put in the rest of the money, because they need the album to promote the show."

The financial burden of a cast recording has bounced back more frequently to the producers who want to enhance the longevity of their properties. *The Last 5 Years,* a two-person chamber musical written by Jason Robert Brown that played Off-Broadway in 1996, is popular in community theaters and universities, and sells a few hundred copies a week for Sh-K-Boom: "I'll take that for the rest of my life, sure. I look at it much more as having a very long shelf life," said Deutsch. An incremental sale, when digital media obviates the need for warehouse shelving or even a physical catalog, makes the economics of a downloadable recording, with enhancement money, a viable proposition. In Deutsch's opinion, "If it's *Book of Mormon*, if it's *Something Rotten*, it starts out with 1,200 people a night, which becomes 10,000 people a week. And then if you're lucky enough, it tours and it's still running on Broadway. Then it grows; it plays worldwide, so you have multiple companies."

In 2011, *The Book of Mormon* rode the crest of the Internet age to see its cast album make it to No. 3 on the *Billboard* 200, the highest-charting position for a cast album since *Hair* held the No. 1 spot for thirteen consecutive weeks in 1969. But that success comes with an asterisk, says Keith Caulfield, because the entire cast album was available for only $1.99 per download on Amazon: "So, yes, it went to No. 3, yes, it was in the Top 10, however, a lot of that was because it was *really* super cheap."[18] But Caulfield attributes the increasing interest in cast albums served up on a digital streaming menu not to technology or even the buzz, necessarily, but because of the audience once deemed non-existent: young people. "Once in a while, you'll get a cast album or a musical that breaks through. When all the stars align and the buzz becomes deafening, then you have a *Book of Mormon*, or a *Rent* or a *Hamilton*, because it breaks the mold in some fashion, it gets a younger audience to pay attention."

If any show of the last half-century got a younger audience to pay attention, it was *Hamilton*. It was born out of both the epic narratives of the pop-opera concept album and the mash-up of the mixtape. In fact, when Lin-Manuel Miranda first contemplated a musical take on the peripatetic life of Alexander Hamilton, he called it *The Hamilton Mixtape*. The show began its uncertain evolution with the performance of one song by Miranda at a 2009 concert at the White House; by the time he performed at a Lincoln Center concert in 2012, he had added a dozen songs to his historical narrative. At that point, its final form as a stage musical was still uncertain, but its roots were very clear; as a kid, Miranda went to Broadway to see "that holy trinity: *Les Miz, Cats, Phantom*."[19] But he also keenly felt the kinship between Broadway tunes and the hip-hop music that was the soundtrack of his life as a grown-up: "What I love about musical theater *and* hip-hop is that everything is fair game: sampling other genres, a fluidity in the service of the moment." As the *New York Times* put it, "In the Venn diagram of contemporary music, hip-hop and musical theater have little overlap, but that is the space in which Lin-Manuel Miranda lives."[20]

By the time *The Hamilton Mixtape* morphed into a fully staged production of *Hamilton: An American Musical* at New York's Public Theatre in early 2015, Miranda had fleshed a full score of almost four dozen numbers, which liberally mixed quotes and samplings from source as diverse as Busta Rhymes, Common, and The Notorious B.I.G. with *Jesus Christ Superstar, Les Misérables*, and *South Pacific*. The production attracted many of the big names of the hip-hop universe during its initial run, including Ahmir "Questlove" Thompson of the hip-hop band the Roots. Questlove had been roped into several proposals for bringing hip-hop to Broadway musicals but always exited wearily, feeling that the projects were more about exploiting hip-hop than exploring it. *Hamilton* struck him as different—*authentic*—and he brought friends and colleagues to check it out: "Is this the most revolutionary thing to happen to Broadway, or the most revolutionary thing to happen to hip-hop?," he wondered.[21]

When the cast album to *Hamilton* was picked up by Atlantic Records (one of its few previous cast albums, *The Wiz* in 1975, was the only one that landed), Questlove and his partner from the Roots, Tariq "Black Thought" Trotter, agreed to produce the recording. The sessions happened over several weeks, with cast members often performing in single sessions, in separate booths, only to have their material mixed by an engineer proficient in the mixing techniques of the hip-hop world. The resulting recording debuted first, not as a two-CD set with an insert book of lyrics (that would come two weeks later), but as a digital download.

When *Hamilton* made its grand entrance on the *Billboard* 200 chart on September 25, 2015, it already had the full winds of cultural approbation backing its sails. "*Hamilton* is not just a great album," says Caulfield. "It's also a phenomenon."[22] It debuted at No. 12, the highest debut for a cast recording since the original Broadway cast recording of *Camelot* debuted at No. 4 in January 1961. In its first week, *Hamilton* also hit an unprecedented trifecta; given its hip-hop provenance, Lin-Manuel Miranda's score landed on three of the granulated *Billboard* charts simultaneously: No. 3 on the Hip-Hop chart, No. 1 on Cast Albums, and No. 9 of all album sales, wreaking complete havoc with the discrete chart categories created in the early 1960s. By November, it had hit No. 1 on the Rap Albums chart—clearly the first cast album ever to do so.

In February 2016, *Hamilton* was the first musical to be invited to perform live during the primetime broadcast of the Grammys; four months later, the week after the show won eleven Tony Awards, the cast album went to No. 3 in album sales, the highest ranking since the *Hair* album in 1969. That week, it sold 30,000 units; comparatively, a huge week for a cast album during the Tonys is 5,000 a week. Unlike most albums of all genres that are bought and downloaded digitally, *Hamilton* has an extraordinarily high number of complete downloads of its score; in other words, consumers want *all* of it, the whole contextual narrative, not just its perceived highlights or selections. Caulfield comments on this outlier to contemporary musical strategies, which value content over context: "Today's consumers tend to experience things in fragmented ways, through viral YouTube videos or a meme—now you can pick and choose exactly what you want to hear. But, cast albums don't work that way—if you skip around, you'll miss the story. With the score to *Hamilton*, there are so *many* moments that people want to hear the whole thing. This is the perfect example of how an album should work."[23] Atlantic Records even released the cast album as a special four-disk boxed set of LPs on vinyl, the most copious set of LPs for a musical since *The Most Happy Fella* six decades earlier.

To the extent that *Hamilton*—the show itself—is a tapestry woven together from dozens of shout-outs, quotes, samplings, and allusions to other songs and shows (or, rather, joined together with the aggressive percussion of a staple gun), the original cast recording is also a mixture—a mixtape—of all the sources and archetypes that came before it, each informing on the tradition of making show tunes from Broadway available to listeners at home. Like *Jesus Christ Superstar*, *Hamilton* was originally conceived as a concept album; like *Hair*, it makes use of contemporary performance and music; like *South Pacific*, the album was produced by an astute musician who had attended the production a dozen times before getting into the recording studio; like *Dreamgirls*, it was produced by a record company outside the Broadway realm; like *Rent*, it was recorded and mixed over several sessions, as opposed to the all-day Sunday pressure cooker; like *Oklahoma!*, it has the full buzz of the zeitgeist behind it before its release; like *My Fair Lady*, it was a pre-sold, highly anticipated release; like *Camelot*, it debuted in the Top 10 on the Album chart; like *Les Misérables*, it makes no concessions of its epic narrative to its listeners; like *The Most Happy Fella*, it contains the entire score and dialogue of the Broadway production (also, like *Most Happy Fella*, its composer, lyricist, and librettist are all the same artist); like *Sweeney Todd*, it included the full lyrics to the score as an insert; like *Wish You Were Here*, it exploited the publicity surrounding its exposure on a prime-time variety show; like *The Phantom of the Opera*, it is successful as an album without the assistance of a pop single; like *Kiss Me, Kate*, it was released in several formats simultaneously.

And, like *Oh Captain!*, it also has a cover album. Fourteen months after the release of the original album, *The Hamilton Mixtape* brought together the top hip-hop and contemporary artists, including Usher, Kelly Clarkson, and Busta Rhymes among others, to perform their own idiosyncratic takes on the *Hamilton* score, after it teased out several of its tracks digitally ahead of its release, whetting appetite among the fan base. When Miranda was devising *Hamilton's* version of George Washington, one of the artists he drew inspiration from was John Legend—so it was only natural to ask Legend to cover one of Washington's most powerful numbers on the *Mixtape*, "History Has Its Eyes on You." Legend returned with a gospel-inspired remix of the song. When *The Hamilton Mixtape*—all two dozen covers—finally dropped in the first week of December 2016, it immediately shot to No. 1 on the *Billboard* 200 charts. Not only was it the highest-charting compilation album in years, it was the first complete album compilation of Broadway material by non-original performers to hit the charts since the days of jazz artists—André Previn, Oscar Peterson—covering Broadway scores in the early 1960s.

▶   Audio Example 14.2, "History Has Its Eyes on You" (John Legend)

Hamilton's across-the-charts success appears to have opened the doors for other comers as well. In February 2017, the Broadway cast album of *Dear Evan Hansen* (also an Atlantic release), with a score by the skyrocketing team of Benj Pasek and Justin Paul, debuted at No. 8, vaulting over *Hamilton*'s debut by a good five positions on the *Billboard* charts. *Dear Evan Hansen*'s contemporary and sympathetic look at a troubled millennial generation accounted for a good deal of its popularity; it probably represented its target demographic even more satisfyingly than *Glee* did. One of the songs from its cast recording, "Waving Through a Window," was remixed and in November 2017 found itself the recipient of a rare honor: the first song from a Broadway show to become a No. 1 hit on *Billboard*'s Dance Club Songs chart. It's worth noting that the cast albums for *Evan Hansen* and *Hamilton* inhabited the Top 20 at the same time; that hadn't happened since

In 1967, Columbia decided to promote its cast album and spoken word catalog by papering over West 45th Street with every record it produced in those categories; astute connoisseurs can catch *The Pajama Game, Juno, Sweet Charity,* and even *Oh Captain!* {left} in the first row. By permission of Sony Music.

Fiddler on the Roof and *Hello, Dolly!* shared the Top 20 more than half a century earlier: an encouraging sign.

Another encouraging sign was the bio entry for Sony Music Masterworks in the *Playbill* of the recent Broadway musical *SpongeBob Square Pants*, which opened in December 2017. Sony is coproducer of the show, along with Viacom/Nickelodeon, and in its brief bio, Sony made reference to the golden days of Goddard Lieberson, when the company (in its Columbia incarnation) produced both the show and the album for *My Fair Lady*. As Scott Farthing, VP for Broadway Masterworks put it, "As our marketing efforts for cast albums help elevate the profile of their shows and lead to more ticket sales, we thought [that] investing in the *SpongeBob SquarePants* production (and potentially others in the future) [made good business sense] along with securing its cast album." Sony's album is technically an "original cast recording"—the "Broadway" part of that equation noticeably absent—as the show was recorded after its earlier Chicago tryout; this allowed for digital streaming of the score six weeks before the first Broadway preview. This was part of Sony's strategy, "a kind of a modern spin on the 'golden age' when pop performers of the day released songs from upcoming Broadway shows and patrons would already be familiar with a song or two before arriving at the theatre," says Farthing.[24] Furthering the retro appeal, Sony has obliged with a two-LP edition (pressed on yellow vinyl, in honor of the musical's eponymous hero), complete with gatefold, color photos, and a lyric sheet insert. It is technically, alas, not a K-series gatefold from the good old days, but it certainly feels like one.

The unprecedented reach of these recent recordings across all formats means that the music of Broadway can go anywhere as well. One part of a new generation of listeners hears *Hamilton* or *Dear Evan Hansen* or *SpongeBob* song by song, carved up into discrete bits of time, while engaged in a variety of activities; another part dedicates the time to listen to the entire score, either on car rides, long subway rides, or quiet afternoons in the park. Technology has taken the appreciation of Broadway scores out of the living room; the mixtape generation is as likely to listen to *Hamilton* while walking along Main Street as their predecessors were likely to listen to *My Fair Lady* in their homes on Main Street. The music of Broadway no longer has any geographic boundaries; it has burst far beyond the Theater District and is as boundless as the soaring breadth and inspiration of its most enchanting creations.

Notes

INTRODUCTION

1. *60 Minutes* broadcast, October 21, 2015.
2. "Clooney Severs Contract," *Variety,* January 11, 1958.
3. "Oh Captain!" "Recent Disks," *Variety,* February 16, 1958.
4. Ibid.

CHAPTER 1

1. "Livingston and Evans," *Variety,* February 3, 1958.
2. "An American Aesthetic," *The New Criterion* (September 2015), 73.
3. David Byrne, *How Music Works* (New York: McSweeney's, 2013), 75.
4. David Byrne, *How Music Works* (New York: McSweeney's, 2013), 76.
5. Interview, *Theater Week,* May 11, 1993.
6. Glenn Gould, "The Prospects of Recording," *High Fidelity,* April 1966.
7. Kander's comment, as well as comments by Stephen Schwartz, are taken from interviews with the author.

CHAPTER 2

1. Richard Rodgers, *Musical Stages: An Autobiography* (New York: Random House, 1975), 17.
2. Ibid., 17.
3. Like many youngsters after him, Rodgers was seduced into a Broadway theater by following the musical-ized escapades of comic strip characters: Li'l Abner, Superman, Charlie Brown, and Little Orphan Annie, in years to come.
4. "Musical of the Month: A Trip to Chinatown" (June 30, 2012) http://www.nypl.org/blog/2012/06/30/musical-month-trip-chinatown.
5. Lynn Wetzel and Carol J. Binokowski, *I Hear America Singing* (New York: Crown Publishing, 1989), 42.
6. Don Tyler, *Hit Songs, 1900–1955: American Popular Music of the Pre-Rock Era* (Jefferson, NC: McFarland, 2007), 7.
7. David Ewen, *The Life and Death of Tin Pan Alley: The Golden Age of American Popular Music* (New York: Funk and Wagnalls/Reader's Digest Books, 1964), 29.
8. Russell Sanjek and David Sanjek, *Pennies from Heaven: The American Popular Music Business in the Twentieth Century* (New York: Da Capo Press, 1996), 39.
9. Richard Rodgers, *Musical Stages: An Autobiography* (New York: Random House, 1975), 34.
10. David Ewen, *All the Years of American Popular Music* (Englewood Cliffs, NJ: Prentice-Hall, 1977), 134.
11. David Ewen, *The Life and Death of Tin Pan Alley: The Golden Age of American Popular Music* (New York: Funk and Wagnalls/Reader's Digest Books, 1964), 152.

12. Max Dreyfus Obituary, *New York Times*, May 16, 1964.

13. Richard Rodgers, *Musical Stages: An Autobiography* (New York: Random House, 1975), 34.

14. Max Dreyfus Obituary, *New York Times*, May 16, 1964.

15. Rodgers, 37.

16. Max Dreyfus Obituary, *New York Times*, May 16, 1964.

CHAPTER 3

1. Brian Rust and Allen G, Debus, *The Complete Entertainment Discography (From 1897 to 1942)*, 2nd Ed. (New York: Da Capo Press, 1989). This essential guide to nearly every recording session by a popular entertainer on either or both sides of the pond provides the context for most of the citations of performers behind a microphone described in this chapter.

2. Frank Hoffman, ed., *The Encyclopedia of Recorded Sound, Volumes I and II* (New York and London: Routledge, 2005), 148.

3. Conversation with the author.

4. But five is a crowd,
   For crying out loud.
   We're crowded in
   My Blue Heaven.

   As quoted in Eddie Cantor, *My Life Is in Your Hands* and *Take My Life: The Autobiographies of Eddie Cantor* (New York: Cooper Square Press, 2000), 157.

5. Larry F. Kiner and Philip D. Evans, *Al Jolson: A Bio-Discography* (Metuchen, NJ: Scarecrow Press, 1992), 47.

6. The latter tune, by the Gershwins, premiered in their 1929 *Show Girl*, where it accompanied Ruby Keeler's tap-dance number; Jolson, who had just married the teenaged Ruby Keeler, would frequently sing along—loudly, no doubt—from the audience.

7. Andre Millard, *America on Record: A History of Recorded Sound* (New York: Cambridge University Press, 2005), 143.

8. George Olsen was more than a mere bandleader: not only did his band play in *The Ziegfeld Follies of 1927*, he met his wife when she starred in the *Follies*: Ethel Shutta, who would go on to stop the show cold with "Broadway Baby" when she was featured in Stephen Sondheim's *Follies* forty-three years later.

9. Richard Rodgers, *Musical Stages*, 31.

10. In his *The Fabulous Phonograph*, Roland Gelatt points to the success of a (British) Columbia recording of a revue at London's Hippodrome in 1915 entitled *Business as Usual*: "To soldiers on leave, the records were a perfect memento of an enchanted evening in London; and they helped push sales into the tens of thousands."

11. Merman eventually recorded "I Got Rhythm" but not until 1949 as a part of a "songs she has made famous" LP for Decca.

12. A 1952 Broadway revival was recorded by Capitol; it is significantly compromised by some updated lyrics and a disappointing Diana Devereaux, which was played by a supremely overtaxed singer who happened to be the producer's girlfriend.

CHAPTER 4

1. Leonard Maltin, *The Great American Broadcast: A Celebration of Radio's Golden Age* (New York: Dutton, 1997), 212.

2. Eddie Cantor, *My Life Is in Your Hands* and *Take My Life: The Autobiographies of Eddie Cantor* (New York: Cooper Square Press, 2000), 216.

3. Philip K. Eberly, *Music in the Air: America's Changing Tastes in Popular Music, 1920–1980* (New York: Hastings House, 1982), 47.

4. Susan J. Douglas, *Listening In: Radio and the American Imagination* (New York: Times Books, Random House, 1999), 121.

5. Eberly, 56.

6. Abel Green and Joe Laurie, Jr., *Show Biz, Variety from Vaude to Video* (New York: Henry Holt, 1951), 331.

7. John Dunning, *On the Air: Encyclopedia of Old-Time Radio* (New York: Oxford University Press, 1998), various.

8. Rudy Vallee and Gil McKean, *My Time Is Your Time: The Story of Rudy Vallee* (New York: Ivan Obolensky, 1962), 67.

9. Douglas, 135. In the opinion of some, Vallee's often combative off-air, off-stage manner was his way of countering criticism that he was a lightweight.

10. Vallee and McKean, 83.

11. Eberly, 233.

12. Lawrence Bergreen, *As Thousands Cheer: The Life of Irving Berlin* (New York: Doubleday, 1988), 231.

13. Maltin, 217.

14. Rodney Greenberg, *George Gershwin* (New York: Phaidon Press, 1998), 78.

15. John Dunning, *On the Air: Encyclopedia of Old-Time Radio* (New York: Oxford University Press, 1998), various.

16. "Radio's New Songwriters," *Time* magazine, September 11, 1934.

17. Howard Dietz, *Dancing in the Dark: Words by Howard Dietz* (New York: Quadrangle/The New York Times Book Co., 1974), 211.

18. Eberly, 234. Tobacco manufacturers were—perhaps ironically—the major sponsors of singing shows.

19. Recording: "You're the Top: A Cole Porter Testimonial," UCLA, 1967 (released on Viper's Nest Records, 1997).

20. Recording: "A Voice on the Air: Frank Sinatra on the Radio 1938–1951" (Columbia Legacy, 2015).

21. Recording provided to the author by Charles Granata.

CHAPTER 5

1. Russell Sanjek and David Sanjek, *Pennies from Heaven: The American Popular Music Business in the Twentieth Century* (New York: Da Capo Press, 1996), 311.

2. Sanjek and Sanjek, 343.

3. Laurence Maslon, ed., *American Musicals (1927–1949)* (New York: Library of America, 2014), 643.

4. Marc Blitzstein, *The Cradle Will Rock* (New York: Random House, 1938), iv.

5. "Cradle to Continue," *New York Times*, October 21, 1937.

6. Sanjek and Sanjek, 176. If the notion of 7½ percent as a wage increase sounds familiar, then you know your *Pajama Game*.

7. David Dachs, *Anything Goes: The World of Popular Music* (Indianapolis, IN: Bobbs-Merrill, 1964), 211.

8. Max Preeo, "Lorenz Hart," *Show Music* (April 1998), 28.

9. Arnold Shaw, *Let's Dance: Popular Music in the 1930s* (New York: Oxford University Press, 1998), 124.

10. "The Music Man," *New Yorker*, August 10, 1940.

11. The commercial value of Rodgers and Hart was also celebrated in a 1940 Columbia album set of four disks entitled *Smash Song Hits,* featuring ten songs by the team. Rodgers himself conducted the studio orchestra, while two forgettable singers handled the lyrics; of main interest is the cover design by the fabled Alex Steinweiss.

12. Sanjek and Sanjek, 218.

13. "Petrillo, At It Again," *New York Times*, July 5, 1948.

14. *The Decca Logs: A Complete Recording Guide* (Jefferson, NC: McFarland, 1988), 311.

15. Samuel J. Brylawski, "Cartoons for the Record: The Jack Kapp Collection," *Library of Congress Journal,* Vol. 2, No. 2, 1981, 5.

16. Max Wilk. *OK! The Story of Oklahoma!* (New York: Grove Press, 1993), 261.

17. *The Decca Logs: A Complete Recording Guide* (Jefferson, NC: McFarland, 1988), 316.

18. Wilk, 262.

19. "OK Gets OK from Buyers," *Variety*, December 6, 1943.

CHAPTER 6

1. "Jack Kapp, Recording Pioneer, Dies at 49," *Variety*, March 28, 1948.
2. Philip Furia, *Skylark: The Life and Times of Johnny Mercer* (New York: St. Martin's Press, 2003), 134.
3. Ibid., 198.
4. "Capitol 10th Anniversary," *Billboard*, June 1952.
5. "Rodgers, Hammerstein, Dreyfus Slow Down 'Allegro'," *Variety*, March 11, 1947.
6. Interview with the author.
7. "Petrillo, At It Again," *New York Times*, July 5, 1948.
8. There is a strong school of critical thought that popular songs *transformed* into three- to four-minute packages in order to accommodate recording technology.
9. Andre Millard, *America on Record: A History of Recorded Sound* (New York: Cambridge University Press, 2005), 163.
10. Travis Elborough, *The Vinyl Countdown: The Album from LP to iPod and Back Again* (Berkeley, CA: Soft Skull Press, 2009), 117.
11. "'South Pacific' Set for the Record," *Variety*, February 15, 1949.
12. *Billboard*, June 11, 1949.
13. From correspondence at the Goddard Lieberson Collection, Gilmore Music Library, Yale University.
14. Certainly Fred Astaire had a hit recording with "Night and Day," back in 1931—but it was a studio recording of a song he just happened to sing in a show (*Gay Divorce*), not really a cast recording. Yvonne Elliman had a hit rendition of "I Don't Know How to Love Him" from *Jesus Christ Superstar*, some twenty-two years after Pinza; she appeared on both the concept album and the Broadway stage.

CHAPTER 7

1. There was a 1941 foxtrot version by Leo Reisman's Orchestra with a limited and bowdlerized vocal by Anita Boyer, and an up-tempo rendition that same year by Benny Goodman and His Orchestra with Helen Forrest.
2. Jule Styne, *Jule* (New York: Broadway Books, 1978), 178.
3. *Variety*, January 12, 1952.
4. David Dachs, *Anything Goes: The World of Popular Music* (Indianapolis, IN: Bobbs-Merrill, 1964), 311.
5. Elijah Wald, *How the Beatles Destroyed Rock 'n' Roll: An Alternative History of American Popular Music* (New York: Oxford University Press, 2009), 151.
6. Gary Marmorstein, *The Label: The Story of Columbia Records* (New York: Thunder's Mouth Press, 2007), 89.
7. Interview with the author.
8. James Kaplan, *Frank: The Voice.* (New York: Doubleday, 2013), 432.
9. Interview with the author.
10. John McDonough, "The History of the Songbooks," *The Complete Ella Fitzgerald Song Books* (New York: Polygram Records, 1993).
11. Ibid.
12. Kaplan, 520.
13. A. H. Weiler, "Pal Joey Is Back on Broadway," *New York Times*, October 28, 1957.

CHAPTER 8

1. Although the punchline to *that* show is that it yielded the standard "Here's That Rainy Day."
2. The correspondence between Lieberson and various writers and performers in this chapter are from the Goddard Lieberson Collection, Gilmore Music Library, Yale University.
3. Ibid.
4. Ibid.
5. *This Is Broadway's Best*, liner notes, 1961.
6. Lieberson Collection, ibid.
7. Ibid.
8. Ibid.

9. *Variety*, July 7, 1955.

10. "Man at the Top," *Business Week,* April, 1961.

11. Comden was speaking at Lieberson's memorial service, June 11, 1977.

12. Conversation with the author.

13. Conversation with the author.

14. From an in-house collection of Lieberson's music writings for the *Saturday Review*.

15. Conversation with the author.

16. Conversation with the author.

17. Lieberson, "Letter to the Editor," *New York Times*, November 11, 1975.

18. "Pygmalion Rights Sought," *Variety*, July 16, 1955.

19. "The Man Behind Columbia," *Business Week*, April 1958.

20. Arthur Gelb, "Oklahoma! and My Fair Lady Make the Grade," *New York Times*, September 29, 1962. This figure has been a slightly slippery one over time, reported—wrongly, I would think—as low as $250,000, or $350,000. The *New York Times*, in 1962, reported a total of $401,207.64 "had been lavished upon it" by the time *My Fair Lady* opened; the sum of $385,000 with an allowance for cost overruns seems right to me.

21. Alan Jay Lerner, *The Street Where I Live* (New York: W.W. Norton, 1978), 186.

22. Bonus tracks, Sony CD release, *My Fair Lady* Original Broadway Cast Recording, 2002.

23. Review of "My Fair Lady" recording, *Billboard*, April 11, 1956.

24. Joel Whitburn, *Top Pop Albums—Seventh Edition: 1955–2009* (Los Angeles: Record Research, 2011).

25. Gary Marmorstein, *The Label: The Story of Columbia Records* (New York: Thunder's Mouth Press, 2007), 89.

26. Travis Elborough, *The Vinyl Countdown: The Album from LP to iPod and Back Again* (Berkeley, CA: Soft Skull Press, 2009), 142.

27. Liner notes, *My Fair Lady* (stereo recording, Columbia Records, 1958).

28. "Sound of Music" file, Sony Archives, New York City.

29. *Billboard*, April 14, 1958.

30. *New York Times*, April 1961.

CHAPTER 9

General note: All information about actual broadcasts of *The Ed Sullivan Show* comes from viewing the programs at the Library of Congress, where an entire set of Sullivan broadcasts—from 1948 to 1971—were donated by Andrew Solt and SOFA Productions. In addition, SOFA Productions graciously provided the author with its meticulous database of more than 15,000 acts, appearances, and artifacts of *The Ed Sullivan Show*.

1. That song would be the only show tune covered by the Beatles—although Paul McCartney was inspired by Peggy Lee's cover version from her 1960 album *Latin ala Lee!*. One additional note on *Oliver!*: the role of the Artful Dodger in this segment was performed by "David Jones," who, as "Davy Jones," would become part of the Monkees, a pop group concoction that would compete with the Beatles two years later.

2. Interview with the author.

3. Interview with Jane Klain, Research Manager at the Paley Center for Media, New York City.

4. Tim Brooks and Earle F. Marsh, *The Complete Directory to Prime Time Network and Cable TV Shows (1946-Present)* (New York: Ballantine Books, 2007), various.

5. Gerald Nachman, *Right Here on Our Stage Tonight! Ed Sullivan's America* (Berkeley: University of California Press, 2009), 213.

6. James Maguire, *Impresario: The Life and Times of Ed Sullivan.* (New York: Billboard Books, 2008), 46.

7. "Wish You Were Here," *Variety*, June 21, 1953.

8. Brooks Atkinson, "Wish You Were Here," *New York Times,* June 27, 1953.

9. Brooks Atkinson, "Once More on the Rialto," *New York Times,* October 11, 1953.

10. Bernie Ilson, *Sundays with Sullivan: How the Ed Sullivan Show Brought Elvis, the Beatles, and Culture to America* (New York: Taylor Trade Publishing, 2009), 32.

11. Courtesy of the SOFA database of *The Ed Sullivan Show*.

12. In 1951, Sullivan nearly ran an uncharacteristically virulent anti-Communist column in which he threatened to out Jerome Robbins as both a Communist and a homosexual; once Robbins named names in 1954, he was reinstated into Sullivan's good graces. His ballets then appeared frequently on the program, as did two particularly lengthy scenes from *West Side Story* on separate broadcasts in 1958. Cf., Amanda Vaill, *Somewhere: The Life of Jerome Robbins* (New York: Broadway Books, 2007), 171–75.

13. Alan Jay Lerner, *The Street Where I Live* (New York: W.W. Norton, 1978), 191.

14. Lerner, 193.

15. Ibid.

16. Not to be outdone, Sullivan opened the second part of the Porter tribute the following week by reporting that "when we mentioned that Cole Porter achieved this eminence despite thirty-three separate operations, we heard from hundreds of shut-ins, army veterans, navy veterans—anyone who has ever been under a handicap."

17. James Maguire, *Impresario: The Life and Times of Ed Sullivan* (New York: Billboard Books, 2008), 46.

18. Liner notes from *The Best of Broadway: The Sullivan Years* (TVT Records, 1996).

CHAPTER 10

1. "An Epilogue," Interview with Theodore H. White, *Life* magazine, December 6, 1963.

2. Laurence Maslon, *The Sound of Music Companion* (London: Anova Press: 2006), 134.

3. Goddard Lieberson Collection, Gilmore Music Library, Yale University.

4. David Dachs, *Anything Goes: The World of Popular Music* (Indianapolis, IN: Bobbs-Merrill, 1964), 381.

5. "My Favorite Things," NPR broadcast, December 11, 2009. The interaction between jazz and show tunes certainly deserves its own chapter, if not its own book. Following the huge success of *My Fair Lady* in 1956, various jazz instrumentalists found a commercially attractive hook on which to hang eight, ten, or twelve interpretations; having a popular musical in the album's title made the LPs more easily identifiable than the typical "So-and-so Plays Prettily" or "Joe Blow Swings Mightily" type of titles associated with jazz albums in the 1950s. *My Fair Lady, West Side Story, Camelot,* and *Fiorello!* were but some of scores sensitively covered by such first-rate jazz instrumentalists as Shelly Manne, André Previn, Oscar Peterson, and Stan Kenton.

6. "Sound of Music to RCA," *Billboard,* November 11, 1964.

7. *Business Week*, October 1963.

8. Interview with the author.

9. Columbia in-house promotion flyer, Sony Archives, 1966.

10. Ibid.

CHAPTER 11

1. Will Friedwald, *A Biographical Guide to the Great Jazz and Pop Singers* (New York: Pantheon Books, 2010), 178–83.

2. Martin Gottfried, *Balancing Act: The Authorized Biography of Angela Lansbury* (New York: Little, Brown and Company, 1999), 343–56.

3. Ibid.

4. Conversation with the author.

5. Conversation with the author.

6. Gottfried, 178.

7. Conversation with the author.

8. Conversation with the author.

9. Conversation with the author.

10. Joel Whitburn, *Adult Contemporary Hits, 1963–1989, Billboard* (Milwaukee, WI: Hal Leonard Publishing, 1995), iii.

11. Fred Hoffman, ed., *The Encyclopedia of Recorded Sound, Volumes I and II* (New York and London: Routledge, 2005), 32.

12. Glenn C. Altschuler, *All Shook Up: How Rock 'n' Roll Changed America* (New York: Oxford University Press, 2003), 156.

13. Altschuler, 158.

14. "Richard Rogers [*sic*] Expresses Views on Rock and Roll," Footage Film, YouTube, posted 2015 (provenance unclear).

15. Paul Ackerman, "Tin Pan Alley Days Fade," *Billboard*, October 15, 1955, 1.

16. David Dachs, *Anything Goes: The World of Popular Music* (Indianapolis, IN: Bobbs-Merrill, 1964), 217.

17. "Songwriters Blast BMI," *Billboard*, March 17, 1958, 9.

18. Conversation with the author.

19. Conversation with the author.

20. Dachs, 234.

21. Conversation with the author.

22. Conversation with the author.

23. Sony Archives, correspondence file, ca. 1961.

24. James Spada, *Barbra Streisand: Her Life* (New York: Crown, 1995), 171.

25. *Boston Sunday Globe*, April 24, 1973.

26. Spada, 183.

27. "Sinatra Launches New Project," *Billboard*, July 12, 1963.

28. Ibid.

29. Ibid.

30. Conversation with the author.

31. Sinatra's version actually comes from the album *The Concert Sinatra* that he recorded four months before the Reprise *South Pacific*.

32. James Kaplan, *Sinatra: The Chairman* (New York: Doubleday, 2015), 351.

33. Conversation with the author.

34. "Herman Finds Hits," *Variety*, October 11, 1964.

35. Conversation with the author. The five renditions of "Cabaret" recorded before its opening were Armstrong's rendition, as well as versions by Marilyn Maye—the first singer to cover it—Don Cherry, Mike Douglas, and bandleader Jo Basile.

CHAPTER 12

1. *Variety*, April 27, 1964, 187.

2. Columbia Masterworks would record *Working* (with a score by Stephen Schwartz and others) in 1978, after a run of twenty-four performances, and RCA would record Sondheim's *Merrily We Roll Along* in 1981, after its sixteen-performance run. Both scores would subsequently be revived around the globe, in no small part due to the inspiration of an archival recording.

3. Courtesy of Ted Chapin, personal collection.

4. Goddard Lieberson Collection, Gilmore Music Library, Yale University.

5. Arthur Gelb, "Record Companies Taking Major Role as Theater Angels," *New York Times*, September 25, 1961, 1.

6. "More Shows on the Bandwagon," *Billboard*, April 6, 1968.

7. Gelb, *New York Times*, September 25, 1961, 18.

8. Gary Marmorstein, *The Label: The Story of Columbia Records* (New York: Thunder's Mouth Press, 2007), 234.

9. "Frisco Sound," *Variety*, August 23, 1967, 1.

10. "Hair Songs Too Hot," *Billboard*, December 28, 1968, 56.

11. Christopher Isherwood, "The Aging of Aquarius," *New York Times*, September 16, 2007.

12. Review of *Henry Sweet Henry*, *New York Times*, December 22, 1967.

13. John S. Wilson, "The New Sound of 'Promises,'" *New York Times*, February 16, 1969, 28D.

14. Mike Gross, "Cast Album on Road Back as Loss Leader," *Billboard*, February 20, 1971, 1.

15. Conversation with the author. Lieberson apparently had an ongoing professional investment in John Barry; when Barry returned to England and wrote a new musical in 1974 called *Billy* (lyrics by Don

Black), Lieberson not only invested CBS money in the show (it was a big hit), but went to London to produce the cast album; Lieberson even got final billing on the album cover.

16. It might have been the second, if Goddard Lieberson had his way back in 1949, when he requested that the newsreel documentary series "The March of Time" be allowed to film the *South Pacific* recording session; the various unions and agents involved squashed it.

17. Conversation with the author.

18. Craig Zadan, *Sondheim & Co.* (New York: Harper and Row, 1985), 176.

19. Conversation with the author.

20. Theodore S. Chapin, *Everything Was Possible: The Birth of the Musical Follies* (New York: Alfred A. Knopf, 2003), 307.

21. Conversation with the author.

22. Conversation with the author.

23. Conversation with the author.

24. Goddard Lieberson archives, Yale University.

25. Chapin, 188.

26. "Jesus Christ Superstar," AllMusic Site.

27. Conversation with the author.

28. Goddard Lieberson archives, "A Little Night Music" file, Yale University.

29. Tom Topor, "'A Little Night Music' in the Studio," *New York Post*, March 20, 1973.

30. Ibid.

31. Ibid.

32. Goddard Lieberson archives, "A Little Night Music" file, Yale University.

33. Ibid.

34. Ibid.

35. David Dachs, *Anything Goes: The World of Popular Music* (Indianapolis, IN: Bobbs-Merrill Company, 1964), 383.

36. Conversation with the author.

37. Conversation with the author.

CHAPTER 13

1. "Diskeries Mine Legiter Lode," *Variety*, May, 25, 1977, 1.

2. Travis Elborough, *The Vinyl Countdown: The Album from LP to iPod and Back Again* (Berkeley, CA: Soft Skull Press, 2009), 312.

3. "Tomorrow Is a Day Away," *Los Angeles Times*, May 18, 1977.

4. Ibid.

5. Bernard Holland, "Making the Music Last," *New York Times*, February 23, 1984.

6. This author remembers *Cyrano* fondly as the favorite cast album of his youth.

7. Conversation with the author.

8. Alan Jay Lerner, *The Street Where I Live* (New York: W.W. Norton, 1978), 25.

9. "Thomas Z. Shepard," *Show Music*, September 1987.

10. One of Shepard's regrets was that space didn't allow for the Act One closer, the highly theatrical "Lion Dance." Conversation with the author.

11. Tom King, *The Operator: David Geffen Builds, Buys, and Sells the New Hollywood* (New York: Random House, 2000), 219.

12. Ibid.

13. "Geffen Launches Geffen Records for Broadway," *Billboard*, October 17, 1982.

14. "David Geffen Returns to Broadway," *New York Times*, October 23, 1982.

15. "Cast Albums or Concept Albums?" *New York Times*, April 24, 1983.

16. Andre Millard, *America on Record: A History of Recorded Sound* (New York: Cambridge University Press, 2005), 355.

17. Conversation with the author.

18. "'Phantom' Sings Through the Air," *USA Today*, February 22, 1988.
19. Conversation with the author.
20. Frank Rich, "Broadway Flops Go to CD Heaven," *New York Times*, October 11, 1993.
21. Conversation with the author.
22. "John McGlinn: Obituary," *The Independent*, March 29, 2009.
23. In 2007, this author nearly got into a fistfight with McGlinn (who passed away in 2009) during a radio interview, while defending Sarah Vaughan's musical "virtue."
24. Laurence Maslon, "Time and the River," *Opera News*, October 2013, 14.
25. Conversation with the author.

CHAPTER 14

1. "The Making of the *Hamilton* Cast Album," *60 Minutes*, October 21, 2015.
2. Those entities have also been particularly clumsy with metadata for Broadway material; songs and scores are often categorized under an incoherent system, frequently highlighting orchestra conductors, orchestrators, arrangers, or secondary and tertiary performers.
3. Conversation with the author.
4. Rebecca Milzoff, "Lin-Manuel Miranda on Jay Z, etc.," *Vulture*, January 15, 2016.
5. "*Rent* Gets Paid—Geffen Takes Album," *Billboard*, November 12, 1997.
6. Ibid.
7. Ibid.
8. Conversation with the author.
9. Stephen Holden, "Barbra Streisand: This Is the Music I Love," *New York Times*, November 10, 1985.
10. Ibid.
11. http://glee.wikia.com/wiki/Glee TV Show Wiki
12. Conversation with the author.
13. Ibid.
14. "The Oral History of Jay Z's 'Annie' Anthem, 'Hard Knock Life'" (December 19, 2014) http://grantland.com/hollywood-prospectus/the-oral-history-of-jay-zs-annie-anthem-hard-knock-life/.
15. Charlotte Alter, "How Do You Solve a Problem Like Carrie Underwood?" *Time*, December 6, 2013.
16. Conversation with the author.
17. Conversation with the author.
18. Conversation with the author.
19. Michael Paulson, "Lin-Manuel Miranda," *New York Times*, August 12, 2015.
20. Ibid.
21. Lin-Manuel Miranda and Jeremy McCarter, *Hamilton: The Revolution* (New York: Grand Central Publishing, 2016), 196.
22. "'Hamilton' Makes Its Own History," *Billboard*, October 12, 2016.
23. Conversation with the author.
24. Conversation with the author.

Bibliography

Altschuler, Glenn C. *All Shook Up: How Rock 'n' Roll Changed America*. New York: Oxford University Press, 2003.

Andrews, Julie. *Home: A Memoir of My Early Years*. New York: Hyperion, 2008.

Aylesworth, Thomas G. *Broadway to Hollywood*. New York: Gallery Books, 1985.

Barrios, Richard. *Dangerous Rhythm: Why Movie Musicals Matter*. New York: Oxford University Press, 2014.

Barrios, Richard. *A Song in the Dark: The Birth of the Musical Film*. New York: Oxford University Press, 1995.

Blitzstein, Marc. *The Cradle Will Rock*. New York: Random House, 1938.

Bowles, Jerry. *A Thousand Sundays. The Story of the Ed Sullivan Show*. New York: G.P. Putnam's Sons, 1980.

Burlingame, Jon. *The Music of James Bond*. New York: Oxford University Press, 2014.

Burton, Jack. *Blue Book of Tin Pan Alley*. Watkins Glen, NY: Century House, 1950.

Cantor, Eddie. *My Life Is in Your Hands* and *Take My Life: The Autobiographies of Eddie Cantor*. New York: Cooper Square Press, 2000.

Chapin, Theodore S. *Everything Was Possible: The Birth of the Musical Follies*. New York: Alfred A. Knopf, 2003.

Dachs, David. *Anything Goes: The World of Popular Music*. Indianapolis, IN: Bobbs-Merrill, 1964.

Dietz, Howard, *Dancing in the Dark: Words by Howard Dietz*. New York: Quadrangle/The New York Times Book Co., 1974.

Douglas, Susan J. *Listening In: Radio and the American Imagination*. New York: Times Books, Random House, 1999.

Eberly, Philip K. *Music in the Air: America's Changing Tastes in Popular Music, 1920–1980*. New York: Hastings House, Publishers, 1982.

Elborough, Travis. *The Vinyl Countdown: The Album from LP to iPod and Back again*. Berkeley, CA: Soft Skull Press, 2009.

Ewen, David. *All the Years of American Popular Music*. Englewood Cliffs, NJ: Prentice-Hall, 1977.

Ewen, David. *The Life and Death of Tin Pan Alley: The Golden Age of American Popular Music*. New York: Funk and Wagnalls/Reader's Digest Books, 1964.

Ewen, David. *New Complete Book of the American Musical Theater*. New York: Holt, Rinehart and Winston, 1970.

Friedwald, Will. *A Biographical Guide to the Great Jazz and Pop Singers*. New York: Pantheon Books, 2010.

Friedwald, Will. *Sinatra: The Song Is You*. New York: Scribner, 1995.

Friedwald, Will. *Stardust Melodies: A Biography of Twelve of America's Most Popular Songs*. New York: Pantheon Books, 2002.

Furia, Philip. *Skylark: The Life and Times of Johnny Mercer*. New York: St. Martin's Press, 2003.

Gabler, Neal. *Winchell: Gossip, Power and the Culture of Celebrity*. New York: Alfred A. Knopf, 1994.

Gammond, Peter. *The Oxford Companion to Popular Music*. New York: Oxford University Press, 1991.

Gelatt, Roland. *The Fabulous Phonograph: From Edison to Stereo*. New York: Appleton-Century, 1965.

Gershwin, Ira. *Lyrics on Several Occasions*. New York: Viking Press, 1973.

Goldberg, Isaac. *George Gershwin: A Study in American Music*. New York: Frederick Ungar Publishing, 1958.

Goldman, William. *The Season: A Candid Look at Broadway*. New York: Harcourt, Brace and World, Limelight Editions, 1969.

Good CD Guide. *Gramophone Musicals*. Suffolk, UK: William Clowes Limited, 1998.

Gottfried, Martin. *Balancing Act: The Authorized Biography of Angela Lansbury*. Little, Brown, 1999.

Granata, Charles L. *Sessions with Sinatra: Frank Sinatra and the Art of Recording*. Chicago: A Capella Books, 1999.

Green, Abel, and Joe Laurie Jr. *Show Biz, from Vaude to Video*. New York: Henry Holt, 1951.

Green, Jesse. "The Song Is Ended." *New York Times Magazine*, June 2, 1996.

Green, Stanley, ed. *Rodgers and Hammerstein Fact Book: A Record of Their Works Together and Other Collaborators*. New York: Lynn Farnol Group, 1980.

Greenberg, Rodney. *George Gershwin*. London: Phaidon Press Limited, 1998.

Groce, Nancy. *New York: Songs of the City*. New York: Watson-Guptill Publications, 1999.

Hamm, Charles. *Yesterdays: Popular Song in America*. New York: W.W. Norton, 1979.

Hammerstein, Oscar, and Amy Asch. *The Complete Lyrics of Oscar Hammerstein II*. New York: Alfred A. Knopf, 2008.

Hardy, Phil, and Dave Laing. *The Faber Companion to 20th-Century Popular Music*. London: Faber and Faber Limited, 1990.

Harris, Michael David. *Always on Sunday: Ed Sullivan: An Inside View*. New York: Meredith Press, 1968.

Haygood, Will. *In Black and White: The Life of Sammy Davis, Jr*. New York: Alfred A. Knopf, 2003.

Hemming, Roy. *The Melody Lingers On: The Great Songwriters and Their Movie Musicals*. New York: Newmarket Press, 1986.

Hoffman, Frank, ed. *The Encyclopedia of Recorded Sound, Volumes I and II*. New York: Routledge, 2005.

Horowitz, Mark Eden. *Sondheim on Music: Minor Details and Major Decisions*. Lanham, MD: Scarecrow Press, 2003.

Hummel, David. *The Collector's Guide to the American Musical Theatre, Volume I: The Shows*. Lanham, MD: Scarecrow Press, 1984.

Hummel, David. *The Collector's Guide to the American Musical Theatre, Volume II: Index*. Lanham, MD: Scarecrow Press, 1984.

Ilson, Bernie. *Sundays with Sullivan: How The Ed Sullivan Show Brought Elvis, the Beatles, and Culture to America*. New York: Taylor Trade Publishing, 2009.

Kander, John, Fred Ebb, and Greg Lawrence. *Colored Lights*. New York: Faber and Faber, 2003.

Kaplan, James. *Frank: The Voice*. New York: Doubleday, 2010.

Kaplan, James. *Sinatra: The Chairman*. New York: Doubleday, 2015.

King, Tom. *The Operator: David Geffen Builds, Buys, and Sells the New Hollywood*. New York: Random House, 2000.

Kreuger, Miles. *Show Boat: The Story of a Classic American Musical*. New York: Oxford University Press, 1977.

Lerner, Alan Jay. *The Street Where I Live*. New York: W.W. Norton, 1978.

Maguire, James. *Impresario: The Life and Times of Ed Sullivan*. New York: Billboard Books, 2008.

Maltin, Leonard. *The Great American Broadcast: A Celebration of Radio's Golden Age*. New York: Dutton, 1997.

Mandelbaum, Ken. *Not Since Carrie: Forty Years of Broadway Musical Flops*. New York: St. Martin's Press, 1991.

Mann, William J. *Hello, Gorgeous: Becoming Barbra Streisand*. Boston, New York: Mariner Books, 2012.

Marmorstein, Gary. *The Label: The Story of Columbia Records*. New York: Thunder's Mouth Press, 2007.

Maslon, Laurence. *The Sound of Music Companion*. New York: Fireside Books, 2007.

McDonough, John. "The History of the Songbooks." Liner notes from *The Complete Ella Fitzgerald Song Books*. New York: Polygram Records, 1993.

Mercer, Johnny, Robert Kimball, Barry Day, and Miles Kreuger. *The Complete Lyrics of Johnny Mercer*. New York: Alfred A. Knopf, 2009.

Millard, Andre. *America on Record: A History of Recorded Sound*. New York: Cambridge University Press, 2005.

Miranda, Lin-Manuel, and Jeremy McCarter. *Hamilton: The Revolution*. New York: Grand Central Books, 2016.

Morris, James R., J. R. Taylor, and Dwight Block Bowers. *American Popular Song*. New York: CBS Special Products/Smithsonian Institute, 1984.

Mustazza, Leonard. *Ol' Blue Eyes: A Frank Sinatra Encyclopedia*. Westport, CT: Greenwood Press, 1998.

Nachman, Gerald. *Right Here on Our Stage Tonight! Ed Sullivan's America*. Berkeley: University of California Press, 2009.

Page, Ted, ed. *The Glenn Gould Reader*. New York: Alfred A. Knopf, 1984.

Pleasants, Henry. *The Great American Popular Singers*. New York: Simon and Schuster, 1974.

Prince, Hal. *Contradictions: Notes on Twenty-Six Years in the Theatre*. New York: Dodd, Mead, 1974.

Raymond, Jack. *Show Music on Record: From the 1890s to the 1980s*. New York: F. Ungar, 1982.

Rich, Frank. *Hot Seat: Theatre Criticism for the New York Times, 1980–1993*. New York: Random House, 1998.

Rodgers, Richard. *Musical Stages: An Autobiography*. New York: Random House, 1975.

Sanjek, Russell, and David Sanjek. *Pennies from Heaven: The American Popular Music Business in the Twentieth Century*. New York: Da Capo Press, 1996.

Shaw, Arnold. *The Jazz Age: Popular Music in the 1920s*. New York: Oxford University Press, 1987.

Shaw, Arnold. *Let's Dance: Popular Music in the 1930s*. New York: Oxford University Press, 1998.

Smithsonian Institution. *I Got Rhythm: The Music of George Gershwin*. Washington, DC: Smithsonian Collection of Recordings, 1995.

Sondheim, Stephen. *Finishing the Hat: Collected Lyrics (1954–1981) with Attendant Comments, Principles, Heresies, Grudges, Whines and Anecdotes*. New York: Alfred A. Knopf, 2010.

Spada, James. *Barbra Streisand: Her Life*. New York: Crown, 1995.

Stanley, Bob. *Yeah! Yeah! Yeah! The Story of Pop Music from Bill Haley to Beyoncé*. New York: W.W. Norton, 2015.

Tyler, Don. *The Great Movie Musicals: A Viewer's Guide to 168 Films That Really Sing*. Jefferson, NC: McFarland Publishers, 2010.

Tyler, Don. *Hit Songs, 1900–1955: American Popular Music of the Pre-Rock Era*. Jefferson, NC: McFarland Publishers, 2007.

Vallee, Rudy, and Gil McKean. *My Time Is Your Time: The Story of Rudy Vallee*. New York: Ivan Obolensky, Inc., 1962.

Wald, Elijah. *How the Beatles Destroyed Rock 'n' Roll: An Alternative History of American Popular Music*. New York: Oxford University Press, 2009.

Wenzel, Lynn, and Carol J. Binokowski. *I Hear America Singing*. New York: Crown Publishing, 1989.

Wilder, Alec. *American Popular Song*. New York: Oxford University Press, 1972.

Wilk, Max. *OK! The Story of Oklahoma!* New York: Grove Press, 1993.

Wilk, Max. *They're Playing Our Song* (expanded). New York: Da Capo Press, 1991.

Zadan, Craig. *Sondheim and Company, 2nd Edition*. New York: Da Capo Press, 1994.

Index

Note: Page references followed by an "*f*" indicate photos or illustrations. **Bold** page references indicate audio links.

"Studio recording" refers to any release of a full or partial score not performed by the show's original Broadway cast.